## The Authors

**Mike Morley** is an awar[...] started in weekly newspap[...] the north-west of England [...] 1983, where he is currently produc[...] produced a number of networked documentaries for the acclaimed *Viewpoint* series, and was winner of the Science Writer of the Year Award for *A Shred of Evidence* – a documentary on the discovery and development of genetic fingerprinting.

**Steve Clark's** career in journalism began with the *Weekly News* on Merseyside, and then at the age of 25 he became editor of the *Nottingham News*. He then went on to write for the *Daily Mirror* and a couple of years later became news editor at ATV and then ITN. For the past three years he has been Controller of Regional Programmes at Central Television where he has produced a series of award-winning network and regional documentaries and features.

*To our wives, for their love
and understanding.*

# MURDER
# IN MIND

## Mindhunting the Serial Killers

STEVE CLARK and MIKE MORLEY

CENTRAL

B⊕XTREE

First published in the UK in 1993 by
Boxtree Limited
Broadwall House
21 Broadwall
London SE1 9PL

10987654321

Cover Design by Head

Printed and bound in Great Britain by
Cox and Wyman Ltd, Reading, Berkshire

A catalogue record for this book is available from the
British Library.

ISBN 1 85283 408 0

# Contents

# Preface

This book investigates some of the world's most horrific crimes and contains exclusive interviews with some of society's most notorious murderers. Sometimes it is graphic and disturbing. It is not the intention of the authors to shock or sensationalize the accounts of men like Dennis Nilsen, who killed 15 people in Britain, or sexual sadist Robert Berdella who drugged, tortured and dismembered six people in America. However, it is inevitable that in discussing their crimes and motivations their language is, at times, profane and their explanations disturbing.

*Murder in Mind* was written from the interviews, notes, tapes and research for the Central Television documentary of the same name. Both projects set-out to try to give an insight into the thoughts of those in society who commit the ultimate crime. From the cot to the courtroom, this book explores the way serial offenders grow up, carry out their killings and are thankfully nearly always caught. It also charts the ever-expanding science of offender profiling and pays tribute to its dedicated practitioners, the detectives, psychologists and psychiatrists, who relentlessly 'mindhunt' the serial killers.

Neither the book nor the documentary would have been possible without the co-operation, advice and encouragement of a number of people. Special thanks to Special Agent Roy Hazelwood of the FBI who over breakfast, lunch and dinner in Australia kindly gave us the benefit of his decades of work as a criminal profiler. Our appreciation also goes to our programme consultants, former FBI Special Agent and VICAP manager Robert K Ressler and Professor David Canter of Surrey University. Kind help with the Dennis Nilsen interview was given by author Brian Masters. Similar assistance was also provided by consultant psychologist Paul Britton who conducted that interview and at times was our guiding light through the complexities of offender profiling in Europe.

We are also appreciative of the support given by the Association of Chief Police Officers and particularly Northumbria's Chief Constable John Stevens and Derbyshire's Assistant Chief Constable Don Dovaston.

In America, we are grateful for the help of the Virginia State Police and its case profiler Larry E McCann, Dr Janet Warren of the FBI and Rochester prosecuting attorney 'Chuck' Siragusa. Our thanks also to the various international police departments and officers who helped with our case studies and to Terry Green, Pete Smeric and Kelly Cibulas who made us so welcome at the FBI Academy and Behavioural Science Unit in Quantico, Virginia.

Within Central Television, our appreciation goes to Andy Allan, Bob Southgate and Roger James who recognized the value of the programme and gave us generous backing and support during its commission. Also to Jill, Liz, Joanna, Deborah and the production crews who behaved so professionally during what were all too often distressing occasions. In the publishing world, our gratitude to Krystyna and Jack.

Our final, and perhaps, most important thanks go to our families, Dianne and Damian and Christine, Lisa and Jack. They have our gratitude for keeping us sane in this study of insanity and evil.

# 1
# Seeds From Despair

*"Kill!"* The only word serial killer Kenneth Erskine uttered
during his attack on one of his victims.

A university professor walks beside a railway line in London.
He is investigating the rapes of more than 20 women and the
murder of at least another three. Their bodies had been bound
and partially burned in a bid to destroy seminal evidence. A
consultant psychologist in Leicestershire breaks from his work.
He is advising police hunting a devil-worshiping sadist who
tortures his victims before mutilating them. Both men are about
to change British policing methods forever.

In the mid 1980s, independently of each other, a number of
psychologists and policemen were laying the foundations of
what is now being called 'offender profiling'. This is quite
simply a system of tracing criminals from the way they behave
during their crimes. Early work in Britain showed that even
when a criminal left no forensic clues at a murder scene they
still left a form of behavioural signature. All that was needed
was special training to decipher that signature.

Offender profiling was not invented in Britain, nor was it just
copied from the FBI's psychological profiling unit in America.
It evolved, almost organically over a period of about ten years.

Unlike America, Britain has had few serial killers. While the
relative size of the two countries has much to do with that, it is
also a tribute to British policing. There are hundreds of people
who have killed twice and then been captured. Few murderers
pass undetected to a third victim, fewer still make it into double
figures. It was the hunt for one of Britain's most notorious serial
murderers which prepared the ground for offender profiling in
the UK. By the time police had bungled their way through the

Yorkshire Ripper case every detective in the country knew there had to be a better way to carry out a major murder investigation.

*********************

The back of a woman's skull caved open with hammer blows, her neck, breasts and stomach lacerated with stab wounds. Another corpse, stabbed and gouged with a screwdriver. More bodies, some disembowelled, some mutilated and one with boot marks stamped upon it. So it was that Peter Sutcliffe announced his 'mission to kill' in the dingy, sodium-lit backstreets of Yorkshire. His reign of terror would span six years, claim 13 lives and see another seven women savagely attacked.

Psychological profiling was not unheard of when the Ripper claimed his first victim in the Autumn of 1975. There were ample opportunities to involve psychologists or American profilers who would certainly have helped a misdirected and, at times, inept investigation. A number of clinical psychiatrists and university psychologists would probably have made valuable educated guesses at the age, sex, occupation and type of person who had killed the Ripper's first victim, mother-of-four Wilma McCann. The fact that the 28-year-old blonde was a prostitute, had not been sexually assaulted and had been cut down just 100 yards from her council home, would have been food enough for thought.

They would have also been interested in the method of attack and the levels of brutality involved. Many assaults, physical and sexual, can be divided into what profilers have now come to recognize as 'con' or 'blitz' style attacks. The smashing open of a woman's skull with a ball-pein hammer is one of the clearest possible examples of a 'blitz' assault.

Wilma McCann's body was left sprawled on its back. In addition to the two hammer blows to the skull, her neck, breasts and stomach had all been stabbed and slashed. In a final act of contempt, her breasts had also been exposed. The nature of the wounds and the way the body was left should certainly have been interpreted as signs of a man who may have been seeking revenge against prostitutes or even women in general.

Like most serial killers, Sutcliffe did not begin his criminal career with a murder. There had been a trial run six years earlier when he cracked a prostitute over the head with a stone-filled sock. As a result he entered the 'system'. That is to say he was given a criminal record. This is of extreme significance, not just because it shows one of the many ways Sutcliffe could have been traced earlier, but because in later years it would be a lesson that profilers would look back upon and learn from. Strangely, that conviction in 1969 at Bradford Magistrate's Court was listed as 'going equipped for theft'. In fact, when he was stopped in the dead of night by an astute policeman in the red light area of Manningham it certainly wasn't theft he had in mind. The 23-year-old had fled the scene but was later found hiding in bushes. Gripped tightly in his hand was a ball-pein hammer. Six years later and only three months before Wilma McCann's killing, Sutcliffe attacked 34-year-old Anna Rogulskyj, another prostitute, in the Keighley area of Yorkshire.

In the early hours of May 5, 1975, the Irish-born divorcee was battered to the point of death. Found haemorrhaging in an alleyway, her injuries were so severe she was given the last rites by a Catholic priest. Only 12 hours of brilliant brain surgery saved her from being the Ripper's first kill.

Two months before the McCann murder, 46-year-old Olive Smelt, the wife of a civil servant and a mother of three, was battered with a hammer and sustained a fractured skull. Like McCann,she was just 100 yards from the safety of her home.

As the New Year festivities of 1976 subsided, five miles west of Chapletown in the posh Leeds suburb of Churwell, 'good time girl' Emily Jackson and her husband Sidney set out for their regular drinking session. They always by-passed the local pubs near their home and headed for The Gaiety in Chapletown. It was best not to go too close to home because of the nature of Emily's 'business'. Away from the trappings of middle-class suburbia, Mrs Jackson was a regular lady-of-the-night. This evening though, the only appointment she kept was a fatal one that stunned not just the local communities but the entire country.

The autopsy showed her head had been virtually obliterated by successive hammer blows. Then her attacker had gone to work with a sharp instrument. Her body was covered with slash wounds and frenzied lacerations around her neck, breasts and stomach. The corpse had then been turned over and a screwdriver used to gouge the 42-year-old's back. As he stood in puddles of Emily Jackson's blood and contemplated the 50 stab wounds he had inflicted, her attacker stamped his size seven boot onto her right thigh. It was a senseless, symbolic gesture of power for him and the final humiliation for his victim.

There had been no mistake with this one. His performance had been that of a consummate psychopath. As intended, this murder left police with little doubt that they were not dealing with the back-street mugger they had attributed the previous murder to. As the pathology reports were passed among investigators they knew they were confronted by a deranged killer who was undoubtedly out to claim more lives.

Throughout the inquiry, detectives worked with seven different photofits and sketches of the wanted man. Ironically, they had their best description at the outset of the hunt in August, 1975. Olive Smelt had survived his bloody attack to go on to very accurately describe her attacker, as aged about 30, 5ft 10ins tall and with a dark beard.

The Ripper hunt, like all murder inquiries before it, was run on what police called a 'manual' or 'card index' system. This meant every suspect, every piece of evidence, every sighting of a car, every report of an attack, every story of a peeping-Tom, etc, was entered on its own card and then filed in giant revolving trays. It was designed to give easy access to the teams who cluttered around the cigarette-burned tables and swopped information and whisky shots long into the early hours. For most murders, this was the traditional, tried and tested system. Cross- referencing came from a mixture of local knowledge by seasoned CID men and index files meticulously prepared by exhibits officers and the Force's intelligence unit.

However, this was not the average murder inquiry. This case was not simply going to generate the traditional pile of paperwork. It would initiate a seemingly endless avalanche of files, photographs, sightings, and other evidence that would engulf, confuse and thwart the team.

Over half a decade, detectives would chase clues across the country, their distracted travels causing considerable concern in the corridors of power. Successive Home Secretaries, Merlyn Rees and William Whitelaw, made visits to the Ripper Task Force headquarters. They discovered a unit that wasn't only hindered by paperwork but was positively paralyzed by it. More than 300 full-time officers had interviewed almost 200,000 people. The 'easy-access' file-trays were choked with almost 13,000 statements. The normally vital check-system on car sightings was bogged down with 10,000 vehicle traces still to be carried out.

The country was simply not prepared for the Yorkshire Ripper. This was one of the UK's rare encounters with a serial killer and its internationally acclaimed police force was left sadly wanting. There were brave attempts to hold order, to organize, to maintain morale, to plan for the mistake everyone knew he would eventually make and to wait for that lucky break the squad so desperately needed.

As the Ripper refined his attacks, the system began to work. On November 2, 1977, detectives interviewed him for the first time. By then he had already killed six women. The lives of Irene Richardson, Patricia Atkinson, Jayne McDonald and Jean Jordan had been added to those of McCann and Jackson. Amazingly, two other women, Maureen Long, in Bradford, and Marcella Claxton, in Leeds, had escaped his attacks.

It was the murder of a 21-year-old in Manchester on October 1, 1977, that brought him face-to-face with a member of the Ripper Squad for the first, but not the last time. Jean Bernadette Jordan climbed into Peter Sutcliffe's latest pride and joy, his new red Ford Corsair. The Scottish born mother of two lived not far from Manchester City Football Club in Manchester's rundown Moss Side District.

It was just around the corner from the flat she shared with her lover when she accepted the £5 offered to her as a downpayment on sex. They made idle chit-chat as the nervous, bearded man followed her directions off the busy inner-city streets to her 'patch'. The journey took a little over five minutes through the clogged shopping traffic. The Corsair pulled up on open land between some allotments and Manchester's Southern Cemetery. For Jean Jordan, as she and the driver clunked the car doors behind them, this was just another 'trick'.

The first hammer blow struck just yards from the car, then another ten rained down upon her head and face. He dragged her into some nearby bushes to complete the ritualistic slashing of the body.

It had been four months since the last murder, the 'mistaken' killing of 16-year-old Jayne McDonald in Leeds. The after-taste of that one had not been so sweet. The public outcry had reached fever pitch with the knowledge that the teenager was not a prostitute. It was a telling barometer of working class opinion that Jayne McDonald would be referred to as an 'inno-cent' victim.

Now, in Manchester, in the heart of 'The Moss', on yet another scrub of waste ground, he was set to finish the task in hand . As the anxieties and excitements swam together, Sutcliffe was denied his further pleasure by a passing car. Enraged, he fled back to Yorkshire. Behind, he left an unful-filled dream and a crisp, brand-new, tell-tale £5 note.

For a week, he scanned newspapers for details about his latest handiwork. On the eighth day he turned his Corsair back along the M62 to Manchester. He found the body undisturbed by humans but already infested with insects. This did not dampen the thrill he felt on returning to the scene and soaking up the memories of the attack. Visiting the area of their murders is now well recognized by psychologists and profilers as among the most pleasurable moments for serial killers.

Now, Sutcliffe was washed again in the fever of the kill but he was also outraged the body had not been discovered. He scattered Jean Jordan's clothing and set about mutilating the torso. He also tried to saw off her head with a broken pane of glass found nearby. When he left, the corpse had been so savaged that the young mother had to be identified from a fingerprint taken from a lemonade bottle in her council home.

Crime scenes are traditionally regarded 'cold' when the murderer has a ten day start on an inquiry team. But this site was hotter than an inferno. As well as the pathological and behavioural evidence that showed the killer had returned to the scene, there was also that new £5 note. It was basic detective work to track down the bank of issue and the branch to which it was distributed. From here detectives traced the companies which could have collected the note as part of a payroll issue.

Manchester officers believed the mutilation of Jean Jordan's body was a sign of anger by her killer, who had returned solely to reclaim the damning evidence he'd left behind. There was a gross misunderstanding by police of the type of individual they were dealing with.

The post-mortem wounds to Jean Jordan were not just signs of frustration, they were also the signs of a psychopathic serial murderer. As well as the skull injuries, four teeth had been smashed out. Across the front of her body there were 18 knife wounds and a cut, running from her left shoulder to her right knee. Another wound was seven inches long, the knife had been plunged so deeply into her flesh it had cut into her backbone; she had also been disembowelled. As these horrific injuries were relayed from the mortuary to senior investigating officers, press releases from Manchester police were playing down any possible links with the hunt for the so-called Yorkshire Ripper.

In private, detectives not only believed the killings were linked, they also hoped they had the vital clue that would put the person responsible behind bars. Within a few hours of finding note AW51 121565, investigators had the information they wanted. The fiver left near Jean Jordan's body was part of a shipment sent from the Bank of England to the Shipley and Bingley branches of the Midland Bank. Staff there came up with a disconcerting shortlist of 5,493 people who could have received the money in their wage packets. Manchester police based themselves in a make-shift incident room in a disused school at Baildon, near Shipley, and whittled down the list to a more manageable 23 factories. Armed with this information and with morale running higher than ever, Lancashire and Yorkshire coppers went 'back on the knocker', more house-to-house inquiries, the backbone of any manhunt.

Only a month after Jean Jordan's death two policemen arrived on the scrupulously clean doorstep of a tree flanked home in Garden Lane, Heaton, a suburb of Bradford, Yorkshire. One knocked on the white painted front door, while the other peered through the bowed lounge windows with their insets of stained glass and pretty white lace curtains. A manicured lawn to the left and rear was in perfect keeping with the quiet lane and its pervasive middle-class respectability. There was nothing out of the ordinary with the polite and courteous man who answered the door. The pro-forma (a standard police question-naire) took only a few moments to fill in and revealed that the householder worked nearby as a driver for T & WH Clark. Of course, there were checks to run on that. Six days later, as a matter of routine, the officers turned up again and confirmed his marital status and place of employment. A five paragraph report was fed into the system, copies were issued both sides of the Pennines and that was that. No breakthrough, no arrest. Nothing. Police had come face-to-face with their man on two occasions and had not realized it. Within a month he struck again.

What is important here, is not the fact that police had descriptions, forensic clues and even first-hand interviews with the killer, but that all their information was lost, solely because of the growing volume of paperwork. It is against this backdrop the next catastrophic blunder must be viewed.

It was 2 pm on Tuesday, June 26, 1979, when Assistant Chief Constable George Oldfield, who was leading the Ripper hunt, began a press conference at the West Yorkshire Police Academy in Bishopgarth, Wakefield. There had been much speculation about the 'presser' and talk of vital new evidence. By now the killer's toll had reached ten and public concern was boiling over.

The rotund and much-respected detective pressed the start button on a large tape recorder that had been set up on a long battered table in front of the television cameras. The tape was poor quality but the words hissed out loudly and ominously around the hushed and expectant conference room: "I'm Jack. I see you are still having no luck catching me. I have the greatest respect for you George but, Lord, you are no nearer catching me than four years ago when I started. I reckon your boys are letting you down, George. You can't be much good, can ya? The only time they came near catching me was a few months back in Chapletown when I was disturbed. Even then it was a uniform copper, not a detective. I warned you in March that I'd strike again. Sorry it wasn't Bradford. I did promise you that but I couldn't get there. I'm not quite sure when I will strike again, but it will be definitely some time this year, maybe September or October, even sooner if I get the chance. I am not sure where, maybe Manchester. I like it there. There's plenty of them knocking about. They never learn do they, George? I bet you've warned them, but they never listen. At the rate I'm going I should be in the Book of Records. I think it's eleven up to now, isn't it? Well, I'll keep on going for quite a while yet. Even if you do get near I'll probably top myself first. Well, it's been nice chatting to you, George. Yours Jack the Ripper. No good looking for fingerprints. You should know by now it's clean as a whistle. See you soon. Bye. Hope you like the catchy tune at the end. Ha.Ha.Ha."

There followed a six-line reprise from one of the pop songs of the time, Andrew Gold's hit 'Thank You For Being A Friend'.

The atmosphere at the end of the chilling recording was electric. The Ripper Squad, via various newspapers, had previously received letters claiming to be from the multiple murderer. But this kind of show of sick bravado was virtually unheard of, in England at least. The tape was played immediately on the next radio and television news bulletins. Newspaper hoardings throughout the country all conveyed the voice of The Ripper to the evening commuters. Television stations world-wide carried pictures of the historic press conference and the mocking tape. Britain's biggest ever manhunt was set to stumble from blunder to blunder, since the tapes were in fact bogus.

By the time of the news conference Peter Sutcliffe's blade and ball-pein hammer had claimed ten lives. The deaths of Jacqueline Hill, Marguerite Walls and Barbara Leach may all have been prevented if so much hadn't been pinned on the bogus tapes. But hindsight is a precise science and the Ripper Squad were not privy to it. Or were they?

In the summer of 1992 in Melbourne, Australia, we were filming a conference on serial murder for a Central Television documentary. In an exclusive interview with a retired FBI agent we were told startling new details about the Yorkshire Ripper investigation. It dated back 13 years, to a purely chance meeting at Bramshill, the police staff training college in England. It shone a disturbing new light on the Sutcliffe case.

Thrown together by unplanned circumstances, were detective John Domaile of the Ripper Task Force and FBI Special Agent Robert K Ressler. Ressler had already made his mark on a number of senior British officers interested in the work he was helping to pioneer with the FBI's Behavioural Science Unit. This, in fact, was why he was in England at the time. One of the founding fathers of offender profiling and the man who first coined the term 'serial killer', Ressler was intrigued by Domaile's accounts of the Ripper hunt. In the course of conversation the tape recording of the now infamous Geordie voice was played to him.

"I told Domaile a number of things," said the FBI man. "Firstly, without hearing the tape, I informed him that I was certain that the killer they were hunting was going to kill again and again until he was caught. There was no way this guy was going to stop. He was enjoying it far too much. Then, when I heard the tape I told him and some other officers who were with him, that the voice on the tape and the killer of those women were not one and the same person."

Domaiie was predictably hooked and pressed Ressler to gauge what type of man he thought they should be looking for. The FBI strongly resist off-the-cuff profiles and Ressler, although a maverick even by Bureau standards, stuck to the rules. He did however, promise co-operation if full details, along with a set of crime-scene pictures and pathology reports were sent over to Quantico, the FBI Behavioural Science Unit's base. The Yorkshire detective was not satisfied and persisted. Eventually, after a jocular 'bribe' of a couple of pints, the American came up with an impromptu profile of the Ripper.

Ressler recalled: "We didn't see the crime scenes because they didn't have any stills with them, but based on their descriptions of the killings, the victims and the circumstances, we felt that the guy would have been a white male, aged between late 20s into the mid-30s. We thought that he would be married. He would be in a vocation where he would have to travel a lot. He would have to travel into the areas where some of the victims disappeared from and we had him pegged as being a truck driver, though we also suggested perhaps a postman."

At the end of a tiring day, after a couple of drinks and with a great deal of reluctance, Ressler had produced a profile that was disturbingly accurate. He had got race, sex, age, marital status and occupation all correct. Compare this to the Geordie composite produced by Assistant Chief Constable George Oldfield, who had a lot more to go on than the five minute briefing Ressler had: "An artisan or manual worker, either skilled or unskilled, with engineering or mechanical connections. He is possibly a machine-tool fitter, electrical or maintenance engineer."

Ressler says his offer of further assistance from the FBI was never followed up. The Ripper Squad subsequently stumbled off in search of the non-existent Sunderland traveller who existed only in George Oldfield's imagination. This refusal to accept help, was not, Ressler believes, because of Domaile's lack of interest but rather his superiors' distaste for involving the Americans. He recalls: "In the Sutcliffe case, the officers that were interested were lower in rank in the inquiry and apparently their superiors were not impressed with the newfangled American criminal profiling process."

Given another two years, police did catch the Ripper. Peter Sutcliffe was cornered in January, 1981, for a motoring offence. It was the night of January 2 when Sergeant Bob Ring and

Police Constable Robert Hyde spotted prostitute Olivia Reivers climbing into a 3.5 litre Rover in Melbourne Avenue, Sheffield. They slipped into the age-old practise of approaching the kerb-crawler and the streetwalker and began the routine booking that accompanies soliciting in red light areas. The driver, who gave his name as Peter Williams, nervously climbed from the car and asked to relieve himself behind some bushes. Once there, he dropped into the undergrowth, a ball-pein hammer and a razor-sharp knife. They were just two of the 50 weapons he had used during his half-decade of murder. By the time Sutcliffe returned to his car the officers had already established it had false number-plates. At Hammerton Road Police Station the man went to the toilet for a second time and hid another knife in a cistern. Here he told officers his real name, Peter William Sutcliffe, and admitted that he had stolen the plates from a scrap-yard in Dewsbury, West Yorkshire.

For some time, his main worry seemed to be that his wife would be told that he had been discovered with a prostitute. Throughout the evening he was calm and helpful and even confided to the officers that he had once been interviewed by detectives in the neighbouring West Yorkshire force in relation to the £5 note found near Jean Jordan's body in Manchester. It was by that time standard practise for all of Britain's 43 police forces to alert the Ripper Squad if they arrested a man in the company of a known prostitute. Sutcliffe was kept in police cells overnight while the procedure was followed. As his name was passed through to office managers in the incident room it became apparent that Sutcliffe had actually been interviewed by police on four occasions and his name had been in the system a total of nine times. Alarm bells began to ring. They became positively deafening when police revisited the scene of the arrest and found the weapons he had been about to use for a further murder.

Peter Sutcliffe sat opposite the Murder Squad's Detective Inspector John Boyle. The policemen mentioned the discovery of the hammer and knife and added: "I think you're in trouble, serious trouble." There was a tense silence. Sutcliffe finally

spoke: "I think you are leading up to the Yorkshire Ripper."
Boyle said: "Well, what about the Yorkshire Ripper?". "Well"
said Sutcliffe, "That's me."

But for sheer chance Sutcliffe, as Ressler had predicted,
would have continued killing. After his conviction there was a
public outcry over how he had managed to avoid capture for so
long. Her Majesty's Chief Inspector of Constabulary, Sir
Lawrence Byford, was called in to report on the deficiencies to
the Home Secretary. Sir Lawrence urged the use of computerization for major inquiries. This would lead to the adoption of
the Home Office Large Major Inquiry System. He was most
concerned that Sutcliffe had slipped through the system so
many times and he also recommended the appointment of a
single officer of the rank of Assistant Chief Constable to head
murder hunts when bodies were found in more than one force
area. More than anything though, the Byford inquiry showed
that British policing had been unable to cope with a modern
serial killer. It had laid the foundations for a new approach,
supported by computerization and new initiatives. That new
approach would be 'offender profiling.'

A year after Peter Sutcliffe was jailed for life, the police
service was thrown into another enormous manhunt. It involved
the murder of three women and the rape of at least 27 other
victims. Scotland Yard, British Transport Police and the
constabularies of Surrey and Hertfordshire were all involved in
a joint inquiry code-named 'Operation Hart'. This time, many
of the mistakes of the Ripper investigation were avoided. A
Chief Superintendent was placed in overall command of the
hunt and new Home Office incident room computers were
brought in to help dam the torrent of paperwork and ensure
proper cross-referencing of suspects. Even with computerization it was a difficult and complex case. Officers were originally unsure of exactly how many murders were linked, there
was evidence to connect dozens of other rapes to the killings
and there was confusion over whether some of the attacks had
been carried out by two men working together or one man on
his own.

In the early series of the rapes, victims identified two
attackers, but towards the end of the series only one was being
reported. It had all the potential problems of the Yorkshire
investigation and more. Here was serial rape and murder, with
sometimes two offenders and sometimes one. More disturbing,
were indications that the attacks were becoming more violent.

As far as detectives could work out, the rapes had started in
1982 and had come before the murders, which didn't commence
until three years later. The inquiry team plotted the offences
across a map of south-east England. Twenty seven pins clustered around the London area, indicating where most of the
attacks had happened. Many of the victims had reported that
one of the men had 'laser beam eyes', a disconcerting stare that
frightened them almost as much as his actions.

In 1985, just four days after Christmas, teenager Alison Day
set out to meet her boyfriend but never arrived on their date.
The 19-year-old's raped body was found in the River Lea close
to her friend's workplace, a photographic laboratory in the
Hackney area of London. The shy, blonde secretary had been
attacked while trying to catch an east London train from the
isolated Hackney Wick station. She had been threatened with a
knife, battered about the head and dragged behind a block of
derelict garages. Her attacker ordered her to strip to the waist
and cut her blouse into ribbons with his razor-sharp knife. He
blindfolded her with the shredded garment and bound her hands
and thumbs together in a praying position but behind her back.
A scarf had been wrapped around her neck and a stick twisted
through it, so that it could be turned like a tourniquet. Closer
examination showed that a knot had been precisely tied on the
scarf, so that it would dig into the windpipe and crush the
Adam's apple. It was an unusual type of garrotting that is sometimes referred to as a 'Spanish windlass'. The offender had also
made an attempt at avoiding detection as Alison's clothing had
been thrown into the river. When divers fished it from the wash,
most but not all of the forensic evidence had been destroyed.
The Metropolitan police crime lab discovered a number of fibres
that they bagged-up, hoping they had come from her killer.

Senior officers in 'Operation Hart' connected this murder to one that happened four months later in April 1986. Just 30 miles from the first murder the raped, strangled and partially burned body of schoolgirl Maartje Tamboezer was found in woods near her home in London's West Horsley district. It became apparent that the 15-year-old had been riding her bicycle back from a local shop along a short-cut running by a railway track. She was thrown from the bike by an outstretched fishing line tied across her path and when she tumbled to the ground, she was grabbed and hauled into the woods where she was battered about the head, raped and killed. She had been tied-up in a similar fashion to Alison Day; only this time the bindings were made from an unusually strong form of paper string called Somyarn, which police subsequently traced back to a factory at Preston in Lancashire.

Just as Alison's murderer had shown a degree of forensic awareness, so too had this killer. Maartje's attacker had strangled her and then after the rape had wiped semen from her dead body with tissues. He set light to these tissues and also to others that he had placed inside her vagina.

The killer had not been careful enough. Scientists microscopically searched every thread of the dead girl's clothing and gathered enough semen traces to give a blood grouping of the attacker. They pinned him down as a 'Type A' (one in three of the population) but also ascertained that he was part of a much smaller group of people classed as 'secretors'. By further analyzing the sample, according to what's known as a PGM (phosphoglucomutase) factor, they filtered his grouping down to one in five. This would be of little use in catching the offender, but could provide vital additional evidence if a suspect were taken to court.

The Tamboezer murder received enormous media coverage and the public response to police appeals for help was considerable. There had been a number of sightings of a stocky but small man running to catch a train to London, near the murder site and at about the time of Maartje's death. Detectives were as thorough as their colleagues in the science labs. They traced more than a million train tickets in the hope of finding his fingerprints. None bore the vital clues they were seeking.

Detective Chief Superintendent Vince McFadden was the Head of Surrey C I D and the officer in overall command of the combined rapes and murders investigation. The pressures that had fallen on the leading officers in the Ripper hunt were now all on his shoulders. He had the added burden of politicians and the media continually warning him about making the same mistakes as the commanding officers in the Sutcliffe case. It was against this intimidating backdrop that he took the unusual step of calling in help from a professor in psychology at Surrey University in Guildford.

"We had a number of incidents running throughout the Home Counties, one of which was at Hendon. On one of my visits there I met Dr David Canter from the University. He had been with a senior Metropolitan Police officer and had been discussing other aspects at the time. He very briefly told me about the kind of work that he did and he made the offer to help us. At that point I knew that I had got a very difficult and complex inquiry on my hands and it was clear that unless we caught the individual or individuals involved, then they would carry on killing and raping. I was conscious of the fact that because it was so complex, there was a chance that at the end of the day, despite our best efforts the case would be undetected. I did not intend to be found wanting, to be accused of being blinkered or having a closed-look on the job and I saw Canter as as an insurance policy. This was just another aspect of the investigation that we could use. It was different to anything that we had done before and if people came along afterwards to look at the inquiry, then I could show that we had used all manner of means to try and detect it."

It was a policy that would pay dividends, not just for this inquiry but for all future policing in Britain. Vince McFadden is a carefully spoken and exceptionally modest man. He writes off the initiative of using a psychologist as though it were purely a selfish way of 'covering his own back'. The truth is far from that as even prior to Canter's involvement, McFadden had been a strong supporter of behavioural science and had pressed the case for psychological profiling with members of the powerful Association of Chief Police Officers. Over the next half decade he would become a vital member of ACPO's offender profiling sub-committee and ultimately a shrewd profiler himself.

In 1986 though, Vince McFadden took his calculated gamble by calling in what other detectives referred to as the 'trick-cyclist' from the local university. His resources were already running thin and economics had almost closed down the Hart inquiry before the Tamboezer murder. Still, he juggled the shifts of his incident room personnel and freed two detectives to help Canter assemble the reports, charts and information he needed.

Detective Constable Rupert Heritage had just returned from holiday when he learned of his new role in the murder squad. "They just told me that I was getting a computer and a professor and I was a stranger to both at the time. I was uncertain which one would give me more trouble." A die-hard, old-fashioned bobby, Heritage found himself strangely fascinated by Canter's academic approach to the rapes and murders. What Canter lacked in police know-how, Heritage supplied with his years of experience. What Heritage lacked in scientific discipline and precision research, Canter readily made up for. It was a perfect partnership and one which continued long after the 'Railway Rapist' had been caught. Heritage stayed at the university on secondment from Surrey Police and also became part of the ACPO profiling group.

The police and the professor made steady progress. No one, David Canter included, really knew what he could contribute to the inquiry. He'd been honest enough to make that plain to McFadden on day one. Until this point, psychiatrists had been held in much the same regard as psychics. Senior officers couldn't afford to ignore their advice if it had been given, but they certainly wouldn't actively seek it, let alone encourage it by detailing officers and resources on such a project.

Canter retraced much of the police paperwork, but he did it in an entirely different manner. Instead of just sticking pins in a map to show where the attacks had taken place, he did it far more scientifically. He dealt with the offences chronologically, starting with what was believed to be the first rape, in the early hours of Thursday, June 10, 1982. He used acetate sheets to build up the sequence of attacks layer upon layer on the map. He immediately began to notice what some detectives in the Ripper inquiry had called 'the centre of gravity' effect. This quite simply meant that the rapes formed a sort of circle, with a few clustered around the middle of it. Surrey police had done a similar exercise but Canter's skills as an environmental psychologist gave him a different perspective. He noticed that the centralized offences were the early attacks. His training told him that everybody does things according to a mental mapping system built up by their knowledge of their local surroundings. Canter used this experience to guess that the first offences were carried out near to the killer's home and then as the offender grew more confident he attacked further and further away. He fixed the killer's address as the Kilburn area of London.

Canter also tore apart every last detail of the victims' statements, scene of crime photographs, post-mortem examination reports and police notes. He looked at the offences of the two men together and of the one man on his own. He concluded that the latest rapes and the two murders had been carried out by just one man. This man would be the dominant and leading personality in the double-handed attacks and it would be his actions, possibly an escalation of the violence in each offence, which had alienated the 'follower'. The boffin, as detectives called him, astutely argued that the degree of sexual maturity shown during the attacks indicated that the killer wasn't a teenager and was probably someone in his late 20s who was, or who had been, married. He also deduced that anyone who could strangle and burn a woman's body must have had a stormy and sometimes violent relationship with his wife.

As Dr Canter began to build up his 'profile', a sequence of tragic events began which would eventually lead to the capture of the 'Railway Rapist'. Exactly a month after the murder of Maartje Tamboezer, John Francis Duffy was arrested for loitering near a railway station. When police searched him, they discovered he was armed with a sharp military style knife. Duffy told them that he was into martial arts and the knife was needed for weapons practise at his lessons in nearby Kilburn. His name was logged into the computer at the murders incident room and he was released. The following day, Sunday, May 18, 1986, he killed again.

His victim this time, was 29-year-old Anne Locke, a newly married secretary who had just returned from her honeymoon. She had been heading home to Hertfordshire after a long day's work at the London Weekend Television studio in the heart of London. Her decomposed body wasn't discovered until ten weeks later. It had been dumped in dense undergrowth near the British rail station at Brookmans Park close to her house.

The few clues that detectives already had, allowed them to make a successful link between this killing and the two other murders. The hands had again been tied behind the back with the characteristic binding of the thumbs and once more there had been an attempt to destroy semen traces by burning the pubic area of the corpse. This horrible attempt to destroy forensic evidence had never been seen in an English murder until these killings. Again, the skilled eyes and fingers of the forensic scientists extracted minuscule semen samples from the dead woman's clothing. They came up with the same blood grouping as the killer of Maartje Tamboezer.

It is believed that around a third of Britain's male population has committed some form of criminal offence and is therefore traceable through police computer records. The office managers of the 'Operation Hart' incident room filtered an enormous list of sex offenders, down to about 5,000 possible suspects. Further inquiries reduced this to a more workable, but still daunting roll-call of 1,999 suspects.

New data was now fed into the computer. It was given the Canter 'profile'. The 17 points the psychologist drew up contained much of the information police were already aware of but also some highly skilled and vital guesswork. Canter fixed the offender's age at mid to late 20s (indicated by sightings of him and his sexual maturity during the offences). He thought he

would have light hair and be about 5ft 9in tall (witness statement information), be right-handed (a guess from police injury
and post-mortem reports) and be blood group 'A' (forensic
report information). Now the profile got bolder. Canter's date
and location analysis of the offences convinced him that the
offender would have lived in the Kilburn area of London since
the time of the first rapes. His age group, the way he talked to
his victims and his level of sexual action during the crimes, led
the professor to guess that he would be married or have a
regular girlfriend but probably no children. To get away with
his crimes for so long, he had to be a 'loner', someone who
didn't mix in a large circle of friends, who might notice any odd
behaviour or regular absences at the times of the rapes and
murders. Apart from his wife or girlfriend, Canter believed he
would have little contact with other women. He also thought he
would have very few men friends and if employed, would be in
a job that did not bring him into regular contact with the public.

The degree of control that he exhibited at the crime scene, in
binding the women and talking to his rape victims before and
after the offences, was indicative of the man's social skills and
possible occupation group. Canter thought he had the intelligence and manual dexterity of someone who might well be in a
skilled or semi-skilled job. The time of the single attacks were
predominantly during the mid to late evenings (when acting on
his own) and usually in the early hours of the morning when
involved in the double-handed rapes, gave the psychologist
clues to a possible working pattern. He also discovered that for
some periods the assaults happened at weekends and at other
times they occurred during the week. This could be indicative
of a change of shift patterns or a period of unemployment. The
profile suggested that the offender would have been employed
in a job that involved weekend working or casual labour from
about June 1984 onwards. It also suggested that he had a
working knowledge of the rail-lines where the attacks happened
and could be or have been employed by British Rail.

The most startling observation contained in the profile, was
the reference to the offender's criminal record. The degree of

forensic awareness at the crime scene (the attempt to destroy semen from the body and clothes) indicated that the attacker had probably been arrested in the past and subjected to police searches. Canter thought the offender would have a fairly recent criminal record but warned that it might not specifically be for a sexual assault. The violence shown during the murders indicated that it could be for another type of offence such as assault.

When all the profile characteristics were typed into the murder squad computer, it cross-referenced the details with the personal files on the 1,999 suspects. Only one name came out. It was John Duffy of Barlow Road, Kilburn. He had been listed as suspect number 1,505. Chief Superintendent McFadden says Duffy was however already the number one suspect for some of the inquiry team. "I had a number of senior investigating officers throughout the south-east of England who were working on a number of suspects and I had to try and decide which suspect was better than the others. The senior investigating officer in Guildford had picked out a number of individuals and one in particular, John Duffy. When you saw the profile produced by David Canter it certainly reaffirmed what the senior officer was saying. When it comes to resources and you have an enormous amount of resources employed in this sort of inquiry, then if you have something which enables you to use a minimum of resources, then it makes the inquiry that bit more efficient and it means the person is likely to be arrested that much quicker." McFadden says he was confident enough in the accuracy of the profile to put Duffy under surveillance, a costly operation that is always a sizable drain on a murder squad's diminishing finances.

At one point the special observations team blew its cover and the suspect realized he was being tailed. As Duffy began jumping on trains at the last second and started to change his personal appearance by shaving off his moustache, police realized that their covert operation had been rumbled. McFadden and his team could not take the chance of Duffy giving them the slip and claiming another life, so he was arrested.

Duffy fitted the Canter profile like a glove. The psychologist had pinpointed the killer's address with more accuracy than a Gulf War Smart missile. The age range of mid to late 20s was tremendously close. Duffy was 30 when arrested and about 25 when he first started raping women. He was certainly a loner and had indeed been involved in a stormy marriage which, by the time of his arrest, had dissolved. Canter's assumption that the offender was childless was also correct. Duffy and his wife had been trying for a child but his sperm count was too low and he grew angry at his infertility, believing it to be a slight on his masculinity. The occupational profile was also close. Duffy had been a British Rail carpenter in Euston but had been made unemployed in 1982. Despite being made redundant he held onto his free rail travel pass and when police examined tickets after the Tamboezer murder, this allowed him to go undetected. In all, David Canter was accurate in 13 of the 17 profile characteristics he had drawn up. The most startling inaccuracy was the offender's height. Drawing on witness statements Canter estimated him to be 5ft 9in, while in fact Duffy was only 5ft 4in and was very sensitive about his small stature. Despite the mistake, a valuable lesson was learned. It was later established that most rape victims considerably over-estimate the size of their attackers and such information is now treated with considerable caution.

From a profiling perspective, John Duffy had been a complex individual to assess. As an offender, he exhibited both caring and sadistic characteristics. During some of his rapes he would tell his victims that he had VD and they were now going to be infected. On other occasions he would sit with the women, during what police call the 'cool down' period after the rape and talk to them as though it had been a consenting sexual affair. While he set alight the pubic area of his murder victims, he would also redress the victim afterwards, so the corpse was not found in too humiliating a position. Like many serial offenders he took items of underwear from his crime scenes as trophies of his conquest and as mementos that would help trigger-off future masturbatory fantasies.

In custody, Duffy said nothing. He took full advantage of his right to silence and held the attitude that the police were going to have to prove their case against him, every step of the way. 'Operation Hart' was more than ready for such a challenge. A search of Duffy's mother's home found incriminating evidence, in the form of the unusual paper string that he had used to bind the hands of his victims. Mrs Duffy had worked in a local laundry and this particular type of wide-edged string, called Somyarn had been used there to bind up clothing. The string was unavailable in shops and was subsequently traced back to a batch made at a factory in Lancashire. All Duffy's clothing was seized and sent to the Metropolitan Police Crime Labs to try to find fibre links to any of the rapes and murders, but it was verbal rather than physical evidence that convinced detectives they had the right man.

Duffy's ex-wife Margaret told the police officers that during a row, Duffy had told her she was frigid and that her sexual coolness towards him had forced him to go out and rape a woman. She said that he had bragged that rape was a natural thing for a man to do and often against her will, he would tie her up and force her to have sex with him. Police always treat such information with caution, it is not unusual for a bitter ex-partner to extract a little revenge by deliberately lying about their former spouse. In Margaret Duffy's case this was not true.

Detectives also interviewed a friend, who carried out martial arts lessons with Duffy. Duffy had told him he was being 'framed' by police for a rape that he hadn't done. He persuaded his friend to punch him in the face, hard enough to cause visible bruising and also slash him across the chest with a razor. The mock attack had taken place in July 1986, the day Duffy had been routinely called in by police to give a blood sample.

After establishing the blood group of the 'Railway Rapist', officers had started a mass 'blooding', working their way through the electoral roll. Duffy had turned up with a solicitor and, as was his legal right, had refused to give the requested sample. He was smaller than witness estimates of their attacker and he had ginger rather than fair hair. Nevertheless, his refusal was enough to make him a prime suspect and Duffy realized this. Within hours of the encounter, he turned up at a police station in Hampstead, claiming to have been mugged. The severe injuries he displayed and his apparent amnesia, led to him being admitted to hospital. When detectives from 'Operation Hart' turned up to carry out a follow-up interview with him, doctors denied them access.

The pressure of the inquiry was such, that manpower was redirected onto the other 1,998 suspects who still had to be cleared. Duffy soon became an out-patient from the hospital and raped his last victim, a 14-year-old schoolgirl. Again he bound her thumbs and hands behind her back in the same fashion as the other victims. He also blindfolded her before the attack but this slipped off during the offence. Inexplicably, the man who had already murdered three times did not kill her, despite realizing that she had seen his face. It is possible that he simply did not have the stomach for another murder and was trying to regulate his own behaviour. Eventually his worst dreams came true and the teenager stood in the witness box at the Old Bailey to identify him.

Being identified was Duffy's long standing fear and possibly more than anything else the reason why he moved from rape to murder. In 1985, Duffy appeared at Hendon Magistrates' Court charged with assaulting his wife, and by accident, he spotted his fifth rape victim in the court building. She did not recognize him but he had no problem recollecting her. He made himself a vow that there would be no other survivors to identify and convict him, 27 days later, he killed Alison Day.

The case against Duffy was a difficult one. Forensic scientists found enough fibre evidence to link his clothes with a sheepskin coat belonging to Alison and the testimonies of his wife and friend were also crucial evidence.

In February, 1988 John Francis Duffy was convicted of four charges of rape and the murders of Alison Day and Maartje Tamboezer. Judge Mr Justice Farquarson described him as "little more than a predatory animal who behaved in a beastly, degrading and disgusting way." He was sentenced to seven life sentences with a recommendation that he serve at least 30 years in jail. The jury was directed by the judge to return a not guilty verdict on the Anne Locke murder charge, on the grounds that there was insufficient evidence. The police however, closed their files on the Locke case and are not seeking another suspect. Duffy's partner in the rape crimes was never prosecuted and although detectives know who he is, they lack evidence to bring him to trial.

Canter was bitten by the profiling bug and with the assistance of some Home Office financing he continued the research he had started. Detective Constable Rupert Heritage stayed on at Surrey University to study the special brand of investigative psychology the professor was pioneering. He was joined by Superintendent Rick Holden from Yorkshire who pursued special research into the rape, murder and assault of elderly people and Anne Davies, a brilliant forensic biologist from the Metropolitan Police Science Labs. Canter soon had the basis for Britain's only Profiling Research Unit and they were inundated with requests for help from other police forces. By 1992 they had been centrally involved in more than 60 rape and murder cases, had helped jail more than a dozen dangerous criminals and had started the world's first MSc course in Investigative Psychology.

Anne Davies had been one of the tenacious forensic biologists working at the Metropolitan Police Science Laboratories on evidence from the Duffy cases. While much of the credit for helping solve the case has gone to David Canter, her role has been somewhat overlooked. She was responsible for originally linking all the rapes together by arduous blood grouping and semen tests. Her later tests linked the murders in with the rapes and also provided the vital information that showed when two men were offending and when Duffy was carrying out attacks on his own. Without the skills of Anne Davies, there simply wouldn't have been enough information to build a viable inquiry upon.

Genetic fingerprinting as it is now known, wasn't used on the 'Railway Rapes' as it was still in its infancy. Davies became actively involved in the development of DNA testing and was the driving force behind the establishment of a computerized Sexual Assaults Index which helps track all serious sexual offenders. Within its first two years more than 3,000 DNA profiles of known offenders had been logged into a computer database. Many of the victim statements were supplied to David Canter and his research team to help develop profiling information on serial rapists.

Working alongside Canter and drawing from the experience of FBI profilers and their work in America, she soon found that when DNA evidence wasn't strong enough to link possible rapes or murders, she could turn to the behavioural science of profiling to establish whether one man was responsible for a series of offences. She realized that criminals leave their psychological signature at the crime scene. Duffy's unique way of garrotting his murder victims and the odd practise of redressing them after death are examples of his 'signature'.

At Hendon Police College, the small blonde who is the Met's Principal Scientific Officer, begins to lecture a class of detectives on the developing art of offender profiling. As the lights dim and the slide projector flickers into life, two young cops struggle to decide who Mrs Davies looks like. They settle on the author Jilly Cooper and pleased with their comparison, pass on their whispered observation to colleagues gathered in the darkness.

The hushed comments are silenced by the white and red image that blazes into the screen like a branding iron. It is the mutilated body of a young woman. Her breasts have been severed and placed ritualistically beside her, her intestines have been ripped out of a giant jagged stomach wound, the head is a jellied mash of battered tissue and bones. The slide is the victim of a 'Lust Murderer', the psychological signature is the explosion of violence seen on the body, it is unmistakable and thankfully rarely seen in Britain. Anne Davies remarks that Peter Sutcliffe was a 'Lust Murderer' and points out that the 'Lust' element is little to do with a passion for sex and far more with a passion for homicide.

The purpose of the lecture is to educate young officers in how to pick up behavioural clues from a crime scene, as well as looking out for the more traditional forensic ones. It is a way of introducing investigative psychology at the roots of the police and Mrs Davies is a polished speaker who holds her audience with a vibrant mix of case studies and scientific theory.

"I run the DNA index, but DNA isn't everything. If you are going to identify serial offenders it has to be multi-disciplinary. If there isn't DNA, there could be conventional fingerprints that link the cases. If the rapist or killer carries out his attacks inside someone's house, then there could be fingerprints on the window. I need to know about those fingerprints. The 'Stockwell Strangler' (Kenneth Erskine) came through windows, he knelt on people's chests and he strangled them one-handedly. So the pathologist's information was very instrumental in proving links in his murder cases."

Through a white haze of dust and smoke the projector fired-up a picture of 24-year-old Erskine, the killer of four men and three women. He targeted pensioners; people who fall into what Anne Davies classifies as a 'vulnerable victim' group. His victims were aged between 67 and 94 and he sexually assaulted and raped them before and after death. The type of victim an offender picks is an important clue to profilers; it is an insight into the personality of the attacker. Erskine picked on old people because they weren't a physical or sexual threat to him. They were easy-pickings he could control and dominate. He was weak and mentally retarded with acute sexual and psychological problems.

Anne Davies spells out to detectives that Erskine's crimes had all the hallmarks of a burglar turned killer, and this is exactly what he was. As well as breaking into the homes he robbed his victims of hundreds of pounds, which he invested in separate building society savings accounts. At his trial, prosecuting counsel James Crespi, QC told the court, "In each case the killing was wanton. It wasn't done for the kind of reason which might induce a burglar in ordinary circumstances to kill. When you put all the circumstances in this case together, there is not only a pattern but a striking one. In our submission the intent of the burglar was to kill and maybe to gratify his sexual inclinations."

The court was told that Erskine had toyed with his victims and enjoyed killing. One survivor, 74-year-old Frederick Prentice, said that Erskine had tried to strangle him at his home in Clapham, south-west London. He remembered that throughout the attack, Erskine had said only one word, "Kill!". Mr Prentice had managed to pick his attacker out of an identity parade following the assault and along with forensic evidence this led to his eventual conviction.

During the 15 day trial at the Old Bailey, Kenneth Erskine, who was said to have the mental age of an 11-year-old, was seen smiling regularly at police officers and witnesses. At one point people in the public gallery complained to court ushers they could see him masturbating in the dock and he had to be forced to stop by prison officers. Detectives who'd interviewed Erskine after his arrest, had also reported that he would start masturbating while they interrogated him about the murders of the elderly people. He told them that he had wanted to be famous but that he couldn't actually recall having carried out any of the killings. He added, "I don't remember killing anyone. I could have done it without knowing it. I am not sure if I did."

He claimed his victims between April and July of 1986 mostly in the Stockwell area of south London, which explains his nickname. As a child he had twice tried to hang his younger brother John. When he was seen by psychiatric nurses for treatment as a youngster he would rub himself against them or expose himself to them. On one occasion he grabbed a nurse and held a pair of scissors to her throat.

He had been educated at a school for maladjusted children and would frequently attack staff and other pupils. He tried to drown other schoolchildren in the swimming baths and stabbed a teacher through the hand with a pair of scissors. His school psychiatric records showed that he lived in a fantasy world where he would play out the role of 'Lawrence of Arabia' and would imagine tying up people and attacking them.

Anne Davies told the detectives the crime scenes had contained many psychological clues to Erskine's mental problems and previous convictions. "One of the habits he had at his murder scenes was to cover up the photographs in his victim's house, the family photographs that would normally be standing on dressing tables or cabinets. You will hear of paedophiles and rapists avoiding eye-contact with their victims but this guy I think was the ultimate in avoiding eye-contact. He would lay the photographs down or he would cover them up. This is what the Americans would call a signature of this man's crimes."

The slide carousel whirls and clicks, Erskine's famous grin beams down from the projector screen. Davies continues: "After killing his victims by kneeling on their chest, breaking their ribs and strangling them one-handed, he would then wash them, tidy them up and put them back in bed. Knowing this, we could work out that he was a necrophile."

The slide changes. An old man, bleached white by death, appears. He's tucked-up in bed as though a caring relative had just left the room. "Sometimes, with his crimes, it was very difficult to determine whether sexual activity took place before or after death. Given that this old man was bedridden and Erskine characteristically came in through windows and strangled his victims while kneeling on them, then you need to look closer at the photograph. You can just make out blood and saliva on the floor and it looks to me as though he was murdered, then buggered on the floor, washed and put back into bed. In fact, you can just make out wounds to his cheek and arm, which are clearly post-mortem wounds. So, there he is, nicely washed up and tidily put back in bed. One of Erskine's other victims was so cleaned up he almost went for burial. In fact it was the son of the victim who was concerned about a bruise on his father's cheek who stopped the burial. They'd actually got the undertakers in, the place had been stripped, washing was in bags and everything was underway, when the son said 'Hold on, I'm not happy about that bruise on his cheek' and the police were called."

Kenneth Erskine, who had an IQ of only 73, was jailed for a minimum of 40 years, the longest recommendation in a British murder trial. Police are convinced that he'd actually murdered many more old men and women than the seven he was tried for. His strange fantasies and the fact that he was excited by the suffering of his victims makes him part of a rare breed of British killers who are classed as sadists. Sadism is just one of the sexually abnormal signs that experts like Anne Davies look for when examining crime scene information.

Erskine was caught because he left a palm print at one of his crime scenes. Detectives reasoned that because the pensioners' homes had been expertly broken into and money and goods had been taken their killer might have previously been a burglar. They were correct and lengthy checks through fingerprint records produced a match. What police had done was perform a basic psychological profile. They had established that their offender was unlikely to have started as a rapist, murderer and necrophile and had probably served an apprentice as a burglar. It seems like little more than common sense (once it has been pointed out) and that is the very essence of offender profiling.

Statistics show that burglars often graduate to rapists, rapists frequently become murderers and then are capable of anything. A similarity to the Erskine case and a practical example of this harsh lesson is the reign of terror by the 'Californian Night Stalker', Richard Ramirez.

Like Erskine, Ramirez was a prolific petty criminal, earning his wages through the art of burglary. Ramirez also had other black interests in the form of the occult. The self-confessed Satanist began adding a new dimension to his break-ins in June 1984. For the next 15 months he would not content himself with stealing other people's money and property – he began to steal their lives and those of their children as well.

Ramirez would pick properties at random and having broken in would then decide his crime. If no one was home, he simply stole. If he came across men they were instantly shot or stabbed. Most were killed while they slept in their beds. Women were his favourite target and they were beaten and tortured before being raped and sexually assaulted. One woman had her eyes gouged out during an attack and Ramirez would frequently leave his 'signature' at the murder, by marking a Black Magic pentagram either on the victim's body or on a wall near to it. Like Erskine, he favoured the psycho-sexual excitement of strangling his women by hand, and if this wasn't possible they were stabbed or shot. Ramirez would also abduct and abuse any children that he found in the households. Some of the boys and girls were as young as six but he would drag them into his car and drive miles away. They would be raped and sodomized and he would then turn them loose to wander the streets.

Just as Erskine was caught through a careless palm print, Ramirez was also arrested because of the skill of fingerprint experts. FBI profilers had predicted that Ramirez would be a former burglar turned rapist and killer. When one of his smudged fingerprints was found on a stolen getaway car, the computerized fingerprint retrieval system in Los Angeles matched Ramirez to the crime. The killer's police mug shot was pulled from the files and circulated to Californian television stations and newspapers.

Richard Ramirez was recognized after he'd attempted to steal a handbag and assault its owner. Her husband attacked him and as he fled he was recognized by a number of people. The mob cornered Ramirez, battered him senseless and held him captive until the police came.

At the end of his trial in September, 1989 he was found guilty of 13 murders, five attempted murders, 11 sexual assaults and 14 burglaries. He showed no remorse and he mocked the jury with his satanic beliefs flashing a pentagram scrawled on his palm at them. He told them, "You maggots make me sick. I will be avenged, Lucifer dwells within us all." When sentenced to death, Ramirez concluded, "Big deal, death comes with the territory" then he jeered at them, "See you in Disneyland!"

Back at Hendon in London, Anne Davies is impressing on detectives, the importance of burglary in the career of aspiring rapists and murderers. She indicates that the type of things stolen from a crime scene can be significant clues to an offender's character. "Theft is a very important category. We need to know what was taken, why and when. If a man steals

£5, then is that all the girl had? Did he take it because he took everything he could get his hands on, or did he take it just because he could? Did he take £5 and leave other money and lots of expensive jewellery? Different types of men from different backgrounds will do different things in those situations. The things that they steal are also important. For example, if you have a rapist that is stealing knickers, then that could be a sign that you are hunting a serial offender." Davies believes the knickers would have been stolen for masturbatory fantasies and as a form of trophy hunting. "Most of the rapists I deal with in an urban population, some 70 or 80 percent, already have criminal records. They are usually for offences such as taking and driving away cars, petty dishonesty, shoplifting and burglary. So, evaluating the importance of theft to an offender can be a clue to their previous convictions."

Before John Duffy began murdering his victims, he and the friend he carried out most of the rapes with, were stopped by traffic police. In the car officers discovered balaclavas, some wire and a box of matches. They mistakenly thought the two men had been stopped on the way to a possible burglary. In fact the odds and ends they'd come across were Duffy's rape kit. The wire was for binding, the tissues were to wipe away his semen and the matches were to burn the tissues and any clothing or areas where semen might have been. Anne Davies has noted that many other rapists are also carrying kits, some far more intricate than Duffy's. "Patrick Riley used to travel the underground in London with his rape kit (see centre illustration). Although his name is Riley, he grew up in Wales and when the Metropolitan Police went back to Wales to look into his background, people there actually said, 'Oh, you mean 'Riley the Rapist',' just as they say 'Jones the Baker, or Jones the Butcher'. Anyway, he was known as 'Riley the Rapist' back in Wales and this is his rape kit; knives to intimidate with, torches for going around at night, things to bind his victims, towels to wipe semen away, woolly hats with different coloured wigs sewn-in, so that victims would give a misleading description of his hair colour and gloves so he could go through their handbags and steal from them without leaving fingerprints. I would imagine that if most police officers stopped him and saw that they would possibly think they've got a burglar and he was going equipped for theft."

There isn't an aspect of an offender's behaviour that the scientist isn't interested in. Anne Davies conveys to the detectives the basic psychological principal that the behaviour of one person is affected by the behaviour of another. This is especially true of victim and attacker. "One of the most important things in your report is to what extent everyone is undressed. If a man takes all his clothes off during a rape then he feels confident about where he is, either perceiving no risk of interruption, no chance of being caught because there is none, or perhaps because he is very inexperienced at this type of crime. Did he tear the woman's clothing off, completely using her as an object, or did he make her undress slowly in front of him. Surprisingly enough, 20 to 30 percent of serial rapists have what is called erectile insufficiency, which is quite a problem if you are taking up a career as a rapist. Others have trouble with premature ejaculation and a few have an inability to ejaculate at all. It's important to know about a man's sexual problems because again it is a clue to what is going on in his mind."

Basic profiling work had been going on long before David Canter's enormous success with the Duffy case. In 1983, Paul Britton, a Consultant Psychologist from a hospital in Leicestershire had been contacted by police to help in a hunt for a murderous sadist. In July of that year 33-year-old pet beautician Caroline Osborne, who had separated from her husband, never returned home after an evening walk in nearby Aylestone Meadows. She had left with her own black labrador and a crossbred labrador belonging to a neighbour. Both dogs were called Tammy. Thirteen hours later her mutilated body was found near a local footpath. Her neighbour's dog was still standing by her side and growled when anyone approached. Her own dog had wandered back to its home in Danvers Road, Leicester.

Her corpse had been found on scrub land near the Grand Union Canal in waist-high grass. There seemed no real motive to the attack, she had not been sexually attacked or robbed. The severity and multiplicity of the stab wounds seemed to suggest that she might have been tortured.

The Head of Leicestershire CID, David Baker recalls: "We contacted Paul Britton and he was very helpful, though at that stage what he was telling us in terms of a profile wasn't of great use because we didn't have any real suspects to test it against. It was only later, unfortunately after we had a second murder, that it all became of particular value."

That next murder came in April 1985. Twenty-one-year-old Amanda Weedon was killed close to the hospital where she worked and lived. The nurse was three months away from getting married and had just arranged to pick up the keys of their new home. Her body was found by a teenage girl. It was crushed into a hedge at the side of a path next to the Groby Road Community Hospital in Leicester. She had been attacked and killed on a Saturday afternoon while her husband-to-be was at a football match. They had seen each other only three hours before her death.

The killing was similar to the Osborne murder. Amanda's body was severely mutilated and again there had been no sexual attack. This time though, a little money and a cheque card had been stolen from her handbag.

David Baker had some important decisions to make. Once more there was that difficult problem of establishing whether the crimes were connected. He telephoned Paul Britton again and asked for his thoughts on the second murder and its relationship with the first killing. The psychologist was skilled in the treatment of rapists, murderers and psychopaths and was also involved in evaluating convicted offenders, to determine whether they could be safely released from prison. He remembers the cases well: "David Baker is one of the most forward-looking detectives I have ever met. What we looked at then, is exactly the same as what we look at now. I was shown post-mortem reports and photographs, scene of crime pictures and aerial photographs of the two murder scenes. We were concerned initially with linkages between the two offences, deciding whether they could be unconnected killings. I was convinced the same man had killed twice." Britton also believed the killer would be a local man and Baker was in agreement on both assumptions.

A profile of the offender was produced by Britton and it detailed some vital areas. "I laid out what I expected in terms of his age, occupation, personal background and sexual history." Britton cited the killer as an athletic, young, local man, unmarried, sexually immature and sadistic, employed in a form of manual work. As in the Duffy case, the profile didn't give police enough to arrest anyone, but it highlighted one of their chief suspects, 19-year-old Paul Bostock.

Bostock lived near to both murders, at Beaumont Leys in Leicester. He was devoted to body-building and known to take long walks on his own. He also had a morbid fascination with horror, the occult and black magic. He was 6ft 5in tall, a strapping youth who stood out wherever he went. So much so, that when his grandmother read a police appeal for information in the local evening paper she immediately recognized her grandson as one of the people detectives wanted to interview.

Detective Superintendent Ian Leecy says it was the break he and the rest of the team had been looking for. "The grandmother told her daughter and husband and the family all had a chat about it. Then they arrived at Blackbird Road police station in Leicester with Paul and asked to see us. They'd just come in to clear his name, but after questioning him for a short while it became obvious that his story just didn't add up."

Paul Bostock did not go home with his parents – instead, Britton was contacted again by the murder squad. "At this time I was asked to come up with a strategy for the interview, to help the youngster admit the murders. At first he was very reluctant to say anything and was completely denying the murders." Leecy says the contribution was crucial, "We were able to go into the interview, ask the questions in a way that Britton had suggested and then review the answers with Britton before going on to the next stage. Eventually we had full admissions to the murders of Caroline Osborne and Amanda Weedon."

When detectives visited Bostock's home they discovered his bedroom was filled with swords, knives, guns and Kung Fu throwing stars. Among the hoard of weapons was a flick-knife that was covered in dried human blood, the knife they believed he had used to torture and murder Caroline Osborne. Detectives seized stacks of drawings that Bostock had made showing women in Black Magic rituals or being bound and tortured. He had also kept a scrapbook of naked women in the bedroom which officers dubbed 'the Devil's den'. When the teenager was arrested, he told detectives he had just left school and was only 16 when he came across Caroline Osborne. He had gone out jogging, complete with a flick-knife and a black magic penta-gram poster in his back pocket. He had stalked the woman with her dogs and then tortured and killed her. Later, when Caroline was buried he visited the cemetery to gloat over her grave. Within months the sadist had claimed his second victim in similar opportunistic circumstances.

David Baker, like Vince McFadden in the Duffy hunt, became a strong supporter of offender profiling. Both men believe that without the help of Canter and Britton they would have still got their men, eventually. The danger is, they could have killed again before police were confident enough to arrest or question them. Baker summed up a feeling felt by many senior officers. "Profiling has its place in some murder investi-gations, especially if there is more than one killing. It won't lead you to someone's front door, but if you've got a good suspect then it gives you confidence to devote more time to him than any others." At the same time Baker was involved in the Weedon and Osborne murders there was another double killing in Leicestershire, that of 15-year-olds Dawn Ashworth and Lynda Mann. Again Paul Britton played a key role in targeting the offender, a bakery worker called Colin Pitchfork. This was another historic investigation, Baker becoming the first investi-gator to use the new science of genetic fingerprinting to eventu-ally prove Pitchfork had raped and killed both girls.

While the Pitchfork inquiry was underway, Paul Bostock was jailed for life in June 1986. Was he mad or just bad?

# 2
# *Mad Or Bad?*

*"End of day, end of drinking, end of person." – Dennis Nilsen*

It is the age-old argument between seasoned police officers and psychiatrists; between prosecuting and defence counsel and between those on either side of the capital punishment debate. Is the killer mad or bad? Is he or she insane or simply evil? There are those who argue that anyone who violently takes the life of another human being cannot be normal. Therefore someone who murders again and again must surely be mad? Others point to the cunning of the serial killer who plans murders with the intricate care and detail an artist invests in his next painting. Surely someone with such rational intent cannot be mad, they argue. How could they evade capture for so long?

Most of us are ill-equipped to judge either way. The serial killer forces us to confront the worst in human nature. It is difficult for us to accept that a killer knew what he was doing, planned it and enjoyed it. It is easier for us to brand the perpetrator of hideous murders as insane. Not to do so could be an admission that we are all capable of such evil.

The 'Mad or Bad?' argument has never been so topically controversial as it is today, particularly in the United States of America. There, as states reintroduce capital punishment, verification or otherwise of insanity can literally mean the difference between life and death.

Although virtually every known serial killer could be placed in the 'Mad or Bad?' category, we have chosen to concentrate on those around whom the debate has been strongest and, in some cases, longest. These include the UK's Yorkshire Ripper and Dennis Nilsen, the USA's Arthur Shawcross and Edmund Kemper and the relatively less-known Arnold Sodeman from Australia.

Sodeman was hanged for murder at the Metropolitan Gaol in Pentridge, Australia, in June, 1936. Today's medical evidence would almost certainly have saved him from the gallows. Sodeman was the image of respectability. Happily married, he was a doting father to his small daughter when he murdered his first victim, a 12-year-old girl in November, 1930. Mena Griffiths had been playing on the swings in Melbourne's Fawkner Park when a man had kept her behind after sending her playmates off to buy sweets. She was never seen alive again. Two days later her body was found in an empty house six miles away. She had been strangled and sexually abused.

Two months later on January 10, 1931, 16-year-old Hazel Wilson was found strangled on wasteland in Melbourne's Ormond district. The sex killing was identical to that of Mena Griffiths. The discovery of Hazel's body led to the release of Bob McMahon who had been charged and actually committed for trial for Mena's murder despite a cast-iron alibi that he had not even been in the state on the day of her murder.

The hunt for a double-killer proved fruitless and after five years had been virtually forgotten until the strangled body of a 12-year-old girl was found near the seaside resort of Anderson's Inlet. Little Ethel Belshaw had been abducted after talking to a man with a bicycle while on a day trip with a party of family and friends. Arnold Sodeman had been among that party. More than 10,000 people were interviewed, including Sodeman. The happily married family man did not arouse the slightest suspicion among detectives.

Once again police had drawn a blank. They knew a child sex killer was on the loose with a precise method of murder but they had no suspect. All they could do was wait until he struck again.

A year later six-year-old June Rushmer was found strangled at Leongatha township. She too had been seen talking to a man with a bicycle. Sodeman, who rode a bicycle to and from his labouring job, had been working at a site just ten miles away from where June's body was found. Some of his workmates pulled his leg by asking if he hadn't been nearby on his bicycle. The reaction was totally out of character. Sodeman threw down his tea mug and stormed off swearing that he had been nowhere near the murder scene. One workmate was disturbed by the reaction. Arnold had developed erratic personality changes over recent years, especially after drinking. The mild-mannered family man had frequently reduced his wife and daughter to tears with his dramatic mood changes, though they never spoke of this outside the home. His workmate went to the police with his suspicions and Sodeman was arrested.

In custody and under prolonged questioning he confessed to all four murders. He described his method of strangulation and even details of his victim's last meals, evidence borne out by the hitherto secret details of the autopsy reports. At his trial he pleaded insanity but despite this he was hanged.

Sodeman's personality disorders were explained following an autopsy on his body. The examination on his opened skull revealed that for years he had suffered from chronic leptomeningitis, an inflammation of the tissue surrounding his brain. The condition was aggravated by alcohol and Sodeman liked a drink. Today's medical technology would have found the illness while Sodeman was alive. It would have provided the defence with the cast iron mitigation it needed to prove their client was not responsible for his actions and he would not have hanged.

********************

Ed Kemper sat in the interview room at Atascadero State Mental Hospital and clearly delighted his psychiatrists. They were assessing his progress since his release a few months earlier. He obviously impressed one psychiatrist who wrote in his file: "I see no psychiatric reason to consider him to be a danger to himself or any other member of society." But 21-year-old Ed, a 6ft 9in giant weighing nearly 300 pounds, was not being entirely honest with the doctors. He had held one thing back during the interview which inspired that optimistic comment. In the boot of his car, parked just outside the medical offices, lay the severed head of his latest victim.

Edmund Emil Kemper the third was described by even his own mother as 'a real weirdo'. It was an acute understatement of a son who would eventually decapitate her, place her larynx in a waste disposal unit and have sex with her dismembered body.

Kemper had been brought up in California by his divorced and domineering mother who had drifted in and out of relationships during his youth. When he was 14 she sent him to live with his grandparents in order to give him some stability. Young Ed had already showed disturbing signs by decapitating his sister's dolls and mutilating the family cat.

Grandma wrote children's books and it was while she was pouring over her latest work on August 27, 1964, that 15-year-old Ed reached for his .22 rifle. He took aim at the old lady's head and fired. He pumped two more bullets into her body before putting the gun down and picking up a large kitchen knife. He stabbed her repeatedly, so many times that doctors could not put an exact figure on it. Then he waited for his grandfather to return to the secluded ranch and gunned him down. After the killings he calmly rang his mother, told her what he had done and waited for the police to arrive. They found him surrounded by the bodies and weapons denying anything to do with the murders. Minutes later the deranged youth made a full confession.

"Why did you do it, son?" asked one detective. Unlike Yorkshire Ripper Peter Sutcliffe or David 'Son of Sam' Berkowitz there was no reference to 'voices from God' or satanic messages from demon-possessed dogs. The answer was childishly simple: "I just wondered how it would feel to shoot grandma."

What had gone on in Kemper's head? What traumatic trigger had left him with murder in mind? Was he 'Mad or Bad?' Or maybe a little of both? Kemper was more than just intelligent. He had an IQ of 136. The average is around 90. But there was no doubt in the minds of prosecutors; in December, 1964. They judged him to be insane. His court report, perhaps the most accurate diagnosis on Kemper, described him as a confused and disfunctioned psychotic who would turn out to be a long-term problem. Despite this some of the medical staff and social workers of the California Youth Authority warmed to their new admission. He was soon to be thought of as not suffering from interference of thought and expressions of delusions.

No psychologists we have interviewed have described the murder of Kemper's grandparents as 'sexual' and yet Kemper was sent to the Atascadero Mental Hospital for the treatment of sex offenders. The only sexual undertone to the murders was Kemper's contemptuous and probably tongue-in-cheek reply when asked if he regretted killing his grandmother: "I was sorry I didn't undress her after I killed her."

There is an argument that more harm than good was done during Kemper's five year term at Atascadero. At a time of developing puberty he was closeted in a sexual pressure-cooker, denied links with females his own age and also bombarded with an array of psychiatric tests. Psychiatrists concluded he gave "the impression of a rather passive, dependent person, rather than one who is overtly aggressive." His personality profile included adjectives such as "suspicious, self-opinionated, artless, apprehensive, non-critical, careless..." But as one learns more about Kemper and his ability to con and manipulate, it seems during his incarceration he learned how to 'play the game'. He returned the psychiatrist's plum phrases during counselling sessions, helping them pigeon-hole his psychosis. He generally stayed out of trouble and ultimately gained early release after five years of 'treatment'. He was paroled into the tender loving care of his mother, the same mother who had ridiculed him throughout childhood and had regularly locked him in the cellar for disappointing her. Clutching his release papers, Kemper went on to become California's notorious 'Co-ed Killer', the murderer of six young college girls. He indulged in an astonishing orgy of sadism, mutilation, necrophilia and cannibalism before running out of steam and surrendering himself to police after a year-long murder spree.

The first murders took place on May 7, 1972. Mary Ann Pesce and Anita Luchessa were room-mates at Fresno State College and Kemper picked them up as they hitch-hiked to campus. He handcuffed Pesce and placed a black plastic bag over her head before stabbing her repeatedly. He then took her friend from the boot of the car where he had bundled her earlier and stabbed her to death. He took both bodies home and photographed them before decapitating them and having sex with various dismembered body parts. He disposed of all the mutilated remains except their heads which he kept for a while as 'trophies'.

FBI Special Agent Roy Hazlewood describes this behaviour as typical of the sexual-sadist. "It's like making movies. First they plan out exactly what they're going to do and how they're going to do it. I guess that's what you call the rehearsal. Then they pick their cast, the unfortunate victim who's going to star in their show. Sometimes there's even a script. The victim is told to say certain things that the killer has fantasized about. Things like 'I love you', 'I'm yours' or whatever. The kill is the 'take'. It's a good word both in the film sense and for what the guy is doing. Quite often there is photography involved during and after death. This is what the sadist uses to keep his masturbatory fantasies alive."

After four months Kemper struck again. His victim was Aiko Koo, a 15-year-old Japanese student who was also hitch-hiking. He taped her mouth and choked her with her own muffler as he raped her and with the body in the boot, he stopped for a few beers. Once home he decapitated the body, indulged in necrophilia and dismembered the remains before burying them in the mountains near Boulder Creek. He kept the head and it was in the boot of his car when two doctors proclaimed him safe to return to society at his psychiatric assessment the next day. After his interview he returned to the car, opened the boot and told the severed head: "They say we're safe. Let's go have some beers."

Another four months went by before he claimed his next victim. He shot student Cindy Schall, took her corpse home and kept it in the closet overnight. After having sex with the body he dismembered it in his shower and later dumped the remains over cliffs at Carmel. Again, he kept the severed head.

On February 5, 1973, two more hitch-hikers made the fatal mistake of accepting a lift from the giant serial killer. He shot

Rosalind Thorpe in the temple as she sat beside him and then spun round with his .22 Ruger pistol and shot Alice Liu three times in the head. After bundling the bodies into the boot he went home. His mother was in so he decapitated both bodies in the boot of the car. The next day he took Liu's headless body into the house and had sex with it. He returned it to the car and amputated the hands before dumping both bodies in Eden Canyon, Alameda, where they were found a week later.

Arguably, in the midst of these murderous moments Kemper's homicidal rages focused not on his victims but on his mother. As a child he had sought love from her but received only rejection or reprimand and he hated the woman. Just before daybreak on Easter Sunday, 1973, he crept into her bedroom and smashed her skull with a hammer. He then carried out the ritualistic decapitation but on this special victim he went one step further. He cut out her larynx and threw it into the garbage disposal machine, bu the machine was faulty and the larynx flew up out of it. "Even when she was dead she was still bitching at me," rued Kemper after his arrest. He placed his mother's torso in the closet and her head on the mantelpiece so he could throw things at it. He later indulged in necrophilia with the body.

To complete his mother's humiliation and deprive her of anyone to mourn her passing, Kemper decided to murder her best friend. He invited neighbour Sarah Hallet round for a surprise dinner with mom. As she sat down he hit her over the head with a brick, choked her and decapitated her body before having sex with it. After putting Mrs Hallet's body to bed he made off in her car leaving a note behind. "Approx. 5.15 am Saturday. No need for her to suffer anymore at the hands of this horrible 'murderous butcher'. It was quick – asleep – the way I wanted it. Not sloppy and incomplete, gents. Just a 'lack of time'. I got things to do!!!"

Kemper, perhaps not knowing what else to do since ridding himself of the nemesis that was his mother, simply drove eastwards. After several hours he stopped – there seemed to be no more reasons to kill. From a public phone box in Pueblo, eastern Colarado the man who had murdered ten people by the age of 25 rang the police and confessed. He had to make several calls before he was taken seriously.

Despite his trail of terror, despite bizarre acts such as cooking flesh from his victims' legs in macaroni casseroles and despite being deemed mentally ill only eight years earlier, Ed Kemper was judged to be sane. His necrophilia seemed to be a classic symptom displayed by psychotics who have spent a lifetime feeling rejected. In Kemper's case it was the rejection by his mother, the woman who had told him he would never get a girlfriend. With a dead person he could feel in control, there could be no ridicule and certainly no rejection, neither could their be any bitching – especially if the head was removed.

He asked to be executed but was jailed for life without any possibility of parole. He is still confusing psychiatrists from his cell at Vaccaville Correctional Centre.

********************

No case in British legal history best illustrates the 'Mad or Bad?' issue more than the Yorkshire Ripper.

From October, 1975, to November, 1980, a gravedigger turned lorry driver terrorized the towns and cities of Yorkshire and beyond with a series of horrific and frenzied murders. Thirteen women aged from 16 to 47 were murdered, their bodies hideously mutilated. Seven other women barely survived the Ripper's attacks.

The hunt for Britain's most prolific serial killer ended on a chilly Friday night on January 2, 1981. A routine police check on a car suspiciously parked in a dark driveway in the Yorkshire city of Sheffield led to the arrest of Peter Sutcliffe. He was a dark-eyed bearded man in his mid-30s and he was minutes away from claiming his 14th victim, Olivia Reivers, a local prostitute he had just picked up. Indeed, he later told detectives: "I would have killed that girl if I hadn't been caught."

Within 48 hours the lorry driver who had been arrested in a red-light area 30 miles from his home in Bradford admitted he was the Yorkshire Ripper. It took him 16 hours to dictate his confession. Of his victims he told detectives John Boyle and Peter Smith: "They are all in my brain, reminding me of the beast I am. Just thinking of them all reminds me of what a monster I am."

Sutcliffe later asked if he could be the one to tell his wife Sonia that he was, in fact, the mass murderer she and every other Yorkshire woman had feared for so many years. "It's me," he told her under the watching gaze of detectives. The intensely private woman stared back at him, her face white, her eyes wide. "Is it?" she asked. "Is it really?"

Four months later on Tuesday, May 5, 1981, the British legal system became embroiled in the Ripper's 'Mad or Bad?' trial in the infamous Number One courtroom of London's Old Bailey. The debate on whether Peter Sutcliffe was a cold and calculating killer or a tormented schizophrenic not responsible for his actions was vital to the accused. It meant the difference between at least 30 years in a maximum security prison, where he would be at constant risk from other inmates, or a more comfortable and perhaps shorter stretch in a secure psychiatric hospital.

In the grand old tradition of the Old Bailey it was to be a sensational court case dominated by the 'Mad or Bad?' argument and despite assurances from the Crown and the judge it soon became apparent that Sutcliffe was not the only person on trial. So too were the psychiatrists.

The prosecution was led by none other than the Attorney General himself, Sir Michael Havers QC and Member of Parliament. He had inadvertently found himself compromized by the first shots of the 'Mad or Bad?' argument a week before the trial began. It was then that Sutcliffe had appeared in the Old Bailey courtroom for the first time to have 13 murder charges put to him. In a slightly high-pitched voice with a broad Yorkshire accent he had replied 13 times the carefully rehearsed line: "Not guilty to murder but guilty to manslaughter on the grounds of diminished responsibility." It was in response to that much repeated phrase that Sir Michael Havers told the judge he was prepared to accept the lesser plea on the grounds of Sutcliffe's 'paranoid schizophrenia'. Sir Michael then went on to detail the medical evidence which, he said, amounted to the fact that this was a case of 'diminished responsibility'.

However, the judge, Mr. Justice Boreham, informed Sir Michael of his grave anxiety over the pleas and announced it would be more appropriate if the case were heard by a jury. This meant that what was to have been a one-day guilty-plea hearing, probably ending in a psychiatric sentence, would now be a full-blown trial lasting weeks. Even though Sutcliffe was not prepared to admit to the murder charges they would still be put to him, but a jury and not the Crown would decide if he was 'Mad or Bad?'. This was now clearly the issue since it was no longer in doubt who had caused the deaths of the 13 women. Sutcliffe had just admitted that.

Such are the peculiar pendulums of the legal profession. Sir Michael, who only a week earlier had been prepared to accept a manslaughter plea on the basis of medical evidence, now set out to discredit that same evidence and press full-steam ahead for murder convictions.

He told the jury it was their job to decide whether Sutcliffe had sought to "pull the wool over the psychiatrists' eyes" or if the doctors had simply been wrong. You could almost feel the medical experts shifting uncomfortably in their seats at what was to await them over the coming weeks.

Sir Michael set about his new strategy with relish. Laid out on a long oak table in the courtroom were the tools of the Ripper's trade: a claw-hammer, seven ball-pein hammers, half-a-dozen carving knives, a hacksaw, eight rusting screwdrivers, some sharpened to points, and a length of rope. Sir Michael, whose son Nigel Havers was at the time starring in the film *Chariots of Fire*, treated each exhibit like a theatrical prop. "Have you ever seen such fiendish weapons?" he would ask before passing them to the jury.

He was quick to get to the principle point of the case. He told the jurors there was a significant difference between what Sutcliffe told the police and what he had told the doctors. "You have to decide whether as a clever, callous murderer he deliber-

ately set out to create a cock-and-bull story to avoid conviction
for murder." Sir Michael said all the psychiatrists believed
Sutcliffe when he told them he had received divine messages
from God to kill prostitutes. Indeed, the accused claimed God
had first started talking to him while he worked as a
gravedigger at Bingley Cemetery in Yorkshire. Yet Sutcliffe
had not mentioned a divine mission to detectives during the two
days he spent confessing to the murders.

Sir Michael told the jury he intended to prove Sutcliffe was a
sadistic killer who had duped the doctors. He said it was up to
the defence to prove otherwise. Unless they could satisfy the
jurors that Sutcliffe really believed he had heard the voice of
God in Bingley Cemetery they would have to find him guilty of
murder – 13 times.

To support the Crown's view that Sutcliffe had manipulated
doctors to pronounce him schizophrenic a succession of prison
officers were called as witnesses. One of them told the court
he'd overheard Sutcliffe talking to his wife during a visit at
Armley Prison while he was on remand. Sutcliffe allegedly told
his wife: "I'm going to do a long time in prison, 30 years or
more unless I can convince people in here I'm mad and maybe
then ten years in the loony bin."

A second prison officer reported finding Sutcliffe very cocky
only a month before the trial. Sutcliffe had claimed an agreement had been reached between the defence and prosecution on
a plea of diminished responsibility. He said a bed had been
reserved for him at Liverpool's Park Lane Hospital and a
psychiatrist had told him he would have to do no more than ten
years to satisfy the public.

A third prison officer described Sutcliffe's mood after his
trial had been transferred from Leeds Crown Court to the Old
Bailey in mid-April. "He was very pleased with that news," said
the officer. Sutcliffe had told him the doctors considered him
disturbed and he was happy and surprised by that. "He said to
me: 'I'm as normal as anyone'."

After a weekend break the defence opened its case with a
surprise and star witness – Peter Sutcliffe himself. The court-

room froze as Britain's most infamous killer was escorted from the dock to the witness box. It was the first time most of the press and spectators had the opportunity to see him head on. He looked quite normal, even friendly.

He then began to describe his 'divine mission' to kill prostitutes. It all began as he was digging a grave one rainy day in 1967 when he was 20 years old. He said he heard a voice echoing from a gravestone. Sutcliffe said it was "very wonderful" and added: "I heard what I believed then and believe now to have been God's voice." The courtroom was deathly silent as he went on. "It had a terrific impact on me...I looked across the valley and all around and thought of heaven and earth and how insignificant we all were but I felt so important at that moment. I felt I had been selected."

It was two years later after a humiliating row with a prostitute that the voice, which he'd secretly heard "hundreds of times" since his experience in the cemetery, began spelling out his purpose. "It kept saying I had to go on with a mission and it had a purpose. It was to remove the prostitutes, to get rid of them." So in September, 1969, armed with a brick in a sock, he clubbed a prostitute over the head in Bradford. The woman did not press charges and Sutcliffe assumed this was a sign that he was to continue with his mission.

Sutcliffe's defence counsel, James Chadwin QC, asked the defendant why he had not mentioned Bingley Cemetery or the voice of God to the police during his long interrogation. The accused said he did not want the police to find out about the mission. "I was by no means convinced it was finished. God was in control of the situation and anything was possible."

Pressed gently by Mr Chadwin, Sutcliffe was asked if he thought he would serve a shorter sentence if people thought there was something wrong with him mentally. Sutcliffe replied immediately: "No. There would be something wrong with me mentally if I thought that."

It was now the turn of the Attorney General to cross-examine. Without hiding the sarcasm in his voice, Sir Michael asked about the voices from God. Why had Sutcliffe never mentioned them to police? And why had he only mentioned them after more than half-a-dozen interviews with psychiatrists in Armley jail barely two months earlier? Sutcliffe stuck to his point that he had not received a direct message from God saying the mission had ended.

After further probing Sir Michael suggested to Sutcliffe that he had already developed a hatred for prostitutes after being humiliated by one in 1969. He accused the defendant of a hatred for that woman and her kind. Sutcliffe admitted it. Sir Michael snapped: "So God jumped on the bandwagon after that and said: 'You have a divine mission, young Peter, to stalk prostitutes and avenge me by killing them'?".

"It's a very colourful speech, sir," said Sutcliffe, "But it does not apply."

Sir Michael remained undiverted from the mission to kill prostitutes. It would provide the prosecution with the main thrust of its attack on the central pillar of the defence's case. Sutcliffe had initially admitted in police custody that later in his killing sprees he knew some of his victims were not prostitutes. Sir Michael put it to Sutcliffe that the whole theory of his mission would collapse if he were to admit to doctors that he had known six of his victims were not prostitutes.

Sutcliffe insisted that all his victims were prostitutes and in police custody he had only made his comments because he couldn't divulge his mission. Sir Michael switched to another crucial tack to dismantle the defence case of mental illness. This was the prosecution's contention, that Sutcliffe was purely and simply an evil sexual sadist.

Sutcliffe was asked why he removed his victims clothes while they were unconscious. He said it was to prevent them hindering him when he stabbed them. Sir Michael suggested he stabbed his victims in sexual areas to derive sexual satisfaction. Sutcliffe denied it. Why then, asked Sir Michael, had he placed a large piece of wood against the vagina of one victim? The defendant claimed he had used the wood to move the body.

Sir Michael then brought up a particularly attractive 18-year-old prostitute, Sutcliffe's eighth murder victim. "Surprise,

surprise. Pretty little Helen Rytka. You went and had sex with her. Why?"

Sutcliffe said he did not have sex. "I entered her but there was no action. It was to persuade her that everything would be alright." He did not add that she was totally oblivious having been struck on the head with a ball-hammer.

Sir Michael ended his cross-examination leaving many seasoned observers with the impression that what had just occurred was merely a rehearsal for a greater courtroom interrogation. The psychiatrists upon whom the defence case rested were about to take the witness stand to confront the lawyers. Two learned professors were on a massive collision course under the voyeuristic glare of the world's press. Only one could emerge the victor in this particular case.

The first of three forensic psychiatrists – or 'lambs to the slaughter', as the press dubbed them – was Dr Hugo Milne, who had interviewed Sutcliffe 11 times while he was awaiting trial. He said he and his two colleagues believed that Sutcliffe was a genuine sufferer of paranoid schizophrenia. Dr Milne, with nearly 30 years experience, told Mr Chadwin he had been especially alert to the defendant feigning mental illness. He stressed there was no evidence that Sutcliffe had simulated mental illness. Indeed Dr Milne believed the accused had been a paranoid schizophrenic since the age of 20. The voices were a classic symptom of the sickness.

As is generally the case in 'big' English trials the barrister leading the prosecution team – in this case Sir Michael Havers – occasionally gives way to one of his 'juniors' to examine witnesses. The term 'junior' belies the status, skill and experience of the lawyer concerned. It is merely a traditional tag. Both the leader and 'junior' are often QCs of exceptional capabilities. In this case the 'junior' was Yorkshire-based Harry Ognall QC, a fearsomely eloquent barrister with the tenacity of a terrier. It was he who was unleashed to cross-examine Dr Milne.

He took up the assertion that Sutcliffe could not have feigned his illness by referring to Sonia Sutcliffe's mental breakdown in the early-1970s. Dr Milne confirmed Sutcliffe's wife had suffered from schizophrenia and had heard voices talking to her. Mr Ognall asked if it wasn't true Sonia thought she was the second Christ. Dr Milne said she had and following Mr Ognall's train of thought admitted that it was just possible Sutcliffe could have 'duped' him into believing he too was schizophrenic. However, Dr Milne maintained that during Sonia's illness she had displayed aggression and restlessness and would change her clothing at odd times. Sutcliffe did not emulate that behaviour even though he had been privy to it.

Mr Ognall went on to suggest it was possible Sutcliffe was alert to what Dr Milne and other psychiatrists wanted to hear. Dr Milne accepted that if the defendant knew the symptoms and signs of schizophrenia and was cool and calculated, then it was possible.

Mr Ognall then cited phrases used by Sutcliffe. "'Morbid depression.' That's a very learned phrase for a lorry driver and so's 'pathological hatred'. That's a rum phrase for a lorry driver to use," he said in typical style.

"He is an intelligent lorry driver," stated Dr Milne.

Mr Ognall wondered why, if Sutcliffe was the hapless victim at God's beck and call, God only called on him to murder on Friday and Saturday nights, the very evenings Sonia worked at a nursing home. Dr Milne said paranoid schizophrenics were cunning and extremely involved in premeditation. He disagreed with Mr Ognall's view that this was the trait of a premeditated killer rather than the schizophrenic.

As Sir Michael had done earlier, Mr Ognall went on to the sexual aspect of the killings. Dr Milne had maintained there was no sexual component to the attacks. "I am of the opinion that he is not primarily a sexual killer," he told the judge.

Mr Ognall put it to the doctor that if Sutcliffe could be shown to pay unhealthy attention to sexual parts of the body it would count against his diagnosis and, indeed, the divine mission. Dr Milne conceded this. Mr Ognall produced the sharpened screwdriver used by Sutcliffe to thrust into a victim's vagina. "That indicates the most fiendish cruelty deliberately done for sexual satisfaction," said the barrister.

Dr Milne denied this was necessarily the case. "Mutilation of the genitalia for sadistic satisfaction would have to be repetitive and there is no evidence, as far as I know, that this man has attacked any of the other victims in this way."

Mr Ognall was not to be put off and demanded to know what else but sexual could the screwdriver attack have been. Dr Milne, who in a report said he believed the screwdriver injury was accidental, eventually conceded the attack, if not accidental, "could not have been anything else other than sexual."

Mr Ognall was intent on proving that Sutcliffe was a sexual killer and to do so would explode the theory that he was schizophrenic and believed he was fulfilling God's will. Fixing Dr Milne once more in his sights, the barrister asked: "If you were to find a number of instances of sexual molestation, the more instances you find, the more it would erode the validity of the diagnosis?" Dr Milne agreed.

Mr Ognall referred to one victim who was stabbed through the breast and another whose bare buttocks were badly scratched with a hacksaw blade. A third who had been left with a length of wood pushed against her vagina; a fourth with whom Sutcliffe had actually had sex as she lay dying and a fifth who Sutcliffe had left with deep fingernail scratches around her vagina.

"I put it to you that the injuries to these women betray quite clear sexual components in the attacks. Do you agree," he demanded of Dr Milne.

"Yes," replied the doctor.

Mr Ognall suggested Sutcliffe was not a missionary of God but a man who got sexual pleasure out of killing women. Dr Milne did not accept that.

Mr Ognall went on: "It is not God telling the tortured soul 'You must kill'. It is a man who craves for it like an addict for the next shot of heroin. What he is saying is: 'I am hooked on it'."

Sutcliffe had told police that by the end of his murderous spree no woman was safe from him, prostitutes or otherwise. He said he had a random and indiscriminate urge to kill any woman. This was borne out by the fact that later in his killing career Sutcliffe did not even bother entering red-light areas to select his victims. He simply parked his car in quiet places and waited.

Mr Ognall suggested to the doctor that if Sutcliffe knew that some of the women he attacked were not prostitutes then the whole divine mission theory along with the doctor's diagnosis lay in smithereens.

The doctor agreed. However, he could not agree with Mr Ognall's additional comments that the defendant "with compelling clarity was a liar and a fake." Two other doctors were called to substantiate the defence's case that Sutcliffe was a paranoid schizophrenic. Dr Malcolm MacCulloch, from Liverpool's Park Lane Special Hospital, said he had concluded Sutcliffe was paranoid after only 30 minutes. Nothing he had seen during the trial had persuaded him otherwise. The other witness was Dr Terence Kay who, ironically, had been brought in to examine Sutcliffe by the Crown. He was convinced the accused believed he had heard the voice of God in Bingley Cemetery. Dr Kay was in no doubt Sutcliffe suffered from paranoid schizophrenia.

In his 90 minute final address to the jury, Sir Michael Havers told them it was their job to decide whether Sutcliffe was mad, as the doctors believed, or "just plain evil." He added: "It is the doctors' belief in what he said about Bingley, the voice of God and the mission which leads them to their diagnosis. If you do not believe that he is telling the truth then the doctors' diagnosis collapses."

For Sutcliffe, Mr Chadwin told the jury how his role as defence counsel had been unusually reversed. He had to prove his case while the prosecution did not have to prove a thing. He asked why Sutcliffe waited six years after his row with a prostitute before he started killing women. A man with a healthy mind would not have waited so long. He did not think there was any sexual significance in the way Sutcliffe attacked the bodies. "He loathed their bodies and he attacked in many cases with excessive violence, one woman having something like 52 stab wounds."

On Friday, May 22, 1981 the jury were sent out to seek a unanimous verdict. More than five hours later they returned to say they could not be unanimous. The judge said in that case he would be prepared to accept a majority. Fifty minutes later they returned with 13 murder verdicts by a majority of ten to two.

Mr Justice Boreham told Sutcliffe: "It is difficult to find words that are adequate to describe the brutality and the gravity of these offences. The sentence for murder is laid down by the law and is immutable. It is a sentence that you be imprisoned for life... I will recommend to the Home Secretary you serve at least 30 years. That is a long period, an unusually long period. But I believe you are an unusually dangerous man. I express the hope when I have said life imprisonment it will mean precisely that."

Nearly two years after his sentence Sutcliffe received a taste of his own medicine from a fellow inmate at Parkhurst Prison on the Isle of Wight. He lost a pint of blood and had to undergo 84 stitches in his face when he was attacked with a broken coffee jar. His attacker, Glaswegian Jimmy Costelloe, was enraged at Sutcliffe's repeated defacings of the prison's copy of the Sun newspaper. The Yorkshireman had branded it 'trash' as he railed against the declining morals of society. He is now in Broadmoor, a scure hospital for the criminally insane.

********************

Detective Inspector Stephen McCusker sat in the back of the unmarked police car as it snaked its way through London's rush-hour traffic on a near-freezing February night. "Are we talking about one body or two?" he asked the pale, thin man sat next to him. "15 or 16 since 1978. I'll tell you everything," replied Dennis Andrew Nilsen.

The arrest of one of the world's most macabre serial killers was initiated by a blocked toilet in the leafy north London suburb of Muswell Hill. Builder Jim Allcock could not flush the toilet in the bedsit he shared with his girlfriend Fiona Bridges at 23 Cranley Gardens. A plumber could not shift the blockage so it was left to a specialist firm to examine the drains outside.

Lumps of grey-white flesh were discovered which were identified within hours as human remains.

Apart from the couple living on the ground floor, three other people shared the semi-detached Edwardian house which had been divided into six bedsits or small apartments. Dental nurse Vivienne McStay and youth worker Monique Van-Rutte shared another ground floor room. The first floor was empty. In the attic rooms, where the windows were strangely never closed, lived an unassuming 37-year-old civil servant, Dennis Nilsen. It was upon him the finger of suspicion fell.

After meeting the consultant pathologist who had confirmed the remains were human, Detective Chief Inspector Peter Jay returned to Cranley Gardens. He awaited Nilsen's return from the Kentish Town job-centre where he worked. "I've come about the drains," was his unlikely introduction. Nilsen said he was surprised the police would be involved in blocked drains. He then feigned shock when told human flesh had been found in them. Jay told him not to "mess about" and asked him where the rest of the body was. "In two plastic bags in my wardrobe," said Nilsen.

Within hours of the chilling car seat confession Jay was back at Nilsen's flat with the pathologist, Professor David Bowen, who specialized in forensic medicine at the University of London. Two large plastic dustbin liners were removed and taken to Hornsey Mortuary. One of the bags contained four smaller carrier bags. In these were found left and right arms attached to parts of the chest, a headless, legless torso and a bag containing intestines and other vital organs. The other dustbin-liner again contained smaller bags in which were found a torso with arms but no hands, a skull with the flesh boiled away and a head which still retained most of the flesh but had been subject to boiling.

The next day Nilsen suggested they examine a tea-chest and also look under the bathroom sink. In the tea-chest Professor Bowen found another torso, a skull and some air fresheners. In the bathroom he found a bag containing the lower half of a man complete with legs.

Over at Hornsey police station on February 11, 1983, Nilsen began a confession that left seasoned detectives ashen with shock and in the months to come would send shockwaves of revulsion around the world.

For nearly five years Scots-born Nilsen, a former policeman, had been picking up young men in London's gay bars, taking them home and strangling them. It did not stop there. Nilsen, a social misfit with no real friends, kept their bodies, sometimes for months, under the floor-boards and brought them out as 'company' during fireside evenings in front of the television. He had murdered three men at Cranley Gardens and "12 or 13", he wasn't sure, at his previous address, 195 Melrose Avenue, Cricklewood, north London.

Names could not be attached to all of his victims. Some were homeless drifters and none of them were known to Nilsen until he picked them up. His method, in most cases, was to ply them with drink once he had got them home, take them to bed and sometime during the night he would strangle them, usually with a crude garrote made from string and a necktie. "I started out with 15 ties. I only have a clip-on left," he later told police. He would bathe the bodies, caress and often sleep with them for the first day or two and then store them beneath the floor-boards. One victim was 'resurrected' four times from beneath the lounge floor at Melrose Avenue. Nilsen would sit him in the armchair next to his own, hold his hand, and discuss the business of the day or television programmes he was watching at the time. Others would be brought up to sit on his knee or join him as he listened to music.

At any one time up to three or four bodies would lie beneath the floor-boards at Melrose Avenue. When asked how many may had lain there at any one time, he replied: "I am not sure. I did not do a stock check." To create space for more victims, Nilsen would light huge bonfires to dispose of the bodies, taking great care to sift through the ashes for tell-tale residue which he would crush.

Seven men escaped death by fleeing or by sheer luck brought about by Nilsen's erratic behaviour. One of them, Carl Stotter, was a teenager when he was lured to Melrose Avenue. Three years later he relived the horror story before a hushed court: "I woke up feeling something round my neck. My head was hurting and I couldn't breathe properly and I wondered what it was. I felt his hand pulling at the zip at the back of my neck. He was saying in a sort of whispered shouting voice 'Stay still. Stay still'.....The pressure was increasing. My head was hurting and I couldn't breathe. I remember vaguely water running. I remember vaguely being carried and then I felt very cold. I knew I was in the water and he was trying to drown me. The third time I came up I said: 'No more. Please, no more' and he pushed me under again. I just thought I was dying. I thought: 'You are drowning. This is what it feels like to die.' I felt very relaxed and I passed out. I couldn't fight any more."

As if miraculously, Stotter awoke on the couch with Nilsen's dog licking his face. He saw in the mirror a red line around his neck and broken blood vessels all over his face. Later he remembered Nilsen cuddling him in bed before he left the house accompanied by Nilsen, who escorted him to a tube station.

Another 'lucky' victim described his night with Nilsen. After leaving a pub they returned to the Cranley Gardens flat and drank some more. He went to bed with Nilsen and woke up at around 2.00 am with a terrible headache. He drank some water and a few hours later, still feeling ill, he went to the bathroom to splash water on his face and was horrified by his reflection in the mirror. His face was very red and his eyes were bloodshot. "There were no whites in my eyes," he said. He had a sore throat and felt quite sick. Nilsen suggested he had perhaps drunk too much the night before. It was only later that day, when his college tutor sent him to hospital, that he realized he had been strangled.

Nilsen's trial was held at the Old Bailey in October, 1983. He sat in the same dock occupied by the Yorkshire Ripper just two-and-a-half years earlier and by Doctor Crippen 70 years before that.

Nilsen faced six murder charges. The prosecution had at first been only able to identify six victims. A seventh had been identified since but this was after the indictment had been drawn up. Three of the victims had met their deaths at Cranley Gardens, the rest at Melrose Avenue, where bone particles from eight bodies had been found in garden ashes. Nilsen also faced two charges of attempted murder.

As in the Yorkshire Ripper trial, there was no doubt who was responsible for the deaths. Nilsen had made a full confession in interviews which lasted more than a week. The jury of eight men and four women had to decide whether Nilsen was guilty of murder or whether, due to abnormality of mind, he was guilty of the lesser crime of manslaughter. Should he serve out his sentence in a secure hospital or a prison?

Mr Alan Green QC was prosecuting and would go on to become Director of Public Prosecutions for a time. Mr Ivan Lawrence QC, a Member of Parliament defended Nilsen. As in the Ripper case, the burden fell upon the defence to prove diminished responsibility.

Nilsen pleaded not guilty to the murders of Stephen Sinclair, whose body had been 'reconstructed' on the mortuary slab from the parts found in Cranley Gardens. Malcolm Barlow, Martin Duffey, John Howlett, Billy Sutherland and Kenneth Ockenden. The latter was a Canadian holidaying in Britain. On December 3, 1979 he had spent the last day of his life sightseeing with Nilsen as his guide. The two had met in a West End pub. Before returning to Melrose Avenue they stocked up with alcohol. Already friends after nine hours together they sat down for an evening of music on the stereo set. Nilsen strangled the Canadian with the headphone flex. He had not experienced such a relaxing and enjoyable friendship in years and could not bear the thought of Ockenden leaving him the next day to fly home. Nilsen did not give evidence in court. In a statement he recalled his actions after killing the young Canadian.

"I bathed his body and laid him on the bed. I kept him in the bed with me for the rest of the night. No sex, only caressing, etc... I put him in the cupboard as I was going to work... That evening I took his body from the cupboard and straightened him... I put body colour on his face to remove the redness from his face. I arranged the body in various positions and took several photos. I lay in bed fully clothed with him lying spread-eagled on top of me. I would sometimes speak to him as though he were still listening... I wrapped him well before putting him under the floorboards. I took him up on about four occasions in the next two weeks... I would sit him in the armchair next to me as I watched an evening's TV, drinking. I thought his body and skin were very beautiful, a sight that almost brought me to tears after a couple of drinks."

In another statement Nilsen recalled the 'company' provided by one victim. "I opened the cupboard and lifted out the body. I cleaned him up. I dressed him and sat him in front of the TV in the armchair next to mine. I took his hand and told him my comments for the day with cynical remarks about the TV programmes. I would also take him on to the armchair with me and hold him safe and secure. I placed him on the table and slowly stripped him. I would always remove his socks last. I would closely examine every part of his anatomy. I would roll him onto his stomach and do likewise to his back. His naked body fascinated me. I remember being thrilled that I had full control and ownership of this beautiful body."

With such evidence it was hardly surprising that Central Criminal Court Number One would once again prove a battle-ground between lawyers and psychiatrists in a bid to establish whether Nilsen was 'Mad or Bad?'.

The prosecution's contention was straightforward. Mr Green maintained Nilsen killed with full awareness and deliberation and therefore was guilty of murder. He said even if there was mental abnormality this was not enough to diminish 'substantially' his mental responsibility for the killings. Mr Green was choosing his words very carefully with Britain's Homicide Act (1957) in mind. He wanted to prove that even if Nilsen was sick he was not sick 'substantially' enough to escape a murder conviction. A key sub-section of the Act states, in typically ponderous fashion, its definition of mental sickness: "Such abnormality of mind (whether arising from a condition of arrested or retarded development of mind or any inherent causes or induced by disease or injury) as substantially impaired his mental responsibility for his acts and omissions in doing or being a party to the killing."

Dr Paul Bowden, psychiatrist for the prosecution, who had interviewed Nilsen 16 times in the eight months since his arrest, was damning of the defendant. He said there was no retarded development of mind, no mental disease or injury and no inherent causes.

Earlier in the trial Mr Lawrence, for the defence, said Nilsen was suffering from an abnormality of mind at the time of each killing. He was therefore incapable of forming the specific intention of murder.

The first psychiatrist called by Mr Lawrence was Dr James MacKeith, who said that during each of the six murders Nilsen was suffering from a severe personality disorder which substantially reduced his responsibilities. He also touched on Nilsen's habit of depersonalization. He was capable of actions without being in full control of them. It was as if he saw himself from a distance. Psychiatrists call this 'dissociation'.

Dr Bowden, for the prosecution, was to later contradict this by saying there was no evidence of 'dissociation'. This invariably involved amnesia whereas Nilsen seemed to remember his crimes in some detail.

Mr Green established that Dr MacKeith's diagnosis was based upon what Nilsen had told him. He suggested Nilsen was nothing more than "a jolly good actor". He did not accept that the killings were the product of a substantially impaired mind because Nilsen planned them. He invited men back to his home for the purpose of killing them. He had attempted to hoodwink the men who survived his attempts at strangulation into thinking that nothing untoward had happened to them. He had collected the belongings of one of his murder victims from the left luggage office at Euston railway station. He had been able to stop himself strangling Stotter and another man. This showed he could employ self-control when he wanted to stop therefore he could also kill when he wanted to. There was also the implication that Nilsen enjoyed this apparent power over life and death.

Dr Patrick Gallwey was the other psychiatric defence witness. He thought Nilsen suffered from arrested development of personality which substantially impaired his responsibility. In his opinion Nilsen was also a victim of the 'False Self' syndrome. This involved Nilsen apparently behaving normally while all the time trying to suppress schizoid or paranoid feelings. The strain caused by this inner turmoil led to periodic breakdowns during which sudden, motiveless, violent and psycho-sexual behaviour manifested itself. He said 'False Self' personalities were kept in place when they were surrounded by affectionate relationships but disintegrated when they were socially isolated. Nilsen was very much an isolated loner, virtually a self-imposed social outcast.

Once again Mr Green insisted Nilsen knew exactly what he was doing. He cited the case of Malcolm Barlow, a retarded epileptic. Nilsen had found him slumped on a pavement, took him in and gave him a coffee before calling an ambulance to take him to hospital. The next day he returned to Nilsen's house and was fed. Later that evening Nilsen let him drink alcohol and the young man fell asleep. He was proving a nuisance so Nilsen strangled him. It was a clear and premeditated decision by the defendant to kill rather than to call a taxi or summon an ambulance, said Mr Green, who knew that even the defence psychiatrists were uncomfortable with the circumstances of this particular murder.

In his summing up, Mr Green said the jury was dealing with a defendant who liked killing and got satisfaction from it. He was resourceful, cunning and articulate, able to bluff his way out of many situations.

Mr Lawrence said they were dealing with a man who, quite simply, was out of his mind. He went through, blow by blow, the horrific details of the case. He said it only needed a sensible jury to see the defendant was 'crazy'.

The judge, Mr Justice Croom-Johnson, said during his four-hour summing up: "There are evil people who do evil things. Committing murder is one them. A mind can be evil without being abnormal." He said if Nilsen suffered from a retarded development of personality that was not something that could be tangibly measured. If it meant 'character' then the jury should not attach too much weight to it. "There must be no excuses for Nilsen if he has moral defects. A nasty nature is not arrested or retarded development of mind."

The jury were sent out to reach their verdicts on the morning of Thursday, November 3, 1983. A relatively quick decision was expected. That afternoon, with still no verdict, the jury foreman was asked by the judge if one was imminent. "No, my lord," he replied. The jury were sent to a hotel for the night and took all the next day before finding Nilsen guilty of all six murders by a majority of ten to two. He was sentenced to life imprisonment with a recommendation he serve a minimum of 25 years.

The details of the Nilsen 'House of Horrors' court case shocked and sickened the country. Splashed across the pages of every national newspaper with photographs of victims and details of their family backgrounds, it was still difficult to accept this had actually happened. It was as if the brain digested the facts and then promptly rejected them, an involuntary reaction to protect our own peace of mind. Did someone really strangle young men and keep them for months under floorboards? Did someone really cut up their bodies once they had served their purpose? Did someone really boil heads in a giant saucepan? Could somebody be so detached from his deeds that he could sum them up as: "End of day, end of drinking, end of person." It was perversion gone mad. Nilsen was surely a one-off, a mass-murderer and mutilator of unfortunate young men whose like would never be seen again?

A disturbing feeling of *déja vous* registered worldwide barely eight years later when, across the Atlantic, a virtually identical catalogue of horror unfolded in the mid-western city of Milwaukee, with the case of 'The Cannibal' Jeffrey Dahmer.

********************

Arthur Shawcross might never have been captured had he not stopped to masturbate on a bridge looking at the body of one of his victims in the river below. With perhaps the most unconventional 'surveillance' arrest in modern times so ended the two year reign of terror of the fat middle-aged killer.

Rochester is a city of 230,000 people in upstate New York. Lying just south of Lake Ontario which forms the border between the USA and Canada, Rochester is 400 miles from New York City. Niagara Falls is 50 miles to the west. The city is well known for its connections with the Eastman Kodak Company and the Xerox Corporation. In the late 1980s and 1990 it became better known for the serial killings of 11 women and a mass-murderer called Arthur Shawcross.

On March 24, 1988, the body of 27-year-old Dorothy Blackburn was found floating face-down in Salmon Creek, Northampton Park, near the Genesee River gorge area of the city. She was well-known in the city's red-light district and she had been strangled a few weeks earlier. There were no leads and as weeks blended into months the death of a hooker was virtually forgotten.

Six months later on September 11, 1988, a second body was found in the Genesee River gorge. It had been well hidden, a trait that was to become a hallmark of the killer. The body had lain undiscovered for months and was virtually a skeleton. Identification was a problem but with the skull intact detectives called in a forensic anthropologist to recreate the face. The scientist had no hair to go by but he went about the facial reconstruction with such skill that when a photograph was issued to the media the victim's father immediately recognized her as his missing daughter. She was 27-year-old Anna Marie Steffen.

More than a year went by without a lead. Thirteen months later on October 21, 1989, skeletal remains were found in the same district. The body had lain undiscovered for four or five months. This time the killer had removed the head. There was to be no facial reconstruction or identification of this victim yet.

Just six days after the headless skeleton was found a group of children playing behind the Maplewood YMCA on Driving Park Avenue, adjacent to the Genesee River gorge area, discovered a woman's body. The decomposed remains were later identified as those of 25-year-old Patricia Ives.

The discovery of a fourth body sent a chill through the police department. There had been muted speculation among officers that perhaps a serial killer was on the loose. Charles Siragusa, Assistant District Attorney, told the media: "Those of us in law enforcement really didn't believe it. We tended to associate serial killers with places like New York City, California, Chicago, but certainly not with our own community. With the discovery of Patricia Ives however, the possibility became probability and speculation reality. Patricia Ives signalled for us that we were dealing with a serial killer."

Police barely had time to catch their breath before another body turned up two weeks later on November 11, 1989. A fisherman in the Genesee River gorge area came across the naked body of Frances Brown. She was 22 and had been strangled only hours earlier.

Two weeks later on November 23, Thanksgiving Day, a sixth body surfaced, this time at Turning Point Park. A man followed his dog into some reeds along the Genesee River to find a human foot protruding from a rolled-up carpet. When police examined the body they were horrified to find she had been mutilated from her chest to her pubic area. Was the killer becoming more frenzied or had other victims, too decomposed to gauge, been subject to the same Ripper-like ordeal? The latest victim was identified as 29-year-old June Stott.

The body count was rising almost as fast as the public outcry. Four days later a deer hunter stumbled across another corpse, face down in neighbouring Wayne County. She had been strangled in the same way as the other victims and was identified as Elizabeth Gibson, 29, a woman familiar with Rochester's red-light district.

Police were coming under mounting criticism for not issuing an earlier warning to prostitutes that a serial killer was on the loose. Behind the scenes every effort was being made to trace the killer who left no clues because his victims, in most cases, had been dead for many weeks or even months before discovery. Detectives were further handicapped by the fact that most bodies had been deposited in a river. Any forensic scientist or pathologist will testify that exposure to river pollutants destroys practically all potentially useful forensic evidence in a body. Surveillance teams were set up in the red-light area and two profilers were enlisted to the hunt, one from New York State Police, the other from the FBI.

Their task was to analyze the type of person responsible for the murders in a bid to reduce the number of suspects. They deduced the killer was a lone male, mid-30s or older, who was capable of female relationships. His occupation would be menial. His appearance would be innocuous and unthreatening and his dress would be functional. He would be familiar with the area and his hobbies would be fishing and hunting. His car would be functional and, strangely, he would be "a potential police buff".

While the profilers added their contribution a prostitute came forward with information about a client who was causing her concern. It seemed he only achieved orgasm when she played dead. She added she had seen the man with Elizabeth Gibson in the days before Gibson's body was discovered and gave police a full description but they were unable to trace the suspect.

Any police officer will vouch that a lucky break will often solve a major inquiry. There are lucky breaks and there are lucky breaks but few are as implausible as what happened during the desperate hunt for the Genessee River gorge killer. If it were written as fiction it would be rejected as too far-fetched.

Another woman had disappeared from Rochester's red-light district. Twenty-year-old Felicia Stephens' clothing had been found near the river. A police helicopter was conducting an aerial search on January 3, 1990. On one of its swoops over the river an officer thought he saw something in the water. The helicopter banked around and sure enough it seemed there was a body beneath a bridge. As the helicopter hovered lower for a better view the officer and pilot saw a grey Chevrolet Celebrity parked on the bridge. Standing beside it was a man holding his penis as he looked down at the woman's body. When he became conscious of the noise of the rotors the man started, looked up, adjusted his trousers, leapt into the car and sped off.

Police who pulled the body from the river found the latest murder victim was not Felicia Stephens but June Cicero, who at the age of 34 had been the acknowledged queen of the red-light district. She had boasted to police that the serial killer would never get her but he had and once again he had resorted to mutilation. He had attacked her genitalia with a knife and like the others she had been strangled.

Meanwhile the helicopter had tracked the grey Chevrolet to the Wedgewood Nursing Home in nearby Spencerport. Uniformed officers were dispatched to the scene and for the first time in the 21 month inquiry the name of Arthur Shawcross surfaced. The pot-bellied 44-year-old married man was visiting his mistress, Clara Neal, who worked at the home. He insisted he had been urinating into a bottle when he noticed the police helicopter.

A police check on Shawcross threw up a chilling discovery. He was still on parole having been convicted of murdering two children 18 years earlier. He had raped and strangled an eight-year-old girl and killed a boy of ten in Watertown, New York state. Shawcross had been allowed to plead guilty to manslaughter in exchange for leading the police to the body of the boy, who had been missing for two months. Shawcross was sentenced to 25 years and had been freed on parole in April, 1987. He began killing within months of his release.

Under state law Rochester police did not have enough evidence to charge Shawcross so he was released under 24 hour surveillance. Detectives, by now paranoid of their suspect, interviewed his wife, his mistress and distributed his photograph among prostitutes in the red-light district. All of the women identified him as a regular 'John'.

The next day, January 4, 1990, another body turned up. This time it was Felicia Stephens. A hunter found her body in the foundation of a farmhouse near Northampton Park, just 300 yards from where the 20-year-old woman's clothes had been found four days earlier. She was strangled and had been dead for a week. At noon Shawcross was brought in by police, who told him they believed he was the serial killer. He vehemently denied it. After police brought in his mistress and allowed him to speak to his wife, Shawcross later confessed to 11 murders.

Indeed, he went even further. Shawcross told detectives about two victims they did not even know about. Later the same day, January 4, 1990, he led them into a wooded area in the Greece district of Rochester to the body of 22-year-old Maria Welch who had been strangled shortly after her disappearance on November 6. He then took them to the town of Clarkson where the body of 32-year-old Darlene Trippi was floating in a culvert. She had been strangled nearly a month earlier.

One detective recalled how during questioning Shawcross shuffled through photographs of dead women. (There had actually been 17 murders in the area.) Shawcross had made a pile of the women he had killed. "It was like he was dealing a deck of cards," said the officer.

Shawcross quickly gave the identity of the mysterious headless corpse as 59-year-old Dorothy Keeler. He had actually returned to the body to sever its head after seeing how one of his earlier victims had been identified from the skull. Keeler was the only victim Shawcross was acquainted with. She was an ageing prostitute who Shawcross and his wife occasionally invited in for a meal. He said he had sex with her down by the river and strangled her after she threatened to tell his wife.

In fact Shawcross had an 'excuse' for the other ten murders. He said he killed Dorothy Blackburn because she bit his penis during sex. Anna Marie Steffen died because, he said, she told him she was pregnant while they were having sex. This was ironic; Anna Steffen, from whose skull the scientist constructed a face, was actually nine months pregnant. The foetus was never found. Patricia Ives died because she refused to be quiet during sex behind the YMCA while children were playing nearby. Frances Brown had to die because she broke his gear-shift during sex in his car. He claimed he killed June Stott because she told him she was a virgin. He said he offered to teach her how to kiss but it soon became apparent she already knew. Elizabeth Gibson was murdered because she went through his wallet. June Cicero, queen of the red-light zone, died because

she called Shawcross a wimp and a faggot and challenged him
with being the serial killer – "the weirdo who would never get
her." It is perhaps significant that Cicero was mutilated, almost
as if Shawcross had gone looking for her. He said he strangled
Felicia Stephens, whose disappearance initiated the helicopter
search, after she approached his car. Maria Welch was
murdered after she tried to take money from his wallet and
Darlene Trippi had to die after taunting him for failing to maintain an erection.

Once police had a confession from Shawcross, prosecutors
prepared themselves for the inevitable plea of insanity. Charles
Siragusa said: "When he was arrested we anticipated an insanity
defence. Steps were taken early on to deal with it." Investigators
were sent to his home town to delve deeply into his background.
Statements were taken from friends and relatives. School
records were studied back to his infancy. "We knew that in
second grade, when he was seven years old, he took an iron
pipe on a school bus to threaten other kids," said Siragusa.
Records were studied from his 25-year term in prison. His 13-
month tour of duty in Vietnam with the United States Army was
closely scrutinized. Shawcross had claimed he had "39
confirmed kills" and "numerous unconfirmed kills" with an M-
16 machine gun. In fact, army records showed Shawcross was a
supply and parts specialist who never saw combat. His
Rochester workmates at a food supply plant were interviewed at
length. They described him as a "bullshitter."

"I would say that by the time Arthur Shawcross came to
trial we knew more about him than he knew about himself,"
said Siragusa.

It is interesting to examine the profile compiled by the FBI
and New York State in the hunt for the Genesee River gorge
killer. This suggested the killer was a lone male, mid-30s or
older (definitely not younger). Shawcross was 44. They said he
was capable of female relationships. Shawcross not only had a
wife but also a mistress. His occupation would be menial.
Shawcross cut up food for a living. The wanted man would
appear "innocuous and unthreatening." Shawcross was a

grubby, bespectacled, balding man, aged beyond his years with a pot-belly – hardly the image of the archetypal serial killer. He would blend into the area and his dress would be functional and not bizarre. This, said Siragusa, "fits him to a tee." The profilers said his car would also be functional and not stylish. In fact, when police arrested Shawcross he was driving an undercover police car he had bought at an auction. A functional vehicle indeed. His profile ended with the comment "a potential police buff." Shawcross was fascinated by police officers and their conversation. He hung around a snack bar called Dunkin' Donuts, a place favoured by police officers. When his picture was flashed across television screens following his arrest, four officers came forward to say they knew him from conversations they had shared at the Dunkin' Donuts.

The trial proper began on October 1, 1990. Shawcross faced ten charges of second degree murder. An 11th charge, involving Elizabeth Gibson, was to be dealt with by a court in neighbouring Wayne County.

Opening for the prosecution, Siragusa said Shawcross' victims were "easy prey, easily approached, easily isolated, easily killed and easily disposed of." He said it was "inescapable" to conclude anyone but Shawcross was responsible for the killings.

Thomas Cocuzzi, one of two lawyers representing Shawcross, focused on the insanity defence. He described the defendant's conduct as a "non-issue." Instead he urged the jury to consider Shawcross' mental state and suggested they might conclude he was "extremely emotionally disturbed." Three weeks later the defence team unveiled new evidence implying that Shawcross suffered from brain damage. This led to a delay in proceedings.

Doctor Dorothy Lewis was called as the defence's chief witness. Dr Lewis said she had discovered Shawcross' brain damage while studying a magnetic image as she prepared for her testimony. She told the court she suspected the defendant suffered from multiple personality disorders. She had hypnotized him to gain a better insight into his childhood.

The court was shown videos of Dr Lewis' hypnosis sessions. Shawcross, sobbing with tears rolling down his cheeks, had apparently been regressed to his childhood. Clutching his groin, he claimed his mother was sexually abusing and hurting him.

In other tapes a 'hypnotized' Shawcross emerged in multiple personalities as himself, his sister Jeannie and his mother, who was witness to this testimony as it was televised daily. In one interview Shawcross emerged as a 12th century cannibal. The name he adopted for this mediaeval character was, by coincidence, his mother's maiden name.

Dr Lewis maintained at the the time of the killings Shawcross was in a pathological condition brought about by extraordinary trauma. He would have been disassociated from his actions. Her diagnosis was that Shawcross had multiple personalities and suffered from post-traumatic stress syndrome. She maintained Shawcross' brain would not have been functioning properly at the time he killed and therefore he would not have had a "conscious will" to commit murder.

Charles Siragusa was unimpressed. Under cross-examination, Dr Lewis admitted Shawcross told "tall tales". Siragusa, who maintained that Dr Lewis had strayed from prescribed guidelines on forensic hypnosis, went on to present letters Shawcross had written from Monroe County Jail while awaiting trial. In one, written to his mistress Clara Neal, Shawcross wrote of the brain scans he had undergone. "There better be something there otherwise my ass is cooked, fried and roasted."

Dr Martin Orne, for the prosecution, said Dr Lewis' leading questions, complicated by her disregard of the recommended guidelines for hypnosis, had made it virtually impossible for him to discern if anything useful had come out of her sessions with Shawcross. Dr Park Dietz, the prosecution's expert witness on forensic psychiatry, did not mince his words. He told the jury Shawcross was faking mental illness. "Mr Shawcross presents to his audience whatever he thinks will benefit him. I don't think we should be surprised that he'd lie or put on a show for doctors in order to avoid prosecution."

Another medical witness for the prosecution was Dr Eric Caine, a neuro-psychiatrist at the University of Rochester. He described Shawcross as a "streetwise, courtwise" criminal who did not suffer from brain damage.

David Murante, the other half of Shawcross' defence team, urged the jury to climb into the defendant's mind. "It's a sick mind that was operating here."

Siragusa flashed his eyes across the jury: "Brand him a murderer, cold, calculating and remorseless, for whom killing was not an emtional disturbance but, in the defendant's own words, 'business as usual'."

The jury agreed with the prosecutor. On December 13, 1990, after retiring for just over six hours, they found Shawcross guilty of second degree murder on all ten counts. Six weeks later on February 1, 1991, Arthur J Shawcross was sentenced to 250 years in prison.

Monroe County Court Judge Donald Wisner asked Shawcross, who had remained silent throughout his 13-week trial, if he wanted to say anything before sentencing.

"No comment at this time," replied Shawcross without looking up from the floor. "Your opportunity will not come at another time. You understand that?" said the judge. "Yes sir," said Shawcross quietly.

Three months later, on May 10, 1991, Shawcross was convicted of the second degree murder of Elizabeth Gibson. He was sentenced to 25 years to life in state prison, this sentence to run concurrently with the previous sentences. He is now in the Sullivan Correctional Facility, New York State. A spokesperson for the state told us ruefully: "Mr Shawcross will be eligible for parole in the year 2240."

# 3

# *Dennis Andrew Nilsen*

*"The bodies are all gone but I still feel a spiritual communion with these people. They are a part of me." – Dennis Nilsen ten years after the murders.*

*Interview recorded with the serial killer by Mike Morley of Central Television.*

Dennis Nilsen stubbed out the dog-end of his cigarette and rose from the hard wooden chair in the unpainted prison office, "However you shoot it, make me look interesting." It was the only thing the biggest multiple killer in British criminal history was concerned with on Monday September 7, 1992 as he returned to his lifer's cell at Albany Prison on the Isle of Wight. The following day he would face video cameras for the first time in his life and talk of the 15 murders he had confessed to.

More than just strangling or drowning his victims, Nilsen had then kept their bodies under floorboards or in cupboards. He would take them out in the evening and wash them, dress them, hold their hands and talk to them. He would masturbate beside the corpses and tried unsuccessfully to have penetrative sex with one of them. He killed them for a variety of reasons, but mainly because he couldn't bare the thought of them leaving.

The extraordinary and historic interview was to be carried out by psychologist and profiler Paul Britton.Just two months earlier Britton had completed an intensive review of the state of offender profiling in the UK and had advised both the Home Office and the Association of Chief Police Officers on how profiling should be developed over the next decade.

Close links had developed between Central Television, Paul Britton and his colleagues and this meant an opportunity arose for a project of joint value. Central's programme had been given complete backing and support from both ACPO (Association of Chief Police Officers) and the Home Office and we were anxious to take part in anything that would be of public value, while at the same time creating priceless television footage. The problem was that a number of serial rapists and killers had directly refused to take part in police or Home Office research and the chances were that Nilsen, with his distrust of authority would do the same. However, it was thought that he might agree to the interview, if it were to be shown on television and have the involvement of some non-Governmental agency.

For the past ten years author Brian Masters has been Nilsen's only link with the outside world, a world he had stunned with acts of murder and necrophilia. Masters wrote the definitive work on Nilsen, *Killing for Company,* and has visited the killer every month since his conviction. In early summer, Central Television approached Nilsen's confidant and asked if he would be supportive of our approach to Nilsen. At the time, the author was deep in work on a book about Jeffrey Dahmer but viewed the concept as important enough to break-off and travel to Albany tó discuss the suggestion with Nilsen. Masters reported back that as we had suspected, Nilsen was indeed wary of the authorities but nevertheless was very interested in Central's proposition. He had agreed to co-operate with us. We then wrote directly to 'Des', as he prefers to be known, at Albany in Newport on the Isle of Wight. There's no doubt that without Brian Masters' face-to-face discussion on Central's behalf, the interview would never have taken place.

As it was, there were still more hurdles to be jumped. Just as Bob Ressler had run into difficulties when he started interviewing serial killers for FBI research in America, now Paul Britton, was finding his route clogged with obstacles. The part of the British Home Office that deals with the police service was supportive of the scheme. The part that deals with the prison service was aghast that it should even be considered. Meetings with Nilsen were delayed, while civil servants stormed the corridors of power, playing internal politics. Here was one of the world's most lucid serial killers, agreeing to talk openly about his crimes and suddenly it was all in danger of collapsing.

After weeks of intense negotiations with prison governors, the prison department and ACPO officials, psychologist Paul Britton and myself from Central Television waited at the gates of Albany Jail. A prison officer squeezed past us, struggling with a stack of red plastic milk crates as our names were checked against an authority list. Presently, we were led through electronically operated inner-gates and were guided towards the Vulnerable Prisoner Unit which houses Dennis Andrew Nilsen.

Nine barred doors had to be unlocked before we reached the end of a corridor marking the joining of 'E' Wing and the jail's Segregation Block. We were taken into a tiny storeroom which had been clumsily converted into a makeshift office. The mandatory cream-painted walls were interrupted by two battered filing cabinets, a couple of chairs, a black plastic bag marked 'confidential waste' and a shelf containing the prison's Suicide Prevention Manuals. Tiny panes of glass in two giant barred windows allowed daylight to filter into the dusty room, creating a long honeycomb of shadows across the floor.

Nilsen entered with his guard-escort. By the time the uniformed hand had closed the door and disappeared, the tall Scot was exchanging confident handshakes and was asking: "Who am I talking to, who's who?" The Nilsen who confronted us was not that of a stalking killer. This was the Nilsen that had been an Executive Officer in the civil service, a man who had conducted hundreds of interviews of his own and was far more accustomed to asking the questions than answering them. We introduced ourselves and Paul Britton settled in behind one of two heavy, metal desks and opened up a large clipboard and notepad. I pulled a chair to within a few feet of 'Des' and asked if he'd known we were arriving that morning. His answer was pointed: "I didn't know a damn thing, they've told me nothing. I expected you to be coming last Thursday and when that didn't happen they said nothing about today." He was justifiably annoyed. Britton explained that we only intended to "chat" today and would return to tape an interview the following morning Nilsen was taken aback. Confusion was now fusing with the initial hostility, "Tomorrow? Oh, well alright, whatever. I'm yours, I've nothing else to do. Have you got any smokes?" We hadn't. It was a blunder. Nilsen is a 20-a-day man, more if he can get them. We vowed to muster some from somewhere.

As the small talk grew bigger, it became clear that Nilsen was antagonized by Britton's line of questioning. At one point he announced: "With no disrespect, I much prefer Dr Anthony Clair. I'm sure you know your job but I'm a fan of his, I listen to him on Radio 4, in what's it called, *In The Psychiatrist's Chair,* that's it, a good programme that, he's got a good way about him." Britton is an affable man, keen never to offend and also a remarkable listener. His priority at this point was to remain aloof; to show his authority and make it plain that he couldn't be manipulated or lied to. It was also important for Britton to avoid asking Nilsen any questions that at this stage might open him up; that process would take place the next day, when the cameras were rolling and an intricate structure for the interview had been laid out. 'Des',who was keen to make friends and desperate for any form of stimulating conversation, found this frustrating. He wanted to begin now.

"In some ways I am ordinary but in most things I'm extraordinary. I don't do what the crowds do, I don't like gangs or groups. When the shit hit the fan at the Old Bailey it was extraordinary, I was extraordinary, I always have been. I think I am a very rare animal indeed, I don't fit in with the herd, I don't do what other people do, not even in here. I don't watch football matches on television or violent karate films, I don't conform." Britton had to bite back the questions. Even uncoached, Nilsen was inviting probing questions into his make-up. Sat before us in a white T-shirt, blue faded jeans with turned down frayed bottoms and scuffed black trainers, he looks everything but the extraordinary man his crimes tell us that he is.

"People in here have said to me, 'Des, with most of your victims you carried out the perfect murder, you'd got away with it'. But I'd never got away with any of them. Right after the first one, I knew I'd done it and I could never get away from that, I could never get away from me knowing. Right after that, I relinquished my union post; I had lost conviction. How could I get up and tell people what they should be doing, after I'd done that? I had such a dark secret to keep, how could I look people in the eyes and make statements about what's right and what's wrong? I just couldn't do it."

As we took in the strange morality that Nilsen was laying out, he fingered a long shiny scar, running from his left ear lobe to his lips. It was a legacy from his brief spell in London's infamous Wormwood Scrubs. "Another inmate did this in 1983. When I'd been convicted, they wanted to isolate me, bang me up as a rule 43 so I told the Governor, 'I'm not having that. I don't want to spend the rest of my life in there with the nonces. I want to go into the general population'.

Then one day I was leaning on the wall having a smoke when this Glaswegian came up to me with a blade and '*Schwish*' he did this." It isn't hard to imagine that the inmate now delights in the twisted fame of being able to claim that he is the man responsible for scarring Dennis Nilsen. After the attack, 11 stitches had to be sewn into the wound to hold the flaps of gaping skin together. Nilsen still refused to embrace the isolation and protection of Rule 43, returning to the exercise yard to show he couldn't be intimidated.

The conversation becomes more personal. The bespectacled man in his mid-40s runs a hand through an untidy mop of greying hair and begins talking about sex and love, in and out of prison. Because of prison rules he has never shared a cell with anyone during his decade in jail and says he's only fallen in love three times. "You could always go in someone else's cell if all you wanted was a quick fuck, a one-night stand, but I've only really been in love three times. You never get over it, when I think about it now, it has exactly the same intensity as it had then." Briefly the subject of religion and personal beliefs comes up; there are strong views here as well: "No, I don't believe in God. God is man-made. Man has fashioned God in his own image."

At 11.30 am the door opens and prison officers insist that Nilsen is taken back to his wing for lunch. Britton had requested that he be allowed to stay with us and share a sandwich, but this is not to be. Earlier, when a guard had brought in cups of tea at a refreshment break, there had been nothing for Nilsen. It was pointed out that this was not bad manners but regulations. There was a chance that he might break one of the pots and use it as a weapon on either of us.

I thought this highly unlikely and offered my mug to Nilsen. He politely declined. It was psychologically important that he felt part of the project, his involvement was vital and little acts of common discourtesy could easily drive a wedge between us. The ruling was that all Category 'A' prisoners have to be fed on their wing between 11.30 am and 1.30 pm and so at exactly 11.30 he was taken back.

Over lunch we collected the packet of Marlboro that 'Des' had set his heart on and Britton summed up what he had learned so far. Nilsen was an egotist, his favourite subject was himself; he wanted to be the centre of attention, to stand out from the crowd and be important. He'd also made considerable efforts to understand why he killed and why he was fascinated with death and dead bodies. He showed no remorse and as importantly, made no pretence about showing remorse. Perhaps this was a private thing, perhaps he felt it churlish to display such a feeling, perhaps it does not exist for him. "What you see is what you get" Nilsen had said. Paul Britton thought this wasn't quite true: "He's working on an image, we're seeing the person he is and the person he'd like to be. From our point of view, that is very important to recognize." Nilsen had presented us with a 500-page insight that he had written on his own sexuality. It was typed on a mixture of coloured notesheets, begged from other prisoners once his own source had dried up. He's also written several plays and corresponded with American professors on a variety of subjects. His energy and frustrations were also keys to his character.

Going back into the prison was a repeat of the tedious but necessary security routine that we had endured in the morning.

Nilsen was kept waiting half an hour longer than seemed necessary. The prison officers simply decided that he would be
'brought down' when they were ready and not when we had
arranged. Nilsen came back at 2.00 pm and was even more
excited and talkative. He swung tirelessly from topic to topic
like a pendulum, not really interested in discussing anything,
more committed to stating his view and having others atten-
tively listen.

"I like being number one. I like being special but I hate
competition, I'll avoid competition like the plague. I hope this
programme is going to be of value to you, I hope you come out
of it with some theory, some knowledge and understanding
because it would be good to know that I'd done something
good. Look at Hitler. Hitler wouldn't have been happy with
Europe, he wouldn't have been happy with the World, he would
have had to have destroyed it eventually. There are similarities
between the two of us, both have personality disorders, it all
goes back to childhood doesn't it?" Nilsen is desperate for
answers, eager for exploration about his 'Hitler Theory' but
Britton won't enter a discussion. Whatever is said today could
influence the freshness of the research tomorrow.

Worse still, Nilsen could simply be testing the ground to see
what pleases the psychologist which could lead to him
distorting the interview by formulating future answers to please
his interviewer. This was a real possibility, especially bearing in
mind Nilsen's admissions about wanting attention and wishing
to be accepted.

Society rejected Dennis Nilsen at 4.25 pm on November 4,
1983. After 12 hours of deliberation the Old Bailey jury
returned to find him guilty of six murders and two attempted
murders. The Judge, Mr Croom-Johnson, sentenced him to life
imprisonment, with a recommendation that he serves at least 25
years in jail. Although he will be eligible for parole in the year
2008, Nilsen believes he will never be released and will die in
prison. He holds a cigarette in one hand and motions towards it:
"I'll probably die of these things before anything else, I'll
smoke myself to death or have a heart attack or just die through

natural causes, but I'm resigned to knowing that I'll spend the rest of my life in here."

More than anything, 'Des' Nilsen does not want us to go. Britton rises and offers an outstretched arm: "Thank you for speaking to us. That's where I'd like to call a halt for today." Nilsen smiles and stands, shakes hands and sits down again. He ignores the cue for the meeting to come to an end.

"So, when's this programme going out then, when will everyone get to see it?" He angles his body around, cutting Britton off completely from the conversation, a little afraid of a rebuff but brave enough to give it a try. It's plain that he will do anything to buy a little more time out of his cell. He's reminiscent of a child that is desperate to stay up at bedtime, stalling on the stairs, inventing headaches or a sudden hunger, anything to gain another few precious moments in the company downstairs. I explain some of the difficulties in giving an exact transmission time, for a programme that is not set to be screened for at least another four months. "I love television, well more the films really, I've watched *Man for All Seasons* over and over. I used to do lots of filming, you know home movie stuff, but good, really good. I burned reels and reels of film, the only stuff that was saved was the the duff bits, the bits I never thought anything of. I never had any training or anything like that but give me a camera and I could look through the frame and know what the camera wanted." He talked with all the enthusiasm of a young film director and I instantly thought of how similar this was to the behaviour of sexual sadists who liked to fantasize, then plan out their attacks like a script; giving victims lines of dialogue to repeat, telling them to perform certain acts then often filming them before, during and after death.

"I hope you're not going to use any of that weird lighting shit." Nilsen brought me back from the theory. "I don't want to look like a bloody monster, I want to look interesting, make me look interesting. However you shoot it, make me look interesting." Throughout the four hours we spent with him, he never asked what type of questions Britton intended to put to him, what the police would do with the interview material or what

value it would be for criminal investigation. He was only interested in the television side of the deal. "I have nothing to do
with the tabloids. I read the shit they wrote about me when I
was arrested. It was real frightening stuff, in fact it was so
damned scary I thought 'Hey, this is a real frightening guy' I
think I'd better stay away from him myself." Brian Masters had
warned me of 'Des's' black sense of humour. In considering co-
operating with a film project about his life, he had given
Masters his full approval but suggested that the end credits
better state: "Cast in Order of Disappearance." He was also
reported to have been instructed to tip some waste food or drink
down a prison wing drain and told the stunned officer, "Are you
sure you want me to do that, I had a bit of bother the last time."

Nilsen was genuinely pained to see us leave. Not because of
any hopes of friendship – I doubt he could even remember our
names – but solely because his audience was disappearing. As
he vanished along the dark corridor it occurred to me that this
was the most successful time of his life. He'd been a policeman,
he'd been in the army and he'd been in the civil service working
in a job centre. He'd joined three old British institutions and had
become what he hated, one of the masses, involved in intrigue
and competition. Now, he had joined yet another institution, the
prison service. Only this time, he was the one name that
everyone knew; he stood out – he was extraordinary.

The following morning Paul Britton and I were joined on the
prison steps by Superintendent Wilf Laidlaw and Detective
Chief Inspector Dennis Clough of Northumbria Police. Laidlaw
is staff officer to Northumbria's Chief Constable John Stevens,
the man who hoisted the wayward train of offender profiling
back onto the workable rails of progress. Clough is a large
Geordie, built like a retired rugby player and has a mischievous
sense of humour. They wore matching Pringle T-shirts and
faded blue jeans. This was their idea of dressing like a television crew, fitting into the scene so as not to look out of place.
They looked more like inmates than anything.

We were soon through the mesh of various internal perimeter
fences and the nine locked gates that separate Britain's most

prolific murderer from the outside world. Instead of the stock-room-cum-office, we'd finally been offered a conference room at the back of a training unit. This was gratefully accepted but it meant a tricky sound and lighting rig and a delay until a prison officer's meeting finished in there.

The large room was filled with echo and nothing else. The concrete block walls had once been economically whitewashed and the bubbling and split cord carpet had once been brown. Thick heating pipes crawled across the skirting boards and up the walls to the flaking plaster of a ceiling that supported three ever-buzzing strip lights. The room had old radiators that looked as though they'd come off Chieftan tanks and it was already at sauna temperature before the camera lights added their own kilowatts of heat. A small square table with black legs and a dirty cream top was wobbily arranged between two chairs of equal size for the interview. It was hardly the perfect setting in which to relax any interviewee, let alone one which was about to be asked the most personal and probing of questions.

I went into the adjoining room and 'Des' Nilsen was already there, hand out, confident and eager. "I've been waiting 20 minutes, no, half an hour." The civil servant was back and was again indignant. I explained the delays, led him in to the pre-set room and introduced him to Laidlaw and Clough. He wasn't really interested in the pleasantries, his eyes had set on the camera and lights. He moved instantly into the empty chair. I handed over a pack of Marlboro, then prepared a radio microphone to fit to the pinstriped blue and white unbuttoned shirt that he wore over a white prison issue T-shirt. Hiding the cable meant pinning the microphone near a buttonhole and then looping the long black wire out of sight around the inside of his shirt. It effectively meant embracing him and I felt a moment of awkwardness. There was a momentary realization, that many others who had been so close to Britain's most prolific killer had died soon afterwards. It was an illogical and embarrassing reaction and Nilsen quickly noticed the hesitation. He gave a knowing smile and began to help with the fitting. By now, he was talking constantly, noticing the equipment and enquiring about its various functions. "I see everything just like a camera, my eyes move like a camera, sometimes in close up sometimes in wide-shot, depending upon how much I want to take in. I was a camera passing through people's lives, they were images flickering before me, behind me and I'd see them like that. I'd know they were people if they'd ask for a light for a cigarette or a drink or something but they were always images. The image was always the most important bit."

As I framed the shot, I realized the extent Nilsen had immersed himself in the production. He'd laid out an ashtray, some notes and cigarettes on the table top and now reclined in a perfect pose behind his props. He didn't squint under the glare of the lights and hardly altered his position. It was a photographer's dream, he was totally at home here. Cigarette lighters aren't allowed in Albany and Nilsen improvised with a makeshift flint and a small metal cog. With amazing dexterity he produced a spark, setting alight the end of a single strand of a cloth mop that he utilized as a wick.

Paul Britton began the interview, starting with Nilsen's childhood in Scotland. He was a war baby; born on November 23, 1945 in the small coastal town of Fraserburgh in the northeast of Scotland. On May 2, 1942 his mother Betty Whyte had married Norwegian Olav Magnus Nilsen, a soldier who had come to Scotland after the German invasion of Norway in 1940. The marriage was a failure. The relationship was so fractured that the young couple never actually lived together. Betty and her children sought refuge in a single bedroom that she tried to turn into a home at her parents' house. The Norwegian met none of his responsibilities as a father or husband and Nilsen says he had no memories of ever meeting him.

"One of my earliest childhood recollections is as a toddler at my grandparents' home in Academy Road. I would be down the path and off down the street. I would scramble under the gate, get caught and be brought back, then I'd scramble under the gate again at any opportunity. I'd always be toddling off down the road, looking for something." Nilsen has acute feelings of loneliness from an early age, believing he didn't fit in at home with his brother Olav and sister Sylvia. "In 1983 when I was arrested, journalists started digging around in Scotland and found my father had divorced my mother on grounds of adultery." He said he'd always thought his mother had 'played around' and believed people in the village might have been aware that he had been sired by a different father than his taller, stronger and blonder brother Olav. He was taunted by other children at school because he didn't have a father and remembered feeling confused about why he only had his mother to go home to. "I remember my mother had this picture taken of her and Olav. It must have cost her a lot of money, it was a proper studio portrait. There she was, with her hair nicely done and this blonde baby sitting proudly on her lap and she was smiling away. When I came along, there was no such picture of me. The only photograph ever taken of me was a snapshot, by an aunty with a Brownie box-camera."

Nilsen experienced many of the childhood influences that FBI research has found common in most serial killers. He was a loner, coming from a one-parent family, unsettled by possible parental infidelity, devoid of deep feelings of love for his mother, and subjected to a great deal of sibling rivalry. He would strive for his mother's attention, constantly washing-up or doing cleaning jobs around the house: "I wanted her to approve, I wanted her to praise me, to notice me." He told Britton he thought she approved of her other children all the time but didn't approve of him unless he did something to gain her attention. Britton put the next question in an emotionless voice: "Did you love your mother?" The reply was just as flat, "No, I didn't love my mother. I was always trying to please her but as a kid there wasn't much you could do. Clean the place up, wash the pots, get a pat on the head. I wanted to be close to her but she was always too busy. I remember her as a dominating presence. She was left with three kids and had to work part-time as a cleaner. She was strong-willed, a very stubborn woman. I think I have a lot of her characteristics, we're very similar in ways."

Nilsen acknowledged the efforts she'd made to keep a roof over the young family's head and provide food for them, but felt cold and uncaring about his relationship with her: "I find it very difficult to cry. If someone walked in here and said your mother's dead in Scotland I wouldn't cry."

The fishing villages that formed Nilsen's childhood community have a history of interbreeding. This created a communal gene-pool that spawned mental problems for many locals. It's been discovered that a number of Nilsen's relatives on his mother's side suffered considerable problems, some ending in suicide. Dennis Nilsen's childhood was a strict one, influenced by religious fundamentalism and dominated by women. At home there was his unapproachable mother, his puritanical grandmother and his sister Sylvia, a rival in his bids for attention. In addition to the lack of love he felt for his mother Betty, he recalled similar feelings towards his grandmother Lily: "There was no love or tenderness with grandmother; it wasn't that kind of relationship at all."

He spoke more glowingly about his grandfather Andrew Whyte. He told us he could remember, "falling asleep in his arms at the end of a long walk along the beach or on the golf course" but Nilsen still wouldn't quantify this as 'love'. "I wouldn't say love for grandfather, more 'attention'. He noticed me and gave me the attention I wanted." Grandad died in 1951 in his bunk on a fishing boat when he was 62, Nilsen was then only six. There's been much speculation that this loss was an emotional trigger that set off Nilsen's fascination with death. Britton started to dismantle this fragile psychological jigsaw: "Did you miss him?" The answer was a little surprising. "I missed the influence of somebody who took an interest in me. Did I weep for him? No, No, never." And what of that traumatic moment when Nilsen was told grandad "had gone to a better place" and young Dennis was shown the old man laid out in his coffin? "I thought, what's he doing in there? You know, I thought it was some kind of crazy stunt or something." He reflected for a moment and then added, "If anything, it perhaps demonstrated for me the power of life and death." It's possible that Nilsen is underplaying the effect Andrew Whyte's death had on him. Certainly Whyte was young Dennis's only male role-model, the only adult to pour attention upon him. In later fantasies, Nilsen would imagine an old man saving a young boy from drowning and vice versa. It is also possible that Nilsen was tired of examining his genealogical roots and didn't wish his crimes to be seen as having been influenced by such an event.

Although he already knew grandad had died at sea, young Des took every opportunity to be terrifyingly near to the water. "Sometimes if I was on my own on the rocks and cliffs I would think about death all the time. I would look out at this innocent stuff called water and wonder how it could kill. I used to court the sea like crazy and I couldn't even swim. The thrill was seducing it, surviving it." This resulted in him spending long, lonely hours on the shores of nearby Broadsea or out at Kinnaird Head on the rocks. When he was about eight years old he says he was rescued from drowning during one of his trips out to Inverallochy. He'd been paddling and got out of his depth and was saved from the pull of the waves by an older boy. Once more, a strong image of a young passive male (him) and an older controlling male (his saviour) had been woven into the fabric of his mind, along with that fascinating threat of death (presented by the sea). Nilsen was in his mid-30s when he began his killings and his targets were always younger men. When he failed in the psycho-sexual act of strangling them with his necktie he resorted to drowning them.

To the young Dennis, his half-brother Olav presented a real identity problem: "I felt that Olav could always out-do me. I had a feeling there was something odd there. I looked at a photograph of him with Betty and thought 'Who is this guy, he looks nothing at all like me?' Olav was destined to succeed – when I was in the 'C' stream he was in the 'A' stream. He took Latin and all that while I was still struggling with mathematics." Nilsen's opinion of himself during these formative years was of "A weak, shy, introverted individual. I wouldn't say boo to a goose."

In awe of the strapping Olav, the feeble Dennis was forced to share a bed with his half-brother, accentuating his own feelings of inadequacy. When Olav was helpless and asleep he would undo his pyjama bottoms and explore his body, handling his penis and stopping when it began to get erect. Nilsen said he didn't find it "sexually exciting," but "interesting." He said Olav never woke up or spoke of the frequent 'explorations' but thought he was aware of them because he chided him for being effeminate and sissy.

Nilsen used to carry out the same 'explorations' on his sister Sylvia, "stroking her private parts as she slept." These ventures were possibly to find what made them more lovable than him in his mother's eyes. They could also have been very basic attempts to elicit feelings of closeness from people he was over-whelmed by as sibling rivals. For a moment he stopped talking and performed the conjuring trick with the flint and mop-wick, producing a lit Marlboro. He sucked deeply, adding: "I felt I could impress Sylvia, I wanted her to feel proud of me, like I wanted my mother to feel proud of me, that's why I joined the army I suppose." He sums up his relationship with his family as "Very shallow."

Britton was not ready to move into those army days and re-directed the interview into the killer's late childhood and teen years. Nilsen remembered being regularly beaten by his history teacher for getting dates wrong and he recalled the daily news-paper and milk rounds that helped supplement his family's poverty-line income and left him tired and inattentive by the time he got to class. Again, like the American research, it seemed an early example of the offender feeling he was being unjustly treated yet was powerless to do anything about it. "Mr Shanks, the history teacher would have this test of history dates and if you got any wrong you got strapped three times. It wasn't the pain that, hurt it was the humiliation. My whole life was a humiliation, the way I was treated at school, the way I dressed, the poverty of the family. I was shabby and undernourished – you were certainly made to feel that you knew your place in society."

Moving away from the people of Nilsen's formative years, Paul Britton began an examination of the twilight world of the young person's imagination. Nilsen quickly recalled his early fantasy life: "From early childhood I'd created this person, he was an observer, he had a passive role and he was a predator: he was two people in one and both people were me. My best friend was me. I was the predator and the victim as well, I could oscillate between the two roles. Life is real to me, but it is not real. All my life has been a fantasy on a theme." Nilsen's thoughts are often complex and it becomes difficult to unravel what is childhood recollection and what might be carefully constructed theory, deliberately designed to intrigue a psychologist.

"I had dreams and daydreams. In my daydreams I was the hero and everything revolved around me, it was a way I suppose for me to get the attention I wanted. I was Robin Hood, I was the leader, I was the top dog, I was the real important person in that scenario."

The picture Nilsen painted seemed suddenly at odds with his comments the previous day that he never wanted to be part of a gang or a clique, that he wanted to be "apart from the herd." The truth might well be that he only wanted to be 'apart' if he couldn't in fact be in charge. He continued: "I was a benevolent hero though, like Gary Cooper in *High Noon*, a firm dictator, firm but fair, the type other people looked up to, respected." This was how Nilsen would view himself in later days as he took positions of branch treasurer and chairman of his local union branch: "In my trade union days when I was fighting for the underdog I was really fighting for myself." Once more he was oscillating between roles: sometimes the underdog, sometimes the dictator, sometimes potent, sometimes impotent but always concerned with the image he was trying to project.

Nilsen the movie-buff recalled the Dracula films of the 1950s. They left him climbing the stairs to bed with images of Nosferatu lurking in shadows on the landing, lying in wait beneath his bed with bony hands ready to grab his naked ankles. He experienced the normal fears of any child that had been gripped by one of the most chilling of all horror stories. For Nilsen though, there was an added fascination. Unlike his grandfather, the blood-sucking Count could rise from the dead. Here was an unkillable hero that could administer death and after-life, who could spread the powerful gospel of immortality.

"I would have nightmares about Dracula, but beforehand I would prepare myself, I would set the scene so that when Dracula would appear I would attack him and pull his head off. I'd decided that I was going to stalk him, that he was going to be the one frightened of me, not the other way round."

It wasn't long before Des Nilsen's thoughts of death were put into practise. Playing alone near a toilet block in Strichen, the seven-year-old caught a kitten. "I hung it up on a piece of wire to see how it died, to see how long it took to die. I hadn't planned it beforehand or fantasized about it, it just sort of occurred to me that I was going to hang it. I did it to see what the process of death was." Nilsen strung the wriggling cat from the toilet cistern. He remembered that it had purred right up until the moment of its execution and he had stood there dry-eyed throughout. There was no remorse afterwards only feelings of guilt, worries about being caught and as he put it, the still unanswered question, "What is death, what is it? I was afraid of death but I thought if you could rationalize it and expose it, then it would be less frightening. If you fear the power of death then you examine the power to see what it is."

Once more, Nilsen fits into the patterns discovered by the FBI. They found that as children, many serial killers displayed cruelty to animals. Nilsen's cat incident also has a parallel with the juvenile experiments that Jeffrey Dahmer carried out on cats and dogs, dissecting them in his father's garage.

Nilsen's masturbatory fantasies as a child revolved around undressing sleeping boys, in the way that he had explored the bodies of his brother and sister. "I had a passive image of them because I knew the only way I could get near to them was for them to be asleep. It was very important for them to be passive and for me to exploit that passivity."

Britton continued the exploration of Nilsen's sexuality as the 15-year-old Des joined the British Army and kept his developing homosexuality in the regimental closet. When the soldiers started talking of 'queers' and 'poofters' Nilsen bit his tongue or even forced himself to laugh along at the jibes that he actually found humiliating and painful. During those vital years

there was a repression of sexual and social skills, pushing
Nilsen back into the auto-erotic world of his own masturbatory
fantasies. His first sexual contact didn't come until he was 21.

Posted to Aden, he was put in charge of catering at a military
prison in Sharjah in the Persian Gulf. Here Nilsen found a
young Arab rent-boy who slept with many of the officers. "I
think he was about 12, somewhere between 12 and 15. This was
the first intercourse that I'd had but it wasn't anything other
than that. The boy would hang around begging everyone to take
him back to England which of course couldn't happen."

Britton discovered that while some of Nilsen's social skills
were underdeveloped, the same certainly could not be said of
his fantasies. They had now become exceptionally complex. As
an NCO Nilsen had acquired the privacy of his own room and
more importantly a large mirror, a new and vital prop in his
masturbatory activities. "I've had a rabid love-affair with a
mirror for years, a form of Narcissism if you like, the oblong
frame is always more powerful for me." He casts a half-glance
at the camera, ensuring we have made the connection with his
previous remarks on photography and film-making. "I'd angle
the mirror so that I couldn't see my head and then I could
imagine that the hands acting upon me were another person and
yet they were still me." In other sex-games with himself Nilsen
would powder his body so it looked drained like a corpse and
then imagine that he was dead.

At this point a prison guard arrived with mugs of tea and this
time there was one for Nilsen. He lit another cigarette and
gulped down the tepid grey liquid. It's a welcome break, a
chance to stop the intensity of the interview and make small talk
for a moment but Nilsen was relentless, unable to stop talking
of himself and his experiences. The cameras stayed rolling and
he recounted waking naked in bed with another man; having
drunk so much the night before he couldn't remember anything.
"I felt really annoyed. Not that it had happened, but that I hadn't
been around to witness it, to enjoy having been in that situation." It seemed that Nilsen only viewed passivity as a turn-on,
providing he was not required to be passive.

He was almost 27 when he left the army and said: "I had only one thing on my mind. To find a partner to share my life with socially and sexually." But to some extent it was a case of 'out of the frying pan and into the fire'. Nilsen left the rigours of the regiment for the homophobia of the Metropolitan Police. PC Q287 was still having to keep his sexuality a secret. "Being a policeman insulted my sense of morality" he told Britton.

At this point he said he was experiencing "increasing desperation. There was that nagging feeling that you are becoming isolated from everybody. The feelings had started as a child but had got increasingly worse." The following year he resigned from his job at the Willesden Green station and found it a struggle to make ends meet. He flitted from a temporary post as a security guard into a very short period of unemployment. He then secured a job as a clerical officer in the Department of Employment, based at a job centre in London's Denmark Street.

Nilsen said he was sexually active, sometimes promiscuous during this spell, but also desperately lonely; finding one-night stands but never the elusive relationship that he had set his post-army sights upon. In November 1975, he came across a young man that perfectly fitted into his blond male fantasies. "I virtually kidnapped David Gallichan" admitted Nilsen, such was his excitement at meeting the unemployed 20-year-old who wore earrings and make-up. Nilsen would nickname him 'Twinkle' and take him in as a lodger at his new flat in Melrose Avenue. They had a two-year affair that blossomed into domesticity. They even acquired a 'family' of sorts – a dog called Bleep, a cat called DD and a budgie named Hamish. For some time there was bliss, with Nilsen being so proud of his new lover that he braved the slings and arrows of heterosexual conformity and took him to a staff party at the job centre. As the matched couples arrived in their suits and best dresses, Des and Twinkle turned up hand in hand. It was a party to celebrate Christmas but Nilsen was also celebrating a public announcement of his homosexuality and the fact that he too had a partner, someone who cared for him.

The balloon burst sometime in 1976. Nilsen said the affair had become one-sided, with Gallichan staying out all hours and seeing other men. "I was dependent upon Dave to live up to his responsibilities and he didn't do that. I wanted him to come back in the evenings, I needed that security, a sense of belonging, that feeling of having someone." Both men started taking other partners back to the flat for sex. Lovers' tiffs turned into unbridgeable differences. In the summer of 1977 Twinkle left their home to go and stay with a new man. Nilsen plunged into drink and headed into heavy depression.

It was 11.30 am and lunch time. It didn't matter that the interview had progressed to the very point where Nilsen's career as a murderer began, Prison rules meant the category 'A' prisoner had to be back on his wing for lunch. Nilsen offered to miss lunch entirely. The authorities would have none of it. He was escorted back to his cell and we were told we could resume two and a half hours later, after all the wing had been fed. Britton's calmness never broke but the irritation was bubbling beneath the surface.

A mile up the road at the Stag Inn in Newport a cage of rabbits amused two toddlers who were wandering in the beer garden. A tethered goat chomped on a wad of grass and the afternoon sun burned down on a party of Isle of Wight holiday-makers. We were so close to the prison and yet so far away from Nilsen's world of murder and necrophilia. As we waited for an order of baked potatoes and sandwiches, the two policemen reflected on the morning's experience. Superintendent Laidlaw disclosed a previous career as a Northumbrian shepherd, and added: "I never saw animals behave like that man; no animal would do anything like the things he did. We have a saying up North, 'There's nowt as queer as folk' and it's certainly true in his case." DCI Dennis Clough had passed the long train journey from Newcastle, reading Brian Masters' book. Now he proferred frequent excerpts to Paul Britton in the hope of helping with the interview. Britton, an expert clinician and brilliant behavioural analyst, graciously accepted the succession of advice, before finally ducking another contribu-

tion by politely declaring that he too had read the publication. In
fact, as well as obtaining Nilsen's consent for the interview,
producers at Central had also provided the psychologist with a
specially taped interview with Brian Masters and a comprehensive dossier of press clippings and reports on Nilsen's crimes.
Nobody could have been better prepared for the horrors that
were about to unfold that Tuesday afternoon.

We had met Brian Masters at St John's College in Oxford on
an August afternoon. He has written more than a dozen books,
including five on French literature. The only time he has turned
his literary skills to the subject of homicide, is the recent
study of Jeffrey Dahmer and his definitive work on Nilsen.
He was to provide us with an invaluable summary of our enig-
matic interviewee.

"I would say that he's mad in the soul, that's the best way I
can think of putting it. He's certainly not mad in the head. Intel-
lectually, he's perfectly able to plan, to devise things and see
things through to fruition. He's working in prison, he paints, he
writes, he composes. He's very articulate when he's talking,
he's very funny, he can make jokes. He was perfectly capable,
when he was on the outside, of catching a bus and going to
work, of walking the dog and doing all those things which show
deliberation and intellectual control. In that sense, he's certainly
not mad, but there is something deeply wrong with his soul.
Now, that's a word I'd never used before I started to work on
this case, because it is indefinable, it's a religious word and one
tries to avoid such words because they are difficult to understand and pin down properly, but there is no other word I can
think of in his case."

Masters wrote to Nilsen when the killer was on remand
awaiting Crown Court trial and has travelled thousands of miles
visiting him in a variety of prisons. Nowadays, they talk of
everything in the world, except the murders. The author clearly
believes he has certain responsibilities to his subject: "I feel a
responsibility to visit. I have no responsibility for his character
or the way he is understood by the world. Whether the world
likes him or loathes him is nothing to do with me. My only

responsibility is to visit him because he was a great help to me in writing a book which won a prize and did me no harm at all. It would be, I think, morally reprehensible, to say to him 'Well, thanks very much for all your help and now you can rot. I will never come and see you again, so goodbye'. I don't think one gross immorality on his part, the killing of 15 men, deserves the minor immorality of me being disloyal towards the help that he gave me in writing the book."

While a friendship has developed between the two men, Masters still believes he is open-minded about Nilsen's case, though he doubts there are any significant stones of personality that he has left unturned. "There are always with people who've done this sort of thing, aspects of the crime that they find peculiarly embarrassing. The fact that they've squeezed the life out of somebody, they can talk about. They can even talk about dismemberment, but it might be a little detail which they won't talk about, something they consider morally repugnant. I suppose masturbating over a corpse is something that a lot of them will hide, and yet Nilsen did admit to doing that and so has Dahmer. Whether he's revealed absolutely everything or not, no one will ever know. My own opinion is that he has told everything that is of importance. I think if he did withhold anything, it might be something like he'd stolen a ring off one of the corpses and kept it. I think he'd probably hide that, because that's something that is against his own morality."

We asked Masters if he thought Nilsen had consumed any of his victims' flesh or blood. It turned out that this was a question he had put to Nilsen in the early days of their interviews. "He made a joke about it. He always takes refuge in a joke if something is embarrassing. I did ask him if he'd ever eaten any human flesh and he said 'Oh no. I'm strictly a bacon and eggs man'. Now, I did laugh. It was a funny response to a serious question and it probably shows that he might have tried it once and didn't want to admit it, but I don't think he did it habitually. The idea of experimentation; even, if you'll forgive the word 'spiritual' experimentation – of taking the spirit of somebody else into your body and making them relive in your flesh, is something they do find attractive. So, it wouldn't surprise me to learn that he had attempted it, but I don't think he made a habit of it. He wasn't cannibalistic by ritual."

Nilsen's crimes were not sadistic. He did not experience any gratification from seeing his victims suffer. There was no ritualistic mutilation of the corpses before or after death and as Brian Masters observed, there was an uncomfortable gentleness to his crimes. "He would treat the bodies, dare I say it, with a certain amount of care and attention. He would carry the body into the bath and wash it, he would dress it and treat it like a private possession, a doll if you like. He would dress it and sit in the armchair. He would undress it at the end of the day and put it to bed and he would even sometimes talk to it. The same has happened to Dahmer. Dahmer did talk to people after he killed them. Usually, Dahmer would say things like, "I'm sorry it had to happen this way. I wish I could have kept you another way.' Nilsen's was much more of a monologue, 'Guess what happened to me today?' and he'd complain about this, that and the other." Masters recalled that Nilsen had a chilling explanation for this bizarre behaviour. "He said that he felt that somehow they were still there, the spirit was still there. He said that 'If I could see them, then they were not entirely lost'. It is hardly convincing but there was not much else he could say. To him, death was not a finality, it was not the end of a relationship but the beginning of one." This was the man we returned to Albany to interview.

When Nilsen returned for the second session, he brought with him a portable Casio keyboard. Over the lunch-break he had composed a minute-long piece of music entitled 'Themes on Childhood'. He played it proudly. It was classic pop, a swirling whirl of synthesized and sampled electronics, evoking strong images of a calm and sometimes raging sea.

The interview recommenced, back in those 'dark days' after Twinkle had deserted him. Nilsen said he had tried to fill an opening social void by immersing himself in union activities with the CPSA, but the feelings of emptiness and loneliness became more and more consuming.

The killing started in the winter of 1978, after a night's drinking at the Cricklewood Arms. Nilsen and an Irish youth returned to 195 Melrose Avenue and fell drunkenly into bed together. In the early light of morning, Des awoke and although no sex had taken place, he felt an enormous attachment to the stranger. He couldn't reconcile himself to the prospect that he would soon be gone. His hands explored the youngster's body, much as he had done with his brother and sister during childhood days. Now, on the spur of the moment he picked up his discarded tie and started to strangle his bed mate. The stranger woke immediately and a struggle began. Nilsen says he pulled the choking man from the bed, straining with the ligature, crashing him into bedroom furniture until he dropped into unconsciousness. Still not certain that he had completely dispatched his drinking companion, he filled a bucket with water and held the man's head in it until the last bubbles of life had stopped rising to the surface.

Nilsen told Britton: "After the killing there was this buzzing, buzzing in my mind. The image of him was buzzing all the time." Nilsen then carried the corpse over his shoulder towards the bathroom, when he says his camera-like eyes caught the act in a mirror. "It was such a powerful sight, so powerful seeing myself carrying him like that." If that was extraordinary, then the ritual that followed of washing, redressing and keeping the body was even more bizarre. "I don't really know why I washed him, perhaps it was just cleanliness. I think I wanted him at his best for my fantasy. Funnily enough, at this point I was him, in my mind I was him as well as me. I'd felt a compulsive necessity to reduce the person into a passive state. I didn't think at this point that the person was gone, I don't think he was ever there as a person to me."

Superintendent Laidlaw and Detective Chief Inspector Clough were sitting together, both leaning forward in their chairs, their faces chiselled with amazement and disbelief. Nilsen recounted the murder in a calm, almost caring voice. He used a tone that would be more suitable for reminiscing about throwing stones on a holiday beach. It was difficult to discern whether he was feeling tenderness at the memories, or experiencing a type of emotion exclusive to him. What was certain was that he was not in the least upset or traumatized by confronting the most awesome crime that man can commit.

Nilsen said he unwrapped a cellophane package of Y-fronts and fitted the underwear to his new flatmate. "I had a frisson of excitement. I imagined him doing to me what I was doing to him. I wanted him to be me. The Y-fronts were brand new, a flawlessness was necessary." At this moment fantasy had fused with reality in the disordered personality of Nilsen. Although the body had now been dead for more than four hours he was romantically aroused by it. He told Paul Britton: "Because of the lighting in Melrose Avenue, there was always a gentle red glow in the room and this fell on his body making him look warm and alive." Britton asked whether Nilsen had tried to have intercourse with the corpse, "I started to have anal sex but I lost my erection because of the coldness of his flesh. It seemed wrong anyway, it spoilt the image of him. It was the visuals that produced the erection." Here again was a practical example of the analogy between murder and filming; Nilsen was fixated with 'the image' that he was creating, he had chosen his cast and had even completed the costuming himself. It was only when the act differed from the fantasy, that he lost his state of sexual arousal. Nilsen withdrew and later resorted to masturbation. He said he considered ejaculation as "a biological release." Many profilers believe that masturbation like this locks the fantasy into the mind of a killer and renders his psychological disorders beyond correction.

He then gave a powerful insight into the strength of his fantasy life, "My imagination had developed by then to such a state that I could conjure up anything that I fancied." His already unbridled imagination now had new horizons to aim for. He had killed for the first time and now believed that anything was possible.

Nilsen tried to dispose of the body. He was what American profilers call a 'disorganized' killer and he was destined to make a mess of it. While he'd spent unhealthy amounts of time sexually fantasizing about having a body, he'd given no clear thought to the task of getting rid of one. Des walked to his local hardware shop to look for tools of dismemberment. As a former army chef, he made a poor choice: "I bought an electric knife and a big cooking pot. I paid £12 for the knife and it was useless. I eventually gave it away to a girl in the office. I said 'Here, have this to cut the turkey up with at Christmas'. It only made a little cut in his skin." Des the chef had the notion that he could chop the corpse into joints and cook them in the stainless steel pot. Then, he could flake the flesh away from the bones and dispose of the body piece by piece.

Before the interview, Paul Britton and I had discussed Brian Masters' belief that Nilsen was not beyond having tried to eat the flesh of his victims. Nilsen was categoric: "No. No, that held no appeal to me. It did not occur to me at all." Despite all the cooking paraphernalia and the boiling of flesh, we could find no evidence to support this concept. It was also apparent that such an act would not have fitted with the fantasy image that Nilsen was bent on creating. If he had indeed carried out such a practise, then even he wasn't yet prepared to confront the enormity of it and has hidden it deep. Nilsen seemed disarmingly honest throughout the interview and subsequent checking of his comments has not revealed any deliberate lies.

The flint and the fags were out once more. It seemed as though Nilsen had timed his lighting-up as a piece of black humour. He'd finished a lengthy sexual discussion and was now almost in post-coition, enjoying a cigarette. He kept the body beneath his floor-boards for the next eight months and insisted that the murder itself did not figure in any of his future masturbatory fantasies.

The killing itself and the body disposal afterwards seem not to have been attractive to Nilsen. While some killers thrill at the power of taking life, or satisfy their mental disorders by mutilating or dismembering their victims, these were merely unattractive prices Nilsen had to pay for the joys of having had a passive and ever-present companion. American research on killers like Nilsen suggests he was driven to exert 'control' over his victims because he felt he had no real control over his own life. In the badly disordered mind of the necrophile, murder is the ultimate weapon of control.

The body of his first victim was kept under the floor-boards and occasionally taken out and washed and dressed while he re-enacted his fantasies. It gradually began to decompose and it's likely some degree of insect infestation would have taken place during the eight months it had become an unexpected lodger in Melrose avenue. "There came a point when he became ugly" said Nilsen uncomfortably "It was the dead-meat syndrome and I had to get rid of him." The landlord built a bonfire in the back-garden and he turned it into a funeral pyre. He added rubbish and rubber to the flames to disguise the sickening smell and smoke from the charring flesh.

It would be a year before Nilsen took a second unpaying guest into his home. During this time, he said he experienced a mixture of feelings ranging from anxiety about being discov-ered to a basic guilt about having taken someone's life. There was no pretence of remorse, simply an acknowledgment that the killing had left him with a dark secret that rankled with his other principles of championing the underdog.

Canadian tourist Kenneth Ockenden, holidaying in London was Dennis Andrew Nilsen's second victim. They met in a pub and after a whistle-stop sight-seeing tour they returned to Nilsen's home and began drinking again. "He was sitting on the sofa and I was thinking 'he'll be gone tomorrow, he'll be flying back to Canada tomorrow' and I just wanted him to stay."

It was after midnight when Nilsen strangled Ockenden with the flex of his stereo-headphones. "I had thought about having sex with him. I wanted a sexual relationship with him, but we had never talked about it." Nilsen carried on drinking and listening to music after the murder. Once he had recovered his composure he discovered that Ockenden had defecated during the strangulation. The washing ritual now began again. Nilsen recounted this stage in such a way, that instead of seeing a killer and his corpse, an image is evoked of a father and his baby. He carried the body to the bathroom, lovingly washed it and carefully dried it. He then took the corpse into his bed and held it in an affectionate embrace until the following morning. This time there was no attempt at anal sex.

The following day Nilsen became the movie-director again. "I got a camera and took photographs of Ken Ockenden lying flat out on the carpet. It was something I had to do, I had to put him in the oblong frame." Having created the image of his fantasies he had to capture that reality by photography. He would then use the reality of the photograph to spark-off even more lavish fantasies. It was a Polaroid camera that Nilsen used, not the home-movie equipment that he loved so dearly. "They were good pictures but there's not much you can do with those types of camera; they're just the flash and take type." Nilsen displayed an air of disappointment. This basic photography hadn't satiated his artistic desires and he felt impelled to alter the image, he had to tweak the fantasy just a little more. "I placed a tissue over his sexual parts to add some mystery to the shots." Like the electric knife, the camera had now outlived his purpose. "I gave it to a guy in the office. I said, 'Here I've got a Polaroid camera, I've got no use for it, you might as well have it'." He seemed to derive some humorous satisfaction from the thought that the staid civil servants in his office would snap-up his free gifts and use them in everyday life for far more mundane tasks.

Ockenden was kept beneath the boards and brought up several times over the next month. Nilsen would wash and dress him like a human sex-doll. There is no doubt that he had completely depersonalized his victims, seeing them as objects rather than human beings. Nilsen said this was necessary, "to keep my sanity." The dehumanization enabled him to consummately move his 'prop' around the 'stage' that had once been his flat and act out a gamut of unbelievable scenes. Yet Nilsen drew an interesting line of distinction here. He said that for the killing to take place it was necessary for him not to view the victim as a specific person, such as 'Ken' or 'Stephen' but for the following fantasies to be excitingly fulfilled, he then had to imagine the bodies as people and not as corpses.

The killer had frictional sex between Ockenden's thighs and he would also talk to the corpse. To the over-garrulous Nilsen, a man obsessed with talking but not listening, here was a perfect companion, unquestioning and always attentive.

For a moment the conversation climbed out of the mire or murder and Nilsen filled in a character sketch of his 'normal' life; as the Des Nilsen that he presented to his unsuspecting colleagues and to the world at large. "I never had sex with anybody when there was someone under the floor. I couldn't get my rocks off like that, I just couldn't do it." He said that he felt sexually re-awakened after cremating one body in the garden. "I put this putrid bundle on the pyre and it was like a cleansing operation. I knew then that I could go out and have sex. It was one-night stand sex, transient and unrewarding. The predominate objective was still to have a real relationship."

On more than half a dozen drunken nights Nilsen had the opportunity and mind to kill, yet he spared his potential victims. "One man woke up while I was taking his trousers off. I had a tie around his neck and was starting to strangle him when he woke. He thought it was all part of some kinky game and said, 'Fuck Me, fuck me'. I just lifted up his legs and had intercourse with him. He thought it was all part of it. He left the next morning." Nilsen allowed himself a thin smile, wondering if his old homosexual partner now realized how close to death he had come.

Another visitor, 21-year-old Carl Stottor, endured a similar ordeal in 1982. After drinking in the local pub, he and 'Des' had gone to bed. He woke from his drunken haze to find his new friend strangling him and shouting at him to be quiet. Next he was being drowned in the bathroom. He blacked out. Because Bleep the dog spotted a spark of life in the dying body, Nilsen the killer turned into Nilsen the saviour. He swaddled Stottor in blankets and took him to bed with him, hugging him close and reviving him with his own body heat.

Stottor only had vague recollections of the nightmare he had survived. Eventually, Nilsen escorted him to the tube station and pleasantly asked him to call again. It's possible that he had saved Stottor because he had become excited by the realization that he could give life as well as take it. This God-like power has proved attractive to many killers but is more common in the peculiar make-up of sexual sadists than it is in necrophilic killers.

Nilsen said he probably attempted to murder at least another seven men and is unsure about why he spared them. The most probable reason was that in some accidental way they broke the pattern of the fantasy that he was acting out. His idea of a passive victim was shattered if they woke or something unplanned disturbed his fantasy – suach as Bleep wandering into the room. Nilsen gave us a clue to this in one of his early comments in the interview, when he explained how he stopped sodomizing his first victim, loosing his erection because "it spoilt the image."

It's uncertain how many more murders followed that of Ken Ockenden. The official total is 15 but Nilsen told Britton that he had confessed to three murders that he hadn't done. He said he made these admissions, simply to fit in with police suggestions and lines of questioning . This may be true, but it must also be remembered that Nilsen didn't even know the names of many of his victims. There could even be a chance that he has killed more than the 15 he readily confessed to.

Just before his arrest, Nilsen's mental condition had deteriorated considerably. Disposing of the mounting toll of rotting corpses was becoming a trauma for him. He says, "I wanted it to stop, but I didn't have the balls to go to the police station and give myself up and I didn't have the balls to stop killing either.

"In the end, when there were two or three bodies stacked up in the house, I knew there would be a smell problem. I worked out that the smell would probably come from their innards, so I decided to do something about that, even though it was totally unpleasant." Nilsen went on to describe how he disembowelled the corpses, scooping out the rancid intestines while still trying to preserve as much of the flesh as possible. "I had to leave every two minutes to be sick on the garden path, then I'd come back in, have another drink and carry on until I was sick again." That was the one moment when a flicker of revulsion crossed

Nilsen's face. The psychologist had started a disturbing investigation into the killer's deepest thoughts. Nilsen added, "It was simply something that had to be done. Man can get used to some disturbing things if you are exposed to them for long enough. People got used to being in the trenches in the First World War and having a friend's brains blown all over them. The remains had no significance to me, they were something untoward and were simply awkward to get rid of."

As already mentioned, there are many interesting similarities between Nilsen and the American homosexual Jeffrey Dahmer. Both were of the same kind of age and sexual predilection, they both killed the same kind of people and kept bodies or body parts around the house. They both talked to their corpses and Dahmer inter-acted with the cadavers to the extent of having sex with their disembowelled intestines. He is reported to have consumed his victim's flesh with the intention of completing an act of total possession. Here, very importantly, he differs strongly from Nilsen. Nilsen said he found the body disposal genuinely disturbing and he extracted no emotional or sexual satisfaction from the act.

Like Dahmer, he still looked back on his victims with a sense of ownership and with a disconcerting feeling of 'possession'. Nilsen told Britton: "The bodies are all gone but I feel a spiritual communion with these people. They are a part of me." Somehow Nilsen's answers haven't completely dispelled the possibility of attempted cannibalism.

The phrase 'spiritual communion' is indicative of Nilsen's strong religious upbringing in Scotland. Many of his remarks were embossed with Biblical or supernatural phraseology. During his trial at the Old Bailey, he told the jury ,"I thought I was in a quasi-God role. I thought I could do anything I wanted while the people next door and upstairs knew nothing." In the interview with Paul Britton, he said of his arrest, "All my demons were exorcised by exposure, I wallowed in it."

The basic instinct to escape detection and carry on living out his fantasies was still the main driving force. This instinct was much stronger than the intoxicating fame that he knew would come with his detailed confession. Nilsen admitted that even when human flesh had been discovered clogging up the drains of his flat, he believed he could still have got away with it. Des joined the other tenants at Cranley Gardens in Muswell Hill in inspecting the mass of rotting flesh that had been uncovered by 29-year-old plumber Mike Cattran. Cattran, a former beach life-guard told police he had pulled bodies out of the sea and had recognized the smell instantly. By this stage Nilsen had developed his body disposal into a practise where he sliced the flesh into four inch pieces after boiling parts in the giant cooking pot.

Because it was dark, Cattran went home and promised to return the following day to complete the job. Nilsen told Britton: "I thought to myself, 'Well Des, you can still pull this off.' I had cleared much of the flesh from the sewer and there were only a few bits left to move. I thought of going down the road and buying some Kentucky Fried Chicken, then I'd break it into similar sized pieces and scatter them down the drain, leaving some of the wings and tips to be found. It was 50 per cent certain that they'd go down the following day and I decided to do nothing. It was a case of heads or tails, if they found pieces then I was through, if not, then I was free."

The odds were really much less than 50/50 and Nilsen by now was battle-tired. "I thought of getting out my passport, buying a plane ticket and going to live in a flat under Ronnie Biggs, but I couldn't be bothered. I knew the police would come." Although Nilsen denied all the murder charges and attempted murder charges levied against him when he appeared in court, he did so, not in an attempt to deny what he had done, but on legal advice that he was "Not guilty on the grounds of diminished responsibility." From the first moments of his arrest, he admitted that he had killed 15 men and tried to kill another seven. He had always held little back, talking freely whenever he believed he had a worthy audience. The only time Nilsen restrained his instinct to 'wallow in it', is if he believed he was going to be misrepresented. Before the interview in Albany he wrote to Central Television and said in the past decade he had only ever been allowed two visitors, Brian Masters and Lord

Longford. He doubted that we would be allowed to see him because there was a chance that in examining his crimes (which he in no way tries to excuse or play down) we may show sides of him that give the impression of someone human and intelligent. Nilsen was both those things and many more. It is his very ordinariness that is the most unsettling.

It is easier for us all to believe that someone so dedicated to death must in all ways be vastly different to the rest of society and stand out from the crowd. It is not so. If that were the case, then there would be no need for forensic science or psychological profiling. Serial killers would be instantly spottable.

Ironically, 'ordinary' is the last thing Nilsen would like to be branded as, and it is his desire to be someone special that is such a contributory factor to his untreatable personality disorders. In the final stages of his interview with Paul Britton, he was asked to summarize "who he is" Nilsen replied: "I did some terrible things but there is some mitigation. I'm ordinary but unique in places. I don't fit in with the herd, I don't do what other people do. I'm different from everyone else, I have a uniqueness but that doesn't make me better than the herd. In some ways I'm definitely more moral, I couldn't be bribed for example. I don't bully people and I don't pick on people."

It comes as no surprise to hear Nilsen include in his summary a lost hope that he would like to have been a film director. He talked guardedly about a brief affair with someone in London's film circles, someone who he believed may have been able to help him get a job as an assistant cameraman. Nilsen thought he should have taken it, then worked his way to the top. "The only thing I could have been good at was making films. I think at the end of the day I could have made it in movies, if only I'd had the guts to leave the civil service."

His last thoughts on the career he chose, that of the UK's most prolific serial killer, show the very reason why Paul Britton began the historic research project into the minds of serial offenders: "Right at the end, the pressure was getting worse and worse and I could see it all accelerating. If I hadn't been caught it could have been one-a-week, there could have been hundreds."

# 4
# Women Who Kill

*"I see no reason why a woman convicted of murder should not hang." – Mr Justice Rayner Goddard to the Royal Commission on Capital Punishment, 1953.*

Women murderers drift readily into criminal folklore. They command a voyeuristic fascination which attracts a sensational and exaggerated degree of interest from the media. Because of this their crimes seem even more horrific and they are often perceived to be more depraved and deviant than male killers.

The very act of a woman committing murder forces us to confront our long-held preconceptions of the female's role in society. It challenges our comforting assumptions of women as mothering protectors, personifications of care and gentleness. It explodes the myths society and tradition have created around little girls in pink who tend to their dolls, adolescent girls as mothers-in-the-making, the young women who will create life and nurture the next generation of husbands and mothers.

It is worth putting female crime into perspective. In Great Britain less than 20 percent of serious crime and less than ten per cent of murders are committed by women, in a society where they outnumber men. In the USA only 12 percent of murders are committed by women.

Ninety percent of the victims of women who kill are men, a statistic which speaks volumes. The vast majority of murders committed by women are, for want of a better phrase, crimes of passion. They are instigated by abuse or jealousy. Women generally are not as violent or physically aggressive as men, who may kill in brawls or during the course of crime. There are different social controls on women which offer them less opportunity to be placed in a position to kill. It is a sign of the times, for instance, that they are not as free to roam the streets and bars at night.

Society in the 20th century has begun to recognize pressures on women that may have driven them to last resort measures. It has been argued, it is easier for the stronger man to kill a woman than vice versa and so the mitigation was greater?

Since 1923 64 women murderers have been sentenced to death in Great Britain. Only nine actually went to the gallows. The execution of Ruth Ellis, who in 1955 was the last woman to be hanged, created such an emotional outrage it provided one of the biggest single arguments for the abolition of capital punishment, which occurred ten years later. It has been argued that courts have since been more prepared to mitigate in the case of a woman facing a murder charge than in that of a man.

Successive governments have pledged tougher penalties for crimes of violence. This generally happens with male offenders but not with women. It is more likely that a non-custodial sentence will be passed on a woman who has murdered her husband or boyfriend. Such sentences may invariably be accompanied by generous social and medical support. The existence of children will also have a significant affect on the sentence a woman receives. Rarely so with men. The law once again assumes it is the woman's role to raise the family so more allowances are made for her than for him.

This is acceptable to society. Women commit far less violent crimes despite suffering greater physical abuse. They have a greater tendency towards tolerance than men and are generally more willing to put their families and relationships before themselves than men are.

So much for the vast majority of murders committed by women. Sometimes, however, society and circumstances throw up a female killer who, because of the nature of her crimes and, indeed, because she is a woman, stuns and sickens us all.

*********************

Superintendent Bob Talbot froze; his ears rang and his blood ran cold as he stared down at one of the photographs on his desk. Reflecting the horror of his own look, a little girl stared out at him. She had tightly curled dark hair, her eyes were wide with terror and her cheeks bulged where a man's scarf was knotted tightly around her mouth. She was naked except for her ankle socks and shoes.

Talbot stared in shock for almost a minute. He recognized that terrified face. It had smiled down from street posters issued after her disappearance ten months earlier on Boxing Day, 1964. It was Lesley Ann Downey, aged ten. He slowly, almost fearfully, thumbed through each pathetic pornographic picture. There were nine in all and he laid them out on the table.

The little girl, confused and innocent, had been made to stand, sit and lie in various poses which to her meant nothing but gave sick gratification to those taking the photographs in the dingy little bedroom. The ninth photograph showed the girl kneeling with her hands clasped in prayer beneath her cruel gag, staring anxiously beyond the camera. Perhaps at someone other than the photographer?

The photographs had been contained in a faded tin marked 'Halibut Oil'. The tin had been among the contents of two suitcases retrieved from a luggage locker at Central Station, Manchester. Among the other contents were pornographic books, a woman's black wig, a number of .45 and .303 bullets, two coshes, more photograph albums and four reels of audio tape. He put the tapes aside, he would listen to them later. When he did, the horror of the photographs would pale in comparison.

Bob Talbot was among the first people to bear witness to the sickening crimes of the killer who would soon become the most reviled woman in British criminal history – moors murderer Myra Hindley.

She was a war baby born mid-way through World War II on July 23, 1942, in the working-class Manchester suburb of Gorton. She was the first of two daughters. Her sister Maureen was born four years later.

Myra Hindley grew up with her grandmother which was not through any parental rejection, in fact far from it. Her mum and dad lived very close by with little Maureen. Myra flitted casually between both houses but favoured her gran's where there was a better chance of being spoilt.

She had a normal post-war upbringing, one of millions of snotty-nosed, grubby, working-class kids who enjoyed endless adventures ferreting about on old bomb sites until the summer nights grew dark. It was still safe for children to roam the streets of Manchester because Myra had not yet grown up.

She attended Peacock Street County Primary School and went on at the age of 11 to Ryder Brow Secondary School, with all the other ordinary boys and girls. She was well-built with long legs and enjoyed most sports, especially swimming, rounders and netball. She had an above average IQ of 109 and was not short of friends.

Searching through her childhood and adolescence there is no incidence of abuse or deprivation, no glaring sign to which an observer could point and say: "There. That was the key that unlocked the monster." But one event did have a dramatic impact on 15-year-old Myra. It was an incident which, if anything, demonstrated the caring and compassionate side of the friendly neighbourhood girl, a girl who made a hobby of baby-sitting, who was seen to hug the laughing toddlers she coaxed to walk towards her. It was her first brush with grief.

Myra loved to mother people, especially those younger than her so she befriended Michael Higgins, a 13-year-old neighbour. He was a delicate child, physically so much younger than his years and easy prey to bullies. Myra protected him and he became her faithful little companion. One sunny mid-June day he urged Myra to accompany him for a swim at the Station Road Reservoir just over a mile away. Myra was a strong swimmer and always handy to have around as unofficial lifeguard in the forbidden and disused pool, but she was not too keen that day so Michael went off without her.

Hours later he failed to return and Myra rushed with his worried mother down to the reservoir. A small crowd had gathered in the early evening light as a stricken Myra gazed down at the gleaming dead body of her little friend.

Those present have never forgotten the depth of her grief. She clasped her hands together and repeated to herself: "Come back Michael." She blamed herself for his death from the outset. It would never have happened if only she had gone with him, she told anyone and everyone. She stood out from the other mourners at Gorton Cemetery, alone and all in black. She withdrew deeply into herself until it seemed she was wallowing in a state of perpetual mourning and her family had to take her black clothes from her. She did not speak of her grief but carried it like a heavy, cold, dark stone for months and months.

She left school at 15 and got a job as a junior clerk, tea-maker and dog's-body at Lawrence, Scott and Electromotors a mile from home. Myra differed from other teenage working girls in her attitude towards boys and sex – she was a prude. She was 'engaged' to Ronnie Sinclair for a while but called it off before the relationship got too physical. Other youths asked what was the point in her having nice legs if her knees were glued together. Her only break with convention was the hair she decided to have dyed blonde which she wore with bright red lipstick. It gave completely the wrong impression and no doubt many would-be gropers were frustrated by it.

She went on to two other clerical jobs before reaching the milestone in her life which can be identified as the crucial turning point. On January 16, 1961, she started her fourth and final job at Millwards Ltd, a small chemical firm across the road from her old school. That was the day she met Ian Brady.

He was a stock clerk who had been in the job for two years when she was introduced to him as the new office typist. He was the illegitimate son of a Glasgow waitress, brought up in the Clydeside slums. His adolescence had been peppered with petty crime and he had spent four years on probation before moving with his mother to Manchester in 1954. Even then the burglaries did not stop and he spent a year in a borstal. At an early age he had acquired a consuming resentment of what he perceived as other people's wealth or good fortune. He had nurtured this over the years and while to others he appeared as merely sullen, his dark brooding masked far more sinister feelings.

Ian Stewart Brady was a budding sociopath. By his late teens he had immersed himself in the study of Nazism. He hated the world around him so much he found comfort in fantasizing about a Hitlerite society where there were no blacks, Jews or religions to spoil things. If only they had won the war! He spent much of his modest earnings on books such as *Mein Kampf* and *The Scourge of the Swastika*. He sent abroad for German marching music from the age of the Nuremberg rallies. He started to learn German and would spend hours alone in his room speaking in odd German phrases into his tape recorder, his favourite machine. He also became absorbed in the works of the Marquis de Sade and pornography. He loved to go alone to the cinemas and engross himself in films of crime and murder.

Gawky, naive Myra mistook his sullenness for sultriness. She thought the black shirts he wore for their Nazi connotations were an Elvis Presley fashion statement – she was 18 and he was 23. Within a few months she had developed a crush on the aloof and moody Scot.

Her girlish diary entrants are a permanent literary reminder of her romantic naivety. July 23: "Haven't spoken to Ian yet." July 27: "Spoken to him. He smiles as though embarrassed. I'm going to change him." July 30: "Ian isn't interested in girls." August 1: "Ian's taking sly looks at me at work." August 2: "Not sure if he likes me." August 8: "Gone off Ian a bit." August 13: "Wonder what 'Misery' will be like tomorrow?" August 14: "I love Ian all over again. He has a cold and I would love to mother him." August 24: "I am in a bad mood because he hasn't spoken to me all day." August 29: "I hope he loves me and will marry me some day."

Myra's August 1 entry in which she has noticed Brady taking "sly" looks at her reveals more about him than her. He was clearly aware of her crush on him and, not entirely comfortable in the real-life role of a ladies' man, the Scot who lived in a lonely, twisted fantasy world was wondering how to play things. He began taking books into the office, mostly *Mein*

*Kampf*, to create the air of a scholar. He sometimes practised his German aloud. All the time he stayed aloof, his faked brilliance dazzling her, fixing her in the headlights of his devious intentions. This game continued through the autumn of 1961 and into the winter. December 2: "I hate Ian. He has killed all the love I had for him." December 15: "I'm in love with Ian all over again." December 22: "Out with Ian!"

Just over a week later on New Year's Eve he took her out again. They went to the cinema to see Charlton Heston's new epic *El Cid*. He took her back to her mother and father's house where they let the New Year in with a bottle of whisky and some German wine he had bought earlier. Ever the gentleman, he walked Myra home to her gran's house. While granny slept upstairs Brady deflowered his breathless girlfriend on the divan in the downstairs front room. Nineteen-year-old Myra Hindley, no longer a virgin, was his forever.

Psychologists call it 'gestalt'. Put simply, this is the coming together of two incomplete personalities to make a whole. The whole is not necessarily perfect and in this case Brady, quite bluntly, was not all there. He was the superman in his own fantasy world. Hindley was a wide-eyed girl ready to be influenced, an open page upon which someone could write either a romance or a horror story.

Their initial courtship was spent exploring the further delights of German wine and their own bodies. Hindley was lavishly indoctrinated with the history of the Nazi movement and Brady, who by now she regarded as an intellectual, talked for hours about the SS and the death camps. He called her Myra Hess and nicknamed her 'Hessie'. She was introduced to the Marquis de Sade and a collection of other pornographic works. At first she was shocked and puzzled by what she read and saw but within a year she was posing as a model for their own pornographic pictures. In one she kneels on all fours smiling over her shoulder at the camera with the faint marks of a whip across her bare bottom. Another, taken with the aid of a timer switch, shows her and Brady apparently having sex and others show them lying naked with hoods over their heads.

Hindley had come a long way in a year and was prepared to go a lot further.

By now Brady had more or less moved in with Hindley and her gran. They had exchanged his motorbike for a Morris Traveller estate car but he couldn't drive so she took lessons. Brady told her he was planning a bank robbery and she would need to drive the getaway car. She even bought guns for the job that Brady never found the nerve to carry out.

Meanwhile, with the back seats folded flat and an old mattress in the back, they would drive out of Greater Manchester to the top of Saddleworth Moor to extend their sex sessions. The moors are sweeping, treeless hills forming part of the Pennines which divide Lancashire and Yorkshire. They are bleak and windswept with occasional rock outcrops and few would describe the area as beautiful. But Brady and Hindley loved the moors, it was their private place. It was also to be the burial ground of four of their young victims.

By 1963 Hindley, under Brady's intense tuition, was desensitized and isolated from her old way of life. There was nothing she would not do for him, no demands she would not meet. In July that year they chose their first victim, one who would not be discovered for more than 20 years and for whose murder they would never be tried.

Sixteen-year-old Pauline Reade lived round the corner from her killers. She left home on July 12 to go to a dance and was never seen again. That same evening Hindley and Brady, who by now had decided to commit the perfect murder to add to their private excesses, were looking for their child victim. Hindley drove the Traveller, with Brady accompanying her. The first youngster they saw was Hindley's next door neighbour, obviously too dangerous to pick up. The next was Pauline Reade, five years younger than Hindley and known to her sister Maureen. Myra offered her a lift home if in exchange she would help her look for a lost glove up on the moor. The girl was also told that she could have some of the records from Myra's collection, which she kept in the back of the car.

The precise details of what happened next are known only to the killers. Hindley's version to police 20 years later was that Brady and Pauline went off to search for the fictitious glove. Brady returned more than an hour later and led his girlfriend back to the teenager's body. Her throat was cut and part of her clothing had been removed and she had also been raped. They buried the body where it lay. On their way home they passed Pauline's frantic mother and brother searching the streets for the missing girl.

Brady contradicted Hindley's version in a letter to the media. He said she had been a willing participant in Pauline Reade's murder and had inflicted injuries to her head and face as well as carrying out a sex assault. In June, 1987, accompanied by prison guards, Hindley led police to the bleak burial place of their first victim.

Four months after Pauline Reade's abduction, which was still baffling the police, the killers were out cruising for their next victim. Britain was still numb from the shock of President Kennedy's assassination a day earlier when the Traveller pulled up alongside 12-year-old John Kilbride as he waited for a bus home from Ashton marketplace. It was six o'clock and he was late so he readily agreed to Hindley's offer of a lift home. His mum had told him never to talk to strangers but it was obviously alright to go with a man and a lady. Again, the exact details of what happened lie locked in the minds of the killers. John Kilbride was taken up to the moors and murdered. When they found his body two years later it was buried face down and he had been strangled. His trousers had been pulled down and his underpants knotted at the knees. He had certainly been sexually abused by one or both of his killers.

In June, 1964, 12-year-old Keith Bennett disappeared and was last seen walking close to the home of Brady's mother. In a virtual carbon-copy of the John Kilbride abduction, Keith Bennett was taken up to the moors by Brady and Hindley, who have since admitted his murder. Hindley says the boy was raped by Brady. The body has never been found despite two days of

searching assisted by Brady nearly a quarter of a century later.
He is the only one of the five known victims to lie undiscovered
and his mother still awaits a decent burial for her son.

After a cooling-off period common to all serial killers, the
moors murderers struck again. It was Boxing Day, 1964. They
were cruising near a fairground in the Ancoats district of
Greater Manchester when they spotted ten-year-old Lesley Ann
Downey. She had been to the Christmas fair and was on her
way home. No doubt reassured by the presence of a woman in
the car, she accepted a lift.

This time the killers did not go straight to the moors with
their victim. They had other plans for this little girl. What
happened in the hours that followed, complete with horrific
documentation, exploded forever in the eyes of the public, any
mitigation since offered by Myra Hindley in her constant
attempts to seek freedom.

Lesley Ann Downey, the bright, curly haired charmer, was
either carried drugged or walked willingly to the couple's new
council home on Wardle Brook Avenue in the Hattersely
district of Manchester. Hindley's gran was with other relatives
during the Christmas break so they had the house to themselves.
The little girl was taken to the back bedroom, stripped, made to
pose for so-called pornographic pictures and, over a period of
hours, teased, tortured, raped and strangled.

Myra Hindley claimed, as in the other three murders, she had
little to do with what happened to Lesley Ann Downey. Years
later she said she had been in the kitchen with her beloved dog,
Puppet, when she heard the girl screaming as Brady forced her
to undress for the photographs. When she went to investigate he
ordered her to leave the bedroom and run the bath. This she did
and waited for up to an hour before returning to the room to
find the child dead.

This was a different story to the one they told police before
their trial in 1966. Then they said Lesley Ann Downey had been
brought to their house by two men so the photographs could be
taken. Once this had been done the couple claimed the girl was
taken away by the men.

But Hindley and Brady, like many serial killers, needed trophies of their victims. It was these trophies, found in the two suitcases at Central Station and first witnessed by Superintendent Talbot, that damned forever both versions of their Downey story.

Talbot had played one tape. It was a mix of martial music, the kind the Nazis might have marched to, and television programmes. He was halfway through the second tape, another collection of musical snatches, when he started at the sound of a child's scream. He wound it back. It was a scream followed by indistinct voices and another scream and a little girl's voice pleading: "Don't... Please God, help me." The girl was gruffly ordered to do as she was told by Brady. There were more plaintive pleas from the child who pathetically told her tormentors her mum expected her home soon. "I got to get back by eight o'clock." A woman's voice, Hindley's, told her harshly: "Don't dally." As the unimaginable suffering continued the tape ended with the eerie playing of *The Little Drummer Boy*.

On April 26, 1966, legal history was made when that tape was played at the moors murderers' trial at Chester Crown Court. Before the machine was switched on the Judge, who said careful consideration had gone into whether the tape should be heard publicly at all, said anyone who did not wish to listen should leave the courtroom. Then came the voice of the helpless child, pleading from beyond the grave for God and her mother to help her. Men and women shook with silent sobs while Brady and Hindley sat impassively in the dock, protected by a bullet-proof screen, another first in a British courtroom.

However there was to be one more murder before their eventual arrest, that of 17-year-old Edward Evans. Brady picked him up at a railway station and Hindley drove them home. Shortly before midnight she went round to her sister's house and asked her brother-in-law, David Smith, to walk her back home. He noticed her hair was tousled and her make-up was smudged. She was also wearing different clothes to the ones she had gone out in earlier in the evening. It is likely, although

Smith would not have been aware of this, that Hindley had joined Brady in a bizarre sex session with Evans. Brady had almost certainly had sex with the teenage boy.

Moments after arriving at Wardle Brook Avenue David Smith heard a scream from the lounge. This was followed by a shout from Hindley: "Dave, help him. Help him." Smith rushed into the lounge and froze. Brady, cursing repeatedly, straddled a screaming youth as he smashed the flat side of an axe over and over again, more than a dozen times, across his skull. After lifting the gurgling head he tightened a length of electric flex around the youth's neck until all was silent. Breathing heavily, he looked up at Smith and passed him the dripping axe. "Feel Dave, feel the weight of that." A mesmerized Smith took the axe in his hand realizing he was suddenly implicated. Brady looked triumphantly at Myra Hindley and said, "That was the messiest yet."

Smith, who like Hindley had always held Brady in awe, was ordered to join them in the clean-up and was instructed to return early the next morning to help dispose of the body. Instead, the terrified youth, who was violently sick when he arrived home, crept out at dawn with Hindley's sister Maureen and called the police. It was October 7, 1965. The horror of 15 months of murder had ended but the nightmare of discovery was about to begin.

A detailed search of the house threw up a series of disturbing pointers to other possible crimes. A notebook, written in Brady's hand, contained a list of names. Many were film stars. Among them was one who wasn't: John Kilbride.

Photographs were found showing Hindley in a series of mysteriously smiling poses up on the moors. Further inquiries revealed that the couple spent long hours picnicking there. A neighbour's 12-year-old daughter told police she was often taken up there by Uncle Ian and Aunt Myra. Could she remember where? Yes.

By October 12, police investigating the two-year-old disappearance of John Kilbride were probing long sticks into the sticky peat and smelling the ends as they withdrew them.

Meanwhile, an officer carrying out another search at Wardle Brook Avenue found a ticket in Myra Hindley's prayer book. It was for a left luggage locker at Central Station containing two suitcases. From then on they realized they were looking for at least two bodies up on the moors.

They found the first on October 16. An officer who had walked off to relieve himself spotted a skeletal arm beckoning him from the peat. It was Lesley Ann Downey.

The photographs of Hindley posing on the moors were studied in intricate detail and some were blown up. They showed her standing and sitting in the same spot, smiling down at the ground as if she harboured a wicked secret. Eventually, detectives and photographers were able to recreate precisely the line up of one of the shots. It showed Myra Hindley holding a puppy, her feet firmly planted on a precise spot, one she had sat upon in another pose. When they dug, detectives found the body of John Kilbride.

Other photographs upon which realignment had been carried out showed that Hindley had also posed upon Lesley Ann Downey's grave. No other bodies of missing children were found at the time. At their trial, which ran from April 19 to May 6, 1966, they denied all three murders. Brady was found guilty of them all and Hindley was found guilty of the murders of Edward Evans and Lesley Ann Downey. She was found not guilty of the murder of John Kilbride but guilty of being an accessory after the killing. They were sentenced to life imprisonment amid calls for the reintroduction of the death penalty which had been abolished only months earlier. Both have since admitted murdering Pauline Reade and Keith Bennett. Allegations linking them with the unsolved murders of vagrants and prostitutes have never been substantiated.

Brady currently resides in a secure mental institution where his faculties have deteriorated over the years.

Hindley, on the other hand, eventually threw herself into studies and obtained a degree. She makes friends easily in prison and has encouraged campaigns for her freedom. She was once again the centre of controversy when her prison governor took her out for a walk in a London park in the 1980s. The friendly neighbourhood girl who was 23 at the time of her arrest celebrated her 50th birthday at the time of writing this book. She is the longest-serving female prisoner in Britain and she may serve many years yet. Politically, it would be a brave Home Secretary who sanctions her release. It might also prove an inhumane gesture in the face of virulent threats which have been made over the years towards her.

She will always be reviled. Many detectives on the moors murder inquiry maintain she was more evil than Brady. This is arguable and partly due to sexism. The thought of a woman participating in the murder of children is more repugnant to most than the thought of a man, although it is equally repugnant.

Myra Hindley became as evil as Brady but there is no doubt he was the dominant personality in this distorted relationship. He was the initial motivator of their crimes; after all, he had been a criminal since adolescence. She turned to crime after they met. She had been a virgin but Brady quickly introduced her to his brand of sex; she said he did not show a lot of interest in her sexually. He made her indulge in anal intercourse which she found painful. He also ordered her to masturbate him or indeed to insert a candle into his backside while he masturbated. He made her aware he had sex with their victims. He sought pleasure irrespective of her needs and if it caused her physical or emotional discomfort, all the better.

These were all signs of his dominance. He came first and she would obey. Eventually she obeyed every order and became a willing accomplice. She procured his victims time after time and helped dispose of their bodies. Perhaps she even took part in their killings. It seems inconceivable that if he had ordered her to do anything she would have disobeyed. Brady maintains she took an active role in the murders of Pauline Reade and Lesley Ann Downey. He said she strangled the ten-year-old girl with a length of nylon cord and often toyed with the cord in front of relatives, smiling at her sinister secret. We will never know the whole truth because there were no other witnesses to the child murders but there was a witness to the Evans murder. David Smith saw both of them in action and one incident he recalls is quite revealing. After Brady had battered and strangled his victim he ordered Hindley and Smith to help him clean up. During the scrubbing of blood from the walls, floor and even the budgie cage, Hindley recoiled at a small portion of bone or brain tissue on the rug. "Pick it up," said Brady. She looked up at him imploringly. "I can't," she said and retched. He scooped it into a plastic bag contemptuously.

We may never know if she gained as much pleasure from the torture and murders as he did. Only that she allowed them to happen, again and again. The evidence of the photographs taken as she posed on the moors graves suggests she derived at least some perverted pleasure from their secret knowledge. This leaves little doubt that had David Smith not shopped them on that bleak October dawn Hindley would have assisted or participated with Brady in more gruesome murders.

Myra was not an uncommon name in the north of England. Nobody calls their daughters Myra anymore.

\*\*\*\*\*\*\*\*\*\*\*\*\*\*\*\*\*\*\*\*

Sex killers tend to operate alone. Only rarely do they stalk in pairs. There are no recorded cases of a man and women teaming up as serial sex murderers until the latter half of this century. The moors murderers are the classic example but since the 1960s such bizarre pairings have not been uncommon. Each case has demonstrated the dominant-subservient relationship in which one partner, usually the woman, does whatever is ordered.

In November, 1986, a half-naked girl who fled hysterical from a house in Fremantle, Australia, led to the arrest of man-and-wife serial killers David and Catherine Birnie. Within hours the 35-year-old couple confessed to the murders of four young women, three buried south of Perth and one to the north. All the victims had been murdered within the last four weeks. Astonishingly, the latest victim had been killed the same day the hysterical girl had been abducted and raped.

The Birnies led police to the graves and during frank discussions it emerged that Catherine Birnie had taken an active role in each murder. Indeed she certainly murdered one of the victims herself by strangulation. She even took photographs of her husband raping the women and of their corpses.

Their method was always the same. The women were taken to the house, held prisoner for at least a day, sometimes three, repeatedly raped by David Birnie while his wife looked on and then murdered.

The first victim, 22-year-old student Mary Neilson, had called at the Birnies' house to buy car tyres. On impulse the husband dragged her into the bedroom, chained her to the bed and raped her whilst his wife was in the same room. They bundled the woman into their car and drove her to the Glen Eagle National Park. Birnie raped her again before he strangled her and with the help of his wife buried her where she lay.

Victim number two was 15-year-old hitch-hiker Susannah Candy. She was kept at the Birnie home for several days and in a macabre twist was made to write two letters to her parents telling them she was safe and well. Perhaps Catherine Birnie suspected her husband was paying too much attention to the young girl because it was she who strangled her. Noelline Patterson was a 31-year-old air hostess known to David Birnie who was taken to their home after her car broke down. Once again she was kept for several days chained to a bed while the husband raped her at will. Catherine became extremely jealous because of his continued interest in the victim and insisted he killed her. He strangled Noelline after drugging her.

The murder of the fourth victim was more traumatic. Denise Brown, a 21-year-old computer operator was picked up while hitch-hiking, and endured two days of rape and imprisonment. Unlike the other victims who were buried in the Glen Eagle National Park, Denise was taken to a pine plantation near Wanneroo. She was stabbed repeatedly but did not die. Catherine Birnie handed her husband a bigger knife but even in her grave the victim put up a fight. Eventually David Birnie clubbed her to death with an axe.

They made the mistake of leaving their fifth would-be murder victim unattended and unchained after her abduction and initial rape. The four-week murder spree was over. Their court case lasted barely an hour and both admitted everything.

David Birnie was oversexed and not averse to sodomy with men if women were unavailable. Catherine Birnie, unlike Myra Hindley, had a desolate and unhappy childhood. Her mother died when she was small and Catherine went to live with her grandmother who would not allow other children in the house. After her gran died in front of her in the throes of a fit she embarked on a teenage life of petty crime with David Birnie. However she married another man with whom she had six children. Birnie, meanwhile, continued his criminal activities, which began to include sex offences. Eighteen years later Catherine abandoned her family after meeting Birnie again. They set up home and, once more, began a life of crime. Experts said they had never encountered anyone so emotionally dependent on another person as she was on him. Had she not met Birnie later in her life and resumed their high dominance versus low dominance relationship one can only assume she would have remained a stable mother to her six children.

*********************

It does not always follow that women are driven to kill by high dominance males. Occasionally a dominant woman may control the actions of her partner.

Jeannace Freeman and Gertrude Jackson were lesbian lovers when Jeannace persuaded her older partner Gertrude that her children were in the way and would have to die. On May 11, 1961, the two women drove into the Peter Skene Ogden State Park in central Oregon with Gertrude's six-year-old son and four-year-old daughter in the back seat. After stopping the car near the edge of Crooked River Canyon, a sheer gorge, 19-year-old Jeannace clubbed her lover's eldest child over the head. She then mutilated his anal region with a tyre lever to make it look like a sex attack before throwing the little boy over the edge of the gorge. Gertrude, who at 37 was nearly twice the age of her teenage lover, mutilated her own daughter before throwing her, naked and still alive, into the river 200 feet below.

The couple then picked up a third lesbian friend and drove back to their apartment, throwing the children's clothes out of the car window as they went. They sold the car and moved out of their apartment.

A statewide alert went out when the children's broken bodies were found by hikers the next day. It was feared for a short while that a crazed sex killer was on the loose. Three days later the children were identified from newspaper photographs by one of Jeannace's relatives. The women were arrested in Oakland.

Jeannace, ever the tomboy with her cropped hair, denied anything to do with the killings. She said the older Gertrude had beaten the children, thrown them into the gorge and threatened her with a similar fate if she said anything. Gertrude said she had left the children with Jeannace for a few minutes and returned to find her son dead. She admitted throwing her daughter into the gorge because she could not bear the thought of the little girl living without her brother. It became apparent that Jeannace was the dominant partner in this relationship even though both had experienced abuse and deprivation as children.

Jeannace was the sixth child of a broken marriage. Her mother's second marriage failed and she began bringing men home, possibly as a prostitute. One drunken client raped four-year-old Jeannace and she was sexually abused by others as she grew up. She associated men with violence and pain and responded positively to the lesbian attentions of an older girl. At 14 Jeannace was living in a county juvenile home where she frequently fought with other boys and girls. Her counsellor regarded her as an urgent case for help and treatment. A psychiatrist's report noted Jeannace's desire to have been born a boy. Not knowing what else to do with a problem tomboy whose only feminine trait seemed to be she liked caring for young children, the authorities eventually sent her to a home for juvenile delinquents. Her behaviour worsened and she dropped out of school.

Gertrude was the youngest of two daughters. Her father killed himself when she was five. Her mother moved with her two daughters to Portland, Oregon, where she worked as a waitress during the day and a prostitute at night. Gertrude's sister, who was five years older, also drifted into prostitution and found she could make even more money by including her younger sister as part of the offer to clients. So it was that at the age of 12 Gertrude was introduced to sex.

At the age of 15 Gertrude ran off with a sailor but she was brought back and placed in a home. When she left, she married a Mexican labourer who needed US citizenship. He beat her and gave her to his friends for sex. When she left him he kept the child, which had been fathered by one of his friends. At 28 she married a building worker, Dempsey Otis Jackson but there was little marital bliss. He also beat her and made her return to prostitution to finance his drug habit. It was with him she had the two children who would die in the gorge.

In 1961 the tired and battered housewife, who had found no tenderness in men, met the slim, boyish Jeannace at a party. They were immediately attracted and Gertrude offered Jeannace the job of babysitter. Within weeks they moved in together, even though Jeannace was having a relationship with another woman. It did not take long for the children to become a problem, so Jeannace demanded her more timid lover did something about it.

Gertrude Jackson was sentenced to life imprisonment but served only seven years because the authorities recognized she was dominated by her younger partner. Jeannace was sentenced to death but after three years on death row, Oregon abolished the death penalty. She proved as rebellious in prison as she did in juvenile homes. She was paroled in 1983 after serving 22 years. Six months later she was back behind bars after she was found living with another woman who had young children. This was strictly against her parole conditions. She was finally released in 1985, aged 44.

\*\*\*\*\*\*\*\*\*\*\*\*\*\*\*\*\*\*\*\*\*

Obviously, women are quite capable of murder without the influence of a dominant partner. Women are driven to kill through jealousy, passion and gain, although with far less frequency than men. But some are motivated by what psychologists have recognized as the power syndrome. This manifests itself differently in women than it does in men.

A man exudes power over his victim through his sheer physical strength or the position in which he has manoeuvred his prey. This materializes in the long drawn-out terror process that a rapist may exercise over his victim. The power-motivated rapist feeds off their fear, it gives him a feeling of power and control. Less than 25 per cent of the motivation of rape is sexual. The rest is the sense of power brought on by force. Robert Berdella, the American homosexual serial-killer, exhibited clear symptoms of the power syndrome, along with a host of others. He kept his young male captives bound and gagged for weeks, to do with as he wished, before killing them.

Women subject to the power syndrome do not have the physical strength to exercise it. Unless their victims are children or the elderly.

A young mother thought there was something odd about nurse Genene Jones following a bizarre encounter in a Texas cemetery in September, 1982. Petti McClellan was lost in her own world of aching grief as she made her way through the headstones to the fresh grave of her 15-month-old daughter, Chelsea Ann. She was distracted by the unchecked sounds of wailing and moaning and was shocked to find a stocky woman kneeling and rocking backwards and forwards at the foot of Chelsea's grave. The 27-year-old bereaved mother recognized her as the nurse who had given Chelsea the immunization injections moments before the infant lapsed into unconsciousness and then death. Petti stared in shock as the nurse, with tears running down her cheeks, wailed the dead baby's name over and over. When Petti spoke, Genene Jones pulled herself to her feet and wandered blankly from the Garden of Memories Cemetery in Kerrville.

Barely a year later 33-year-old Genene Jones was on trial for Chelsea's murder. Police and medical authorities had become concerned by the number of emergencies occurring at a paediatric clinic where she worked. Children had been collapsing into seizures for no apparent reason and had to be rushed to intensive care. Some had come perilously close to death. Little Chelsea had not been so lucky.

Their concern became outright alarm when it was discovered that nurse Jones had been at the centre of a hushed-up inquiry at the Bexar County Hospital, San Antonio, where 20 infants had died under her care between May and December, 1981. Emergencies always occurred on the three to 11 shift, her shift. It was nicknamed the Death Shift.

Genene Jones was an intimidating and emotional woman. She had two children, a broken marriage and several unstable relationships. She was also given to pretending to fall ill. To many she was a dedicated, if not know-it-all, LVN (licenced vocational nurse). She was not averse to haranguing colleagues about how the job should be done.

Staff at Bexar County were at first baffled and then suspicious by the constant emergencies in the paediatric intensive care unit whenever Jones was on shift. Stable infants would go into relapse within hours of her taking over the ward. This took the form of seizures, erratic heart movements, heart stoppages, sudden and heavy bleeding and all too often death. Whenever danger signs were spotted hospital staff sounded an alarm, or 'code'. Medical staff rushed to the scene from all parts of the hospital and with Genene Jones in the thick of the action the fight for the baby's life would begin. All too often it failed. Twenty babies died on the three to 11 shift. Genene Jones clutching an infant to her breast as she made her way sobbing to the hospital mortuary became a familiar sight and she was always on hand to comfort or cry along with broken-hearted parents.

Because of her intimidating manner and lack of supervision or both, Jones seemed to escape effective disciplinary action. She appeared drunk in the intensive care unit at 5 am and tampered with a babies drip unit. She was caught administering a massive overdose of an anti-clotting drug to one child but no definite action was ever taken to remove her from the paediatric unit.

Eventually most of her colleagues suspected her. One went as far as to say aloud to her superior: "Genene's killing kids." A whispering campaign began and she was nicknamed the 'death nurse'. An inquiry was held comprising experts from Canada and the USA. They too were told by one nurse that Jones was killing infants. A doctor said there seemed to be a problem with one nurse in particular. Amid fears of a legal suit against the hospital following angry outbursts from Jones there were no firm recommendations singling her out. Instead she was allowed to leave with a warm letter of recommendation. Indeed if prospective employers contacted the hospital personnel department they were to be told Jones was eligible to reapply for employment.

She went on to work at the paediatrics clinic in Kerrville, Texas, where she injected certain death into healthy Chelsea Ann McClellan while her trusting mother held her still. Jones vehemently denied causing any deaths, especially little Chelsea's. "I would have given my life for hers. Goodbye ·Chelsea," she wrote on the infant's medical chart. She attended the baby's funeral and even received special thanks in the Kerrville Daily Times from the baby's distraught parents, who praised her sensitive care. "A care which extended beyond our loss and helped us more than anyone could ever know."

Medical staff suspected Jones had injected the drug succinylcholine into Chelsea. This is often called the 'doctor's poison' because it is quick and hard to trace. Eight months after her death, Chelsea's body was exhumed and tissue tests carried out in Sweden showed traces of the drug. Jones was charged with her murder. There were calls for her to be charged with up to 40 other baby killings but there was an understandable reluctance to exhume so many infants' bodies.

Jones was found guilty and sentenced to 159 years in prison. Her parole date was set for 1993, after being rejected in 1989 when a campaign by Chelsea's parents led to hundreds of protest letters.

Power was one of the prime motives which drove Genene Jones to murder. By administering potentially lethal drugs to babies she created life and death situations in which she played a key role.

But that was not the only motive. In the 1950s a British doctor, Richard Asher, writing in *The Lancet* medical journal identified a condition he called 'Munchausen's Syndrome'. He named it after an 18th century German Baron who enjoyed telling far-fetched stories to get attention. Dr Asher attributed the condition to patients who sought admission to hospitals claiming a variety of serious ailments. The motivation behind this, said the doctor, was the desire for attention and a grudge against hospitals and doctors which instigated an urge to deceive them.

In 1977 another British doctor, Roy Meadow, took this theory even further with a condition he identified as 'Munchausen's Syndrome by Proxy'. This centred on mothers who induced illnesses in their children, such as seizures and bleeding. The mothers not only had a knowledge of medicine but enjoyed the hospital environment and the prospect of friendship with medical staff. Many also suffered from hysterical personalities and were easily depressed.

'Munchausen's Syndrome by Proxy' also applies to those who induce medical problems in children in their care. Genene Jones is a classic example. In a childhood which she felt was devoid of adequate attention she grew up lying to attract it. As an unattractive teenager she lied to win friends. She was obsessed with medicine and disease and exagerrated her own illnesses and those of her children and other relatives to gain sympathy and attention.

There was no greater opportunity to be the centre of attention than by creating a life and death drama around a sick baby. She would almost brag to colleagues that she had "lost" another infant and how much it had destroyed her. She always insisted on carrying the dead babies to the morgue rather than hand over the bodies to porters. She wallowed in the attention of the long, slow, tearful walks through the corridors down to the basement. She had to be the centre of attention even among grieving parents who she would invariably out-grieve. In turn they recognized her as a caring angel and tower of strength. She was in her element.

Those who witnessed Genene Jones during code emergencies remember her as the loudest person on the scene. Many recalled her as sweaty and excited, almost sexually euphoric.

Power syndromes involving female nurses are not uncommon around the world. In 1989 Michaela Roeder, a nursing sister from Wuppertal in Germany was charged with the murders of 17 patients. The public prosecutor accused her of playing mistress over life and death amid claims she had injected patients with overdoses of the drug Catapresan. As in the Jones case it was other medical staff who pointed the finger, concerned at the high death rate on her ward. They had nicknamed her the 'angel of death'. Twenty-eight bodies were exhumed and 17 were found to contain traces of Catapresan.

In the same year in Austria four nurses working at Vienna's Lainz Hospital were charged with the multiple murders of elderly patients. At least 49 serial killings were suspected. The nurses at first claimed the deaths were mercy killings but Dr Stacher, head of Vienna's hospital system, vehemently dismissed this defence. "These nurses enjoyed killing because it gave them extraordinary power over life and death," he said. "They killed patients who had become a nuisance to them."

Once again it was a suspicious colleague who raised the alarm. She was surprised at the death rates of elderly patients. At first it was one every few months, then it became one a month. The nurses used different killing techniques including sleeping pills and injections of insulin and glucose. Their favourite method was the 'mouthwash'. This involved drowning the old folk by holding their noses and forcing water down their throats. Dr Stacher observed: "This is a painful death." It was also a convenient death as Dr Stacher pointed out: "Water in the lungs of an elderly person is considered quite normal."

All four nurses were jailed for a total of 20 murders in March, 1991. The ringleader, 32-year-old Waltraud Wagner was convicted of 15 murders and 17 attempted murders. The mistress of the deadly mouthwashes, she was jailed for life. Irene Leidolf, 29, was also jailed for life after being found guilty of five murders and two attempted murders. Stefanija Mayer, 52, was jailed for 20 years for seven murders and Maria Gruber, 29, was sentenced to 15 years, later reduced to 12 at an appeal in May, 1992.

Waltraud Wagner held her co-accused in awe of her on the ward and they generally did as she ordered. Her nerve however, failed her during sentencing. While the other three women sat in silence, she collapsed sobbing and had to be carried from the courtroom.

While this book was going to press a trial with bizarre similarities to the Genene Jones case was beginning in the United Kingdom. British nurse Beverley Allitt faced 26 charges, four of murder, 11 of attempted murder and 11 of causing grievous bodily harm. The four murder charges related to children at Grantham Hospital in Lincolnshire. Three were babies and one was an 11-year-old handicapped child.

The 24-year-old nurse allegedly committed the offences in 1991 and 1992. It is alleged that most of her child victims were admitted to hospital with routine ailments but suffered inexplicable cardiac or respiratory attacks. Many were rushed to the Queen's Medical Centre teaching hospital in Nottingham. Staff there raised the alarm when a child was found with massive overdoses of insulin.

While awaiting trial Allitt was switched from a remand prison to a top security hospital after being found with self-inflicted wounds.

*********************

In documenting examples of women who kill we have concentrated only on serial murders, accepting that dozens of women each year commit one-off murders, predominantly crimes of domestic frustration or passion. The examples listed in this chapter are either crimes motivated by dominant personalities or power-cum-attention-seeking killings.

Dorothea Puente was 57 when she offered her home as a lodging house to social services in Sacramento, California, in 1986. Regarding her home as "the best the system had to offer," social workers sent her 19 lodgers over the next two years. Most of them were never seen again. Neighbours first started complaining of a sickly smell from her property in May, 1988. On November 7, that year, police visited Puente to check on the whereabouts of a male lodger who had not been seen for three months. Unconvinced by her explanation that he had returned to Mexico they returned with spades a few days later.

The first body was found on November 11. Two more were dug up the next day. By November 14 the body count had risen to seven. Extensive digging revealed no more corpses on the premises but police were swamped by anxious calls about relatives who had stayed at the Puente home and disappeared. Up to 25 former residents were missing. Not all the bodies they had discovered were identified as some had been decapitated and their limbs severed. To date eight bodies have been found. Detectives have attributed a middle-aged man found in a box two years earlier to the Puente inquiry.

Police believe Puente murdered lodgers for their social security cheques. She was due to stand trial as this book went to press.

# 5

# *Killer In Profile*

*"Some of us go to a ball game, some of us sit down and have a beer and watch TV. And some people kill, just for the thrill of killing." – FBI profiler Larry E McCann.*

July 23, 1992, Richmond, Virginia, USA. The sun beats down on the blistered tarmac ribbon of Interstate 64, a buzz of American FM radio stations concur that it's 96 degrees, humidity is high and in Richmond, thunderstorms are on the way. Special Agent Larry McCann steps from the air-conditioned cool of his specially adapted State Trooper's car and walks into the shaded light of dense woodland.

"This is a lover's lane, you have to have local knowledge to know it's here." He walks on through the undergrowth, past the rotting remains of a gutted deer and through a cloud of flies. "This is where the skeletons were found, we couldn't find a cause of death on the male but we think the woman had her throat cut. There was a deep slash through the bones on her hand, the sign of a defence wound. It looks as though she'd been protecting her neck from the knife and her killer caught her as he slit her throat. We think the boyfriend may have been forced to look on as she was murdered, it may be one of the 'kicks' that was going down here."

McCann is investigating a series of murders that began in 1986 and have continued ever since. He's certain they're a series because they're all double murders, all white victims, all of the couples were together by mutual consent, all the locations were lovers' lanes, the killer had always taken a weapon to the scene rather than improvized when he was there, and no bindings were found at the abduction sites or murder spots – in fact hardly any clues had been found. Another linking aspect is the fact that it seemed that after they had been abducted, the victims had been made to drive or walk to other locations where they were killed.

The first two to be murdered were lesbian lovers Rebecca Dowski, just 21, and her friend 27-year-old stockbroker Cathleen, Thomas, one of a hundred female graduates of the US Naval Academy. Part of their courtship was routinely spent in Thomas' white Honda hatchback, parked up in a quiet spot off the Colonial Parkway. On October 9, 1986 they were interrupted by their killer.

When their car was found three days later, Dowski and Thomas had both been strangled and had their throats cut. Autopsy reports showed Dowski had been choked to death and the knife used as an afterthought. Her body was stuffed into the back seat of the Honda. Thomas' corpse was dumped into the hatchback, the blood-soaked vehicle was then doused in petrol, set aflame and rolled down a steep banking into the York River.

Twenty-year-old David Lee Knobling and a girl he'd just met, teenager Robin Edwards, were the next victims in what became known as the Parkway Killings. The two had crept out late one September evening to a party together. Three days later their bullet-ridden bodies were discovered 50 yards apart from each other on a beach off one of the main local roads called the Colonial Parkway. Detectives were able to work out that the young couple had been made to walk for 25 minutes from their parked vehicle to the sands where they were both shot in the back of the head. When the Black Ford Ranger pick-up, Knobling's pride and joy, was found, the keys were still in the ignition and the radio was still playing. From the nature of the wounds, detectives speculated that the 14-year-old girl was killed first and then as Knobling ran for his life he too was shot.

Eighteen-year-old Cassandra Hailey and 20-year-old Keith Call were also on their first date, when they were killed in April 1988. The couple left a party at the University Square Apartments in the Newport Mews college community in the early hours of the morning, and they were never seen again. Police have no doubt their disappearance was connected to the other killings. Keith Call's father Richard was on his way to work at Anheuser-Busch when he spotted his son's car with its personal plate KEIFS. It was parked at a beauty spot less than three miles east of where Dowski and Thomas were found.

Eighteen months later the Parkway Killer added another two victims to his death tally. Twenty-one-year-old Danny Lauer and 18-year-old Annamaria Phelps had decided to cement their relationship by moving in together. After dropping off friends near Virginia Beach, they went to Lauer's home and gathered up some belongings, then stopped at Phelps' parents home and watched a late movie. They left just before midnight and headed towards the beach. They weren't be seen again for another six weeks. Their bodies were discovered in dense woodland off a lovers' lane near Interstate 64 in New Kent County.

It was back at these woods that Larry McCann now stood, recalling that Lauer's 1973 gold Chevy had been found abandoned in the rest area on the opposite side of the Interstate. Not just abandoned, but left in front of the restrooms where the telephones are and most people come and go. It was also left across two parking spaces with the front wheels up on the pavement; in other words it was left deliberately for the police to find.

McCann's theory is that the couple were accosted here, made to drive onto the next exit and then off onto the old logging road where they were murdered. The killer then drove the Chevy back to the rest area and left it at an angle. "It's like he's saying, 'I'm smarter than you, come and get me if you can'," observed the seasoned detective.

Quietly spoken, quick thinking, Larry McCann is a fellow of the FBI's Behavioral Science Unit, one of the élite trained in the art of drawing up psychological profiles. Walking through the undergrowth, sun-dried branches breaking under his feet, he begins his task: "Because of the fact that we've got eight young, healthy, strong individuals who went to their deaths without a struggle and because of the control that's necessary to move two people at a time around to areas like this, I'm sure we're looking for a person who worked in connection with another individual.

"When you think that some of the victims were made to drive miles before they were killed, I'm positive we're hunting two murderers not one. One is a natural leader, the other a born follower – you couldn't have any arguments over this kind of thing, one fella would have to be making all the ground. When you draw up a profile in situations like this you concentrate on the characteristics of the leader, the one that's in charge; the one that's done all of the planning and the one that's got so much control that he is able to get someone else to go along and carry out these crimes with him."

For a while McCann says nothing. He walks among the dense foliage, awakening the hidden animals of the under-growth. He's now far off the grit-track once used by giant trucks heading towards a distant lumber mill. Within minutes he's lost, not geographically, but back in time, back in the final moments of the night of the murders.

It's early afternoon and the temperature is now chasing the 100 degree mark. The sun is high but the shadows from the sentry-straight pines are still long enough to checkerboard the forest floor. Occasionally, McCann's immaculate white shirt appears out of the darkness. He breaks the drama of the silence with a phrase little heard outside of America: "Recreational Homicide. That's what's been going on with these fellas, that's what we are seeing here. Someone who is killing just for the sake of killing. Someone that enjoys inflicting pain, suffering and finally death upon another individual. Someone who doesn't care about the welfare of society; someone who holds life in no great regard at all. They'll kill again, for them this is recreation. Some of us go to a ball game, some of us sit down and have a beer and watch TV and some people kill, just for the thrill of killing."

McCann is now out of the sombre trance that had engulfed him, the personal reflection on the young people that had been killed is over and now he's talking quickly, a stream of thought: "I envision someone who has very good control of himself, who has planned, plotted and fantasized in great detail and for a long period of time before he has committed these crimes. I think he cons the victims when he approaches their car. I think he pretends to be a policeman or some authority figure. I think the fella that is doing this is wearing some type of uniform and is catching his victims unawares and off-guard. This would explain how he manages to split up the couple and get control of one victim before their partner comes along. Again, remember they're in lovers' lanes; these victims aren't aware of what's going on around them, they're paying absolute attention to each other."

The thoughts of the profiler now begin to focus into hard detail. "Statistically, white males kill white individuals, blacks kill blacks, that's what we find with our studies. So here is a white male, probably around 30-years-old when he started this series back in 1986 and someone who is familiar with this area. Someone who feels comfortable on the Colonial Parkway, on Interstate 64 and Route 154 and feels comfortable pulling into little dirt by-ways that lead to nowhere. I'm sure both murderers live locally, they need to have done surveillance on places where they attacked, killed and disposed of their victims."

Attention turns again to the leader and what kind of job he might do, "Could be a butcher, a meat cutter, knows about animals, could be a hunter, feels comfortable in the woods, feels comfortable with a knife in his hands. The leader is certainly an under-achiever, he may even have applied to have joined the police force and have been rejected."

A graduate in psychology and a serving officer for 20 years, Larry McCann can't bear to think that the eight murders might actually have been carried out by a serving officer, but he won't discount it. "I hope, I really hope that we manage to weed all the psychos out."

He reflects on the cold, calculating violence, how organized the attacks must have been and the thought of a young man being made to watch his girlfriend die: "The goal for the serial killer is the power to kill or spare. What we're seeing here is the manifestation of the ultimate power trip, complete power over life and death. The fantasy that has been going on here is one of control, domination, superiority, anger at the world. He's mad at the world and he believes he's smarter than anybody else. He certainly believes that he is smarter than me; smarter than the Virginia State Police; smarter than the New Kent County Sheriff's Office; smarter than the FBI and now it's a game for him. Dominion over other people, dominance, that's the key."

McCann's observations on the killers are a combination of logic, common sense and behavioural analysis. The 'profile' that he has come up with is basically a social-sketch equivalent of an artist's impression of the 'wanted man'. While the police artist may depict the offender as white, 5ft 11in tall, slim, dark-hair and blue-eyed; the profiler may well describe the man detectives are hunting as white, semi-skilled, living alone with sexual problems and aged 18 to 25. Seldom are people caught by the artist's impression alone, even fewer are caught by a solitary profile. Both can be amazingly accurate or completely misleading. At best they are simply investigative sieves that detectives can use to eliminate vast amounts of suspects and so concentrate their men and minds on those most likely to have committed the crime. The artist's sketch and the profile are also determined by other things. The sketch accuracy depends upon the recall of witnesses and the skill of the artist. Profile accuracy relies firstly on the clumsiness of the offender and secondly, the proficiency of the profiler to recognize that the way an offender behaves during a crime says something about the type of person he or she is in everyday life.

Larry McCann, the Virginia State Police and in fact most police forces throughout the world, have now moved away from the term 'psychological profiling'. There are many reasons why. After the film *Silence of the Lambs* practitioners were anxious to dissociate themselves from the Hollywood hype and get back to reality. More importantly, the system has now developed a long way from its original roots in psychology and psychiatry. Statistical based programmes, where thousands of past murders are fed into computers for cross-referencing, are currently having their largest ever impact on profiling groups.

The terms that are currently used in the UK, Europe and North America are 'offender profiling' or Criminal Investigative Analysis. This encompasses the growing work of psychologists and the data-input from statistical caseloads. Whatever the type of profiling employed, profilers such as Larry McCann are concerned with the same areas of the criminal's activity. These can basically be divided into three main areas: Pre-crime, Crime and Post-crime.

Pre-crime involves what the individual did or didn't do, prior to the murder. This area is vital in establishing whether the offender has killed before and whether he has a criminal record for other offences and consequently can then be traced through police files. It is generally agreed that as serial killers get more and more experienced, they refine their behaviour with the explicit intention of leaving fewer clues. A badly planned murder would be an indication of a first killing and not perhaps number three in another linked series. McCann is sure that in the Parkway Killings, the killers were on what he calls a vertical learning curve, "More than anything they learnt what to do with the bodies. You can see the progression; from leaving the corpses in a burned out car to eventually hiding them so we don't find anything for more than six weeks, by which time decomposition has taken everything away that could have been of forensic use to us. In one of the later killings, we still haven't found the bodies. Yeah, these fellas were learning alright."

Crime – here the concern is centred upon the type of victim chosen and how it was chosen. How the murder took place and what injuries and sexual assaults were inflicted before death. This would include vaginal and anal rape, torture and enslavement. Victims fall into two main groups, 'High Risk' and 'Low Risk'. The choice of a 'Low Risk' victim, such as a housewife at home in a middle-class housing estate, rather than a 'High Risk' victim, like a prostitute in a red-light area, shows where the offender feels comfortable and is often a sign of his own social status and background.

Post-crime deals with the injuries to the body, especially when they are inflicted after death and are particularly useful signs to a profiler. Using the prostitute example again, it's worthwhile considering an attack in which a streetwalker is battered unconscious, isn't sexually interfered with but is then mutilated after death. Profilers may conclude that they are looking for someone who hates women in general or prostitutes in particular, has some form of sexual dysfunction and either lives in an area close to his victim or frequents a kerb-crawling location. Emphasis would also be placed on dismemberment and disposal of the body and also the taking away of any body-parts or victim's possessions as souvenirs or trophies. Most revealing is what attempts have been made to conceal possible forensic evidence and move or conceal the body itself. In developing the profile, constant attention is drawn to 'The Big Picture', an American way of saying that everything must be taken into account, no matter how ridiculous or insignificant it seems. It is in these three main areas (Pre-crime, Crime and Post-crime) that the offender's 'behavioural signature' is left and can best be interpreted by the graphology of profiling.

In the smoked-glass tower-block of the Virginia State Police Headquarters in Richmond, an answerphone clicks into life. Larry McCann has been away from his desk for more than a week. He listens to the messages, a mingle of familiar family voices and intense inquiries from other police forces. After a quick call to his father and a check that his son, wife and daughter made it to the local soccer game, he looks up, takes off his glasses and rubs the bridge of his slightly sunburned nose. "There are 43 cases on this desk" he says very matter-of-factly, "More than a hundred victims, and they are all homicides that other agencies have failed to solve. Now they expect me to look into some crystal ball and come up with a profile that will catch them their killer." McCann knows that profiling is not, and probably never will be, a precise science. Indeed, in many cases, it turns out to be far more of an art, carried out by an expert who skillfully uses his or her own theories, along with crime scene reports, photographs, information from past cases that have similarities and any forensic evidence that is available from the current case. It is most effective, not in the everyday routine of domestic murder (husband kills wife etc) where clues are usually plentiful, but in the dark world of 'stranger murder' where kidnapping, paedophilia, necrophilia, cannibalism and sadism rear their evil heads.

McCann shrugs at the enormity of the workload facing him, secure in the knowledge that he's already used his expertise in more than a hundred homicide cases and has saved the lives of dozens of potential victims. Heading back across the giant parking lot to his unmarked car, he looks out through the thin Virginia air to the high mountains on the horizon. "The burnout rate is high among profilers. To be successful you've got to slip into the mind of the killer, understand his gratifications, what turns him on, what annoys him; you've got to become him during those moments when he carries out the most inhumane of crimes."

The detective has vowed to see out five more years before he heads for the hills and retirement with his family. "In developing a profile, I look for a description which will help me distinguish him from any other member of society. I look at the crime scene, the photographs, the autopsy and forensic reports and I interpret these into information about the offender's race, sex, age and whether I think they're married or not. I ask myself, does the crime scene suggest the perpetrator has got any previous convictions. For example was their evidence of a professional break-in before the murder? We could be looking for someone who already has a burglary record. I go on to look at how intelligent I think they are, what's their possible lifestyle and socio-economic status; how socially adjusted I think they are, will they be loners, are they sexually competent and could this be contributory to motive?" McCann's list goes on forever, covering every aspect of human emotion and behaviour. He ends with his assessment of how he thinks possible suspects would react to police questioning and how he thinks they should be handled during any intense interviewing. It's easy to see why he gets so many of the cases that no one else wants.

The FBI claims a 70 to 80 percent accuracy rate in its profiles, but that doesn't mean that in 80 percent of cases where a profile was produced, it lead directly to the capture of the killer. It means that when the killer was caught, he fitted the profile more than three quarters of the time. He may well have been arrested for a different crime, police may have been tipped off by an informer or he may well have simply given himself up.

A three hour drive north from Richmond brings you into the Marine-based town of Quantico. Nestled in the acres of woodland that surround the military camps are the biscuit coloured buildings of the FBI Academy. Sixty feet below the lush green lawns that get trampled hourly by Academy joggers and route-marchers is a honeycomb of offices in what was once a nuclear bunker. This is the headquarters of America's National Centre for the Analysis of Violent Crime (NCAVC).

Housed in tiny rooms that are filled with the heavy whine of ancient air-conditioning, are two of the most important criminal units in the world, the FBI's Behavioural Science Unit and its Violent Criminal Apprehension Programme (VICAP).

The 'profiling' system developed by the mindhunters of the FBI, is to date the most effective and proven way of criminal analysis that is currently in existence. Other countries borrow from it, some deride it but none ignore it. Its power comes in its simplicity. It is deliberately simple, as Senior Supervisory Agent Roy Hazelwood told us: "It has to be simple, it's got to be understood by police officers." The remark is tongue-in-cheek. Hazelwood, in his light-coloured suits and dark glasses, is the archetypal detective and believes himself to be first and foremost "a cop", but the system has been expertly developed with complete emphasis on ease of learning and ease of use.

Hazelwood and his FBI colleague John Douglas, divided murderers into two specific groups: 'organized' and 'disorganized'. This means quite basically, that their behaviour in planning the crime, carrying it out and avoiding detection afterwards (Pre-crime, Crime and Post-crime), fits them 'shoebox' style into one of those two categories. There is now a third and more unusual category, that of the 'mixed' offender or 'mixed' crime scene. This is where patterns of behaviour are confused, either by a number of offenders being involved, or because unconnected crimes have been included in a series.

There are mistakes, there always are in any labelling system, especially when offenders progress from rape to murder. They often become more sophisticated in living out their fantasies and perhaps even start laying false clues for police to follow. More than anything though, this 'organized', 'disorganized' and 'mixed' system, enables detectives, from square one, to have at least an idea about the type of person they are hunting. It is a starting point for investigators.

Hazelwood rightly points out: "You've got to remember that not all police officers have a long history of investigating dozens of serial crimes. Many come into an investigation as senior members of the inquiry with little previous homicide experience. Some are thrown in without any at all." The categorizations that he arrived at came while he and John Douglas were examining 'lust murders'. These are killings, not of passion, but of particular ferocity where the offender has mutilated the victim's sexual areas. In many cases there will be amputation of breasts, buttocks or genitalia.

"Those two terms" Hazelwood explains, "'Organized' and 'disorganized', were developed because we were trying to come up with classifications of killers in lust murders specifically but it has now broadened to include homicide in general. We were trying to provide classifications that were simple to understand and would bring to mind immediately things about the offender. So, we came up with the 'organized' and 'disorganized' terms. We were even told at the time by some people, 'You can't use those terms, they're too simplistic. No one will ever buy those terms' but we said the purpose isn't to 'sell' those terms. The purpose is for the police officer to be able to relate to what we are trying to impart. 'This person is very 'organized'.' Now what does that mean to the common person?

"It means that he is methodical. It means that he is planned and has planned his crimes well. It means that he is careful. It means that he is exhibiting concern and control over himself. Now, what does the term 'disorganized' mean? It means that the crime is unplanned, that it is spontaneous and sloppy. It means that the offender will leave evidence at the crime scene.

So, we chose those terms because they are simplistic terms and easily understandable. We never imagined that they would come to be utilized as widely as they have."

Research by the Behavioral Science Unit shows 48 per cent of murders are by 'disorganized' offenders, 32 per cent by 'organized' killers and only 14 per cent fit into the 'mixed' classification. The remaining six per cent of cases fall out of the typology range, because either the body was too decomposed or the crime scene was too old for proper analysis.

An 'organized' offender is expected to display the following traits. He is of average to above average intelligence, he will fit into society in the sense that he will have a job and a home. He is actually more likely to be employed in some skilled work other than menial labour but will be underachieving at work and will consider himself hard done by and capable of much greater things. He will come from a fairly good home and will not have experienced undue poverty as a child; he may however have been troubled as a youngster and his parents will have been inconsistent in their punishment/disciplining of him as a child. In carrying out the crime, he will show that he is in control of both the situation and his own moods. This may well be in spite of him having to have drunk heavily to have mustered the courage to carry out the crime in the first place. The attack is likely to have been triggered off by extreme stress such as a partner's infidelity and subsequent departure. Situational stress, such as financial problems or unemployment can either be contributory or in some cases reasons on their own to spark off an attack or killing.

The profile ascertains that he will most likely be, or until recently have been, involved in a marriage or long-term relationship with a partner. He will drive a car and it will be kept in good condition. He will also be well informed, following news bulletins and particularly crime shows on television. He is certain to follow his own crimes in the media and may change jobs or leave town during a series of offences.

FBI categorizations also lay out how an 'organized' offender is likely to behave at the crime scene. There is expected to be some semblance of order. The abduction or killing area has probably been checked-out before the attack, so while the victim is picked at random, the attack area, or what the FBI call the 'comfort zone' usually isn't.

It follows that an 'organized' offender will have planned the attack and the victim will have been a stranger until the offence itself, but then, the killer will make attempts to personalize the victim, almost as though some kind of relationship could be developed between them.

The murderer will be calm and controlled throughout the crime and this will show in signs of little disruption and struggle at the scene. He is quite likely to have bound and possibly gagged his victim beforehand. Acts of sex and violence may well take place while the victim is still alive and then afterwards the corpse is usually well hidden. It is often transported by car or van to a different scene from either the abduction area or the murder scene.

It's normally found that the killer will also have taken a specific weapon with him to carry out the killing – like a knife, gun or noose, rather than have improvized with something found to hand at one of the crime scenes, such as a rock, piece of broken glass or discarded rope. The final aspect of 'organized' offending will be an absence of evidence. Extreme care will have been taken to avoid leaving blood, semen, hair, fibres or fingerprints at any of the crime scenes. It's what police are now calling 'forensic awareness'.

So, who are 'organized' offenders and how does their behaviour fit their crimes? A classic example is the 1970s serial killer Theodore Robert Bundy. The illegitimate son of a Philadelphia secretary, he was inappropriately called Theodore because it means 'gift of God' – Bundy grew up to rape and kill at least 30 women. A good-looking, highly intelligent student, he studied psychology and Chinese, making his way through the Universities of Washington and Stanford. Professors graded him among the top one per cent of pupils and there seemed little doubt that he'd achieve his aim of carving-out a successful life as a lawyer or high-flying law enforcement officer.

As he climbed the career ladder he worked as a political canvasser, joined the Department of Justice Planning and even worked for the Crime Commission. He was the 'American Dream' personified, complete with charm, sophistication and a beautiful, long-term girlfriend from a wealthy, well respected family.

When Bundy turned to crime he did so in a typically 'organized' way. He targeted college girls, those of a social status who he believed considered themselves to be too good for him. As a consequence, they were what he considered 'worthy victims'. He even planned his initial attacks and learned from each crime. His first victim was Seattle student Sharon Clarke in 1974. Bundy crept into her unlocked home, battered her unconscious with an iron bar and then left, leaving the bar lodged in her vagina. Sharon Clarke had not been raped and survived the savage ordeal, but emerged from a week-long coma with brain-damage. This clumsy, 'blitz' style of attack bore all the psychological hallmarks of an immature offender who was about to embark upon a sexually violent career as a serial murderer.

Bundy's second victim was also a student and this time his attack was far more thorough. When police investigated the disappearance of 21-year-old psychology student Lynda Healy they were bemused. There had been no sign of a break-in at her home and her bed was disturbed but had been re-made. When the sheets were pulled back they were drenched in blood. In the wardrobe was Lynda's nightdress, again soaked in blood. With the body gone and everything else in its place, detectives remarked that it was one of the tidiest crime scenes they'd ever encountered, Bundy was learning quickly. Within six months he had abducted and murdered six young women and he'd left police with no substantial forensic evidence – except that a couple of witnesses could recall hearing the name "Ted."

When Bundy was questioned in house-to-house inquiries, his fine public stature and charisma meant that he was quickly discounted from a list of more than 3,000 suspects. In September, 1974, the Seattle murders stopped and the local task force no doubt breathed a tentative sigh of relief. True to the 'organized' profile, Bundy simply moved towns, as he would continue to do throughout his series of murders.

Ted Bundy signed on as a law student at the University of Utah, 100 miles south-east of his killing ground in Seattle.

The Mormon community of Salt Lake City now had one of America's most famous killers in its midst. Autumn clouds gathered in the blue skies, the deep red mountains could still be clearly seen, jutting up high above the city skyline and college-girl killer Ted Bundy had now graduated in first degree murder. Gone was the unsophisticated 'blitz' attack, in its place a much more subtle 'con' and kidnap style of operation. He approached women with his arm in plaster and a sling, asking for help to get to his car. He even posed as a policeman, complete with a look-alike police badge and handcuffs. The new wave of victims were being sodomized, strangled to death while being raped, then twigs, dirt and other objects thrust into their vaginas. With each fresh killing came an escalation in the violence, as Bundy searched for more and more satisfaction. Some of the bodies were kept, washed and new make-up applied before necrophilia was carried out.

When Bundy's behaviour is listed, it's interesting to see how accurate the 'organized' profile is. The profile says average to above average intelligence. Bundy was a psychology graduate turned law student. It expects a level of social competence – this was an offender who was described by his peers as charming. When on the run from prison, he even managed to persuade people who knew he was an escapee, to take him in and look after him. The profile said he will be sexually experienced – none of his string of girlfriends complained on this score. However, Bundy's long-time lover Meg Anders stated that Bundy had insisted on trying sodomy and bondage games, during which he once half-choked her. She also remarked that she would wake up sometimes at night and find him staring strangely at her body under the bedclothes.

The 'organized' profile purports that the offender will follow news of his crimes in the media and will change jobs or leave town. When he escaped from prison in Salt Lake City, the FBI issued a wanted report on him and listed his jobs as: bellboy, busboy, cook's helper, dishwasher, janitor, law school student, office worker, political campaign worker, psychiatric social worker, salesman and security guard. In all, he killed in five different States: Washington, Oregon, Utah, Colorado and Florida.

The profile suggests the offender will consume alcohol prior to crimes, will remain in a controlled state during the crimes themselves and will have a functional car in good condition. Bundy's survivors all reported the heavy smell of alcohol on his breath. The killer was so composed during his crimes that after almost being caught attacking 17-year-old Carol DaRonch, he slipped into a School Hall to avoid detection, watched the school play *The Redhead* and then targeted another victim. As 17-year-old Debbie Kent left the hall, Bundy abducted her on the parking lot and later murdered her. Bundy certainly had the functional car that experts had expected. He drove a distinctive, orange VW Beetle.

The profile also holds up pretty well when the killer's behaviour at the crime scenes is analyzed. Experts predict a planned offence against a stranger, during which the offender will exhibit controlled/authoritative conversation. Bundy's victimology was to always pick strangers, never anyone he knew or who might know him. His attacks were always thought out and he used his intelligence to pretend to be a law enforcement officer or fake disability to a level which allowed him to manipulate his victims. The profile predicts the use of restraints, aggressive acts prior to death and an absence of evidence and possibly the body itself. Bundy used restraints, not only in the sex games that his girlfriend spoke of but also as a practical way of controlling terrified victims.

On July 14, 1974 Bundy captured two women. Using the arm-in-a-sling ruse, he parked up near Lake Sammamish in Seattle's State Park. He then asked 23-year-old blonde Janice Ott to help him lift his boat onto a trailer at the back of his VW. Taken in by his conversational skills she went with him and never returned. Hours later teenager Denise Naslund was caught by the same trick. When their bodies were discovered two months later, bits of a third skeleton were also collected. During this murderous spree Bundy used his powers of authority and control to their limits, no doubt aided by some firm ropes or ties. The absence of any bindings at the scene, the removal of the bodies to a place ten miles from the abduction site and the complete lack of any forensic clues at any of the scenes conforms to the profile for 'organized' offenders.

Profiles never fit perfectly and even in this classic case there are examples where Bundy strayed out of the expected matrix. For example, the 'organized' profile would predict that an offender would be subject to 'precipitating situational stress'. There is little evidence of this in Bundy's case, though some efforts have been made to establish his break-up with a long-time girlfriend as the emotional trigger for the killings. This is slightly confusing because he was eventually re-united with the woman and then Bundy curtailed the affair himself. As an illegitimate child no real relevance can be placed on the profile's suggestion that "the offender's father will be in stable full-time employment." Similarly, while Bundy planned his crimes well, the last series (for which he was caught) was a complete and uncontrolled mess.

On the run in Florida, 2,500 miles from his first fumbled attack in Seattle, Theodore Robert Bundy was subject to what he would eventually describe as "the urge drive." A fortnight earlier he had escaped from captivity in Colorado and under the alias Chris Hagen had blended into the student life of Tallahassee like a chameleon. In the early hours of Sunday, January 15, 1978 he slipped into the Chi Omega Sorority House, a residence which was exclusively for a female equivalent of the American fraternity organizations. His behaviour in here was far from the controlled style he exhibited in other attacks, when he kidnapped victims and disposed of their bodies without a trace of evidence.

A little after 3 am student Karen Chandler was discovered staggering around the lodgings with blood pumping from head wounds. A second lodger, Kathy Kleiner was found swaying on the edge of her bed with blood streaming down her face and neck. As the lights went on and a search began, 21-year-old Margaret Bowman was found. Her underwear had been torn off so violently that her skin had been grazed and she had been choked to death with her own stockings. Some rooms away, another victim was discovered, 20-year-old Lisa Levy. Blood was running from her anal and vaginal passages and again she had been choked with a stocking. Lisa, who sustained horrendous bites, including the severing of a nipple, died on the way to hospital. After this frenzied attack Bundy had strolled on another six blocks to another rooming-house and clubbed youngster Cheryl Thomas into unconsciousness before being disturbed by some of her friends.

Bundy would stay at large for some more months living on what he could steal from local stores and even claiming more victims, but the Sorority House spree would prove to be his undoing. He had left a perfect set of teeth marks in Lisa Levy's buttock. When dental experts proved the match, it was the only real evidence in an otherwise circumstantial case against him. That night of uncontrolled murder was enough to send him to the electric chair. At 7:07 am on January 24, 1989 at Starke Prison, Florida, he was executed. Right to the end, Bundy tried to use his manipulative skills. After his appeal had been turned down, he offered to make a complete confession and own up to all the killings (believed at the time to possibly be double those he had been charged with) in return for a sentence commuted to life in prison.

The fact that Bundy doesn't fit 'the profile' perfectly, is a clear example of the quandary investigators face. If only part of the behavioural analysis is focused upon, then an investigation can be completely misled. Practitioners constantly remind themselves and those they teach their skills to, that like Bundy, offenders can often change their behaviour throughout a series of killings.

In teaching profiling to agents and law enforcement officers, profilers from the FBI emphasize that the 'organized' offender is dominated by fantasy and ritual with obsessive and compulsive traits surfacing in his behaviour at the crime scene. Sometimes the murder is not planned, rape is planned as part of the fantasy and when rape is carried out murder is a possibility. Agents are often quoted the following real-case scenario of five rape-murders as a way of trying out the skills they've been learning as analysts.

The first victim, a woman in her late 20s was sexually attacked and killed, after she drove home to her high-rise apartment block at the end of a late night at work. Her body was found about 150 yards from her home, in a wooded culvert yet her car was parked outside the apartments. The body was semi-naked, found in a stream with no sign of mutilation before or after death. The victim had been partly strangled and had died from drowning. Her attacker had held her head in the running water of the stream. There were some bruises and defence wounds but nothing to indicate that she had been battered prior to death. Her shoes were missing from the body, but were later found elsewhere in the woodland, as were footprints that are believed to belong to her attacker. There were no signs of tyre-marks and detectives were certain that although a ring had been taken from the woman's hand, nothing else of value was missing.

The second victim in the series was found less than a quarter of a mile away in an area of similar woodland. This time, a woman in her late 20s had died after being stabbed repeatedly in the chest but there was no mutilation and no water at hand. Similarities with the first attack included the fact both women had been returning home late at night in the same area. Both had parked their cars but never reached their apartments and both had been sexually assaulted.

The third victim died in similar circumstances and was of comparable age and looks to the first two women. In this case though, after the rape there was evidence to show that the victim had been mainly re-dressed after death. A stocking had been taken from the murder scene.

Several months later, a fourth victim was claimed in the same area. This time the woman was black, in her early 30s and like the others had been returning home to an apartment block in the early hours of the morning after a late night at work. Like the first victim, she had been strangled and drowned.

The fifth and final victim was again a woman in her mid-20s. She was attacked as she left a party at around half past one in the morning and was found in the same wooded culvert as previous victims. She'd been stabbed several times in the chest, but unlike the other women had been partly buried.

In this case, the FBI profile that follows was instrumental in a successful arrest and prosecution. This is the profiling summary: "The offender selects victims who are returning home during the late evening or early morning hours. The assaults generally take place near the victims' homes, as they are walking from their parked cars. The offender is watching the parking areas for single women returning during these times. He takes the victims from the apartment complex to wooded areas close by for the assaults. He chooses the time and place of assault.

Since no scream or resistance is evident, one must assume the assailant carries a weapon and instructs the victims to accompany him to the secluded area. This indicates a persuasive, articulate person who convinces them no harm will come to them if they 'do as he instructs'. He would be manipulative and have a history of anti-social traits and behaviour. He is youthful and aggressive, probably macho.

"Since he uses the same MO (*Modus Operandi*) in each assault, one must assume he knows the territory well, both the travelled built-up areas and the surrounding woods. He probably lives in the area, is youthful and has grown up and played in the woods as a child. He is a long-term resident.

Medical examination and crime scene assessment show rape prior to death, and death is sudden with minimal mutilation, again indicating the well-planned crime by the 'organized' anti-social criminal. The victims are 'sized up' prior to the approach, and the killer knows they will not resist if he promises release after the rape. He has raped before the killing started, but some life trauma has triggered the taking of the life of victim number one. The offender has had past problems with law enforcement and once he has killed he feels he must continue to kill to avoid victims testifying against him. He does not value the life of a victim over the chance that she may identify him to the police.

"In summary, the assailant in the five homicides is an 'organized', anti-social personality. He is a youthful, white male, has good intelligence, is articulate and manipulative. He fits into the community and has lived there for many years. He lives in close proximity to all his victims. He precipitates his crimes with alcohol and or drugs, possibly is first born in his family and is sexually competent. He probably has a girlfriend but had a recent problem with her prior to the first killing. Considering his age, he would live with a single parent and would have no car, since he selects his victims on foot, sometimes using their cars in the assault. He probably would follow the media reports of the crime and may be in a crowd of onlookers when the police locate the bodies."

In this case, the profile helped lead to the arrest of a 17-year-old white youth who lived close to all the victims and also within a one mile radius of a large city suburb. As predicted, he was bright, yet didn't excel at school. He lived with his mother and had a girlfriend whom he referred to as "his fiancée." She had broken up their relationship to go away to college, the bust-up coming just before the series of rape-murders began. House-to-house inquiries revealed that he thought of himself as macho and a bit of 'a ladies' man', although many of his peers regarded him as 'a con artist'. He had a lengthy juvenile record, which included offences of sexual assault and rape. He used to drink beer or smoke marijuana before he targeted victims in the area he had grown up in.

The opposite of the 'organized' offender is the 'disorganized' and both in terms of the type of person he is and the way he leaves the crime scene, the traits of this criminal are distinctly inverse to those of the Bundy-type killer.

The 'disorganized' offender is likely to be of below average intelligence and may even fall into the category of being classed as socially inadequate. Unlike Ted Bundy, you won't find him studying Chinese or law. If he's employed at all then it will be in unskilled work. There'll be no string of girlfriends, he's expected to be sexually incompetent and will almost certainly always live alone or with a parent. His home, and if he works his workspace too, will be near to where he carries out his crimes. He will also become very anxious while carrying out the offences. While the 'organized' offender is likely to be the first born in a family, his 'disorganized' counterpart is likely to be the youngest. He will have experienced particularly harsh discipline, possibly emotional, physical or sexual abuse as a child and his father will not have enjoyed stable employment. He won't be reliant on alcohol before carrying out an attack and will be impulsive, especially while carrying out his crimes.

The 'disorganized' crime scene will reflect the spontaneity of the offender's behaviour. He is likely to be familiar with the location and even the victim, though during the attack he will attempt to depersonalize the victim and will only exchange a bare minimum of words, if any. There is a probability of sudden violence to the victim and a high possibility of sexual acts being carried out on the body after death.

The crime scene will be very random and sloppy and the body itself is likely to be left uncovered where the murder took place. It is usual that the scene will provide some good evidence for investigators and the murder weapon itself is often found here as well.

Just as Bundy fitted almost perfectly into the 'organized' profile category, then Edward Gein, one of the most celebrated of all serial killers, fits similarly into that of the 'disorganized' criminal. Gein, who coincidentally shared Bundy's other Christian name, Theodore, committed grisly acts of murder, mutilation and cannibalism. His distorted and psychopathic life inspired the Hitchcock thriller *Psycho* and proved source material for the Buffalo Bill character in Thomas Harris's novel and film *The Silence of the Lambs*.

Born in Wisconsin in Midwest America on August 27, 1906, Edward Gein was the second son of a domineering, Lutheran mother and an unloving, drunken father. He grew up on a small farm with little contact with the outside world. His elder brother Henry died in mysterious circumstances in the spring of 1944 and his father had died of natural causes some four years earlier. When Augusta Gein died of a stroke in 1945, Edward Theodore was left alone in a world that was a complete stranger to him. Straight after her death, and burial, he turned her bedroom into a mausoleum, leaving everything as she'd always had it, then boarded up the ground-floor room with planks. He was 39 years of age, but barely had the intelligence of a child.

Gein never had any sexual partners and engrossed himself in a fantasy world of violent comics and magazines such as *Tales from the Crypt*, *Vault of Horrors* and *War Criminals*. He poured over soft-porn, masturbating to pictures and stories of corpses, whippings and sadism. As a result, he became more and more introverted. The only factual books he read were medical text-books featuring exploded-diagrams of the female anatomy.

It wasn't until the Christmas of 1954 that police in Plainfield had any reason to suspect that Ed Gein was anything other than the mild-mannered, slightly eccentric local handyman that he'd always appeared to be. Mary Hogan, the fat 54-year-old land-lady of Hogan's Tavern vanished on the freezing afternoon of December 8. A local farmer calling in for a drink noticed that she had gone and after then discovering bloodstains in a doorway, he alerted the Sheriff's department. When a proper forensic search was carried out, a spent .32 calibre rifle cartridge was found in the bar and it was evident that the German-born landlady had been dragged through the tavern, out of the back door and onto the parking lot outside. Investigators simply followed a trail of blood out into the snow. Freshly-made tyre-tracks also indicated the general direction in which Hogan's killer had made off with her body.

As the local crime-lab and Sheriff began to piece together Hogan's last moments, Ed Gein was virtually making a confession to one of his few acquaintances. Out on his farm, six miles west of Plainfield, he discussed the murder with local sawmill owner Elmo Ueeck. Ueeck was ribbing Gein about "having had a soft spot" for Old Mary, perhaps even being in love with her. When the visitor suggested that if Gein had been more confident about himself and had told Mary about his feelings, then instead of going missing she might still have been around. Ed replied strangely: "She isn't missing... she's at the farm right now." Amazingly, Ueeck put the remark down to his friend's weird sense of humour, as did several other townsfolk he repeated the claim to.

With small resources and lots of other business to attend to, the small town Sheriff's office filed the Mary Hogan murder in their unsolved homicides drawer. Three years would pass before they needed to dust it down, re-open the case and discover a series of monstrous acts that shook America.

Bernice Worden was the same kind of size and age as Mary Hogan, but there the similarities stopped. In her late 50s she was a devout Methodist, ran the town's hardware store and was considered a pillar of the local community. For weeks before her death she had been pestered in the store by Ed Gein, who used to pretend to be interested in buying things but really came into the single-storey shop just to stare at her.

Eventually, tiny, feeble Ed asked Big Berni if she'd go out on a date with him. She laughed at his suggestion and rebuffed him in an embarrassing way that clearly upset Gein. She mentioned the incident to her son Frank who was a Deputy Sheriff and he added that he had also seen Gein gazing strangely at her from his truck.

On Saturday, November 16, 1957, Ed Gein made a date with Mrs Worden that she couldn't refuse. While looking over a .22 rifle for sale in the hardware store, he slipped in some shells of his own, took aim and blew a bewildered Bernice across her own firearms display cabinet. He then dragged her corpse to his pick-up truck and returned to his broken-down farmhouse where he began to disembowel and decapitate her.

When Frank Worden discovered that his mother was missing and there were bloodstains throughout the back of the shop he immediately suspected Gein. Within an hour he and the County Sheriff that he had called in from Wautoma, 15 miles away, were heading out towards the farmstead. In fact, Gein had already been arrested by two traffic cops as he was spotted leaving a friend's home where he'd been sharing an evening meal. When one of the officers, without mentioning the murder, asked the handyman where he'd been that day, he replied: "Somebody framed me." "Framed you for what?" inquired the official. Gein then unnecessarily committed himself further, "Well, about Mrs Worden." "What about Mrs Worden?" pressed the officer. "Well, she's dead isn't she," Gein went on. At this point no one other than him could have known that Bernice Worden had only been reported as a missing person.

When County Sheriff Art Schley and his officers entered the pitch-blackness of Gein's farmhouse, he shouldered into something and immediately flicked the beam of his spotlight upwards. There, hanging from the rafters was the headless body of Bernice Worden, with a gaping hole in her stomach where she had been disembowelled. Adjusting their eyes to the bright light and the dangling body, the men could also make out, but couldn't believe, that the corpse had been skinned of its flesh. Their journey around what local youngsters had always referred to as 'The Haunted House' had only just begun.

Inside the rest of Gein's home, they discovered boxes of pornography and rows of teeth, meticulously laid out on a mantelpiece. As they made their way through the ramshackle, old white building, they found a number of human skulls that had been hacked in half and used as bowls and ashtrays. A chair in the kitchen had a seat that had been made out of strips of human skin, while human remains had also been used to make lampshades, waste-baskets, bracelets and a drum.

Gein's fridge was stocked with human organs, and other boxes around the house contained body parts that had been clinically cut away with the skill of a surgeon. Gein's bedroom was a Chamber of Horrors. The bed itself was supported on severed heads, while around it hung four masks that had been made from the hair and faces of his victims. Another five masks, which had been fashioned by stripping away the flesh from women's skulls and then stuffing the inside with crumpled-up newspaper balls, were also found. They'd all been displayed as trophies, just as a Big Game Hunter would have mounted and shown-off the heads of slaughtered deer or buffalo. Investigators also found a sort of vest, made out of the skin of his victims. Gein had carefully sown the pieces together and during his necrophilic fantasies would wear the garment to heighten his stimulation.

The body parts of at least 15 corpses were found in the house but the middle-aged simpleton was not responsible for all those deaths and it's probable that he only killed Worden and Hogan. During a confused confession he admitted that the other cadavers had come straight from the cemetery. After the burial, often of someone that he knew, Gein would return in the dead of night to dig the body up and take it home.

In summary then, how does Gein fit the profile characteristics for a 'disorganized' offender? The profile says a 'disorganized' offender will be of below average intelligence. This certainly applied, as does the suggestion that the criminal would be socially inadequate. Until middle-age, Gein hardly mixed with anyone. The profile predicts an unskilled worker who will be sexually incompetent and have low birth order status. Ed was the youngest in the family and when the others died he let the farm turn into a ruin. He collected a subsidy because the land was fallow whilst he had resorted to doing odd jobs as a handyman to earn a living. No one in Plainfield could ever remember him having any relationship with anyone of either sex and it is not unreasonable to expect that with such a background he would be sexually dysfunctional.

It is predicted that this type of offender will live alone, near to the crime scene (as he did) and will have experienced harsh discipline as a child. Records show that Mrs Gein, who came from an austere German-immigrant family, was herself a strict disciplinarian who frequently beat her children and was not too quick to forgive them. It's also suggested that this type of offender's father will not be in full-time employment and this certainly applied in Gein's case. His father George drifted in and out of jobs and drank away what little money he earned at any bar that was open. Conversely, experts predict that the 'disorganized' offender will make "minimal use of alcohol" in relation to his crimes, will experience minimal situational stress but will be particularly anxious when he carries out an offence. Again, all three assumptions are smack on target with Gein. In his confession, there is no reference to drinking alcohol, even in the murder of tavern landlady Mary Hogan. Gein was noted for only having a rare glass of beer and sitting shyly at the bar. With him working only when it suited him and mixing with only a handful of people, Gein was definitely not subject to any clear situational stress. It is also reasonable to assume from the careless way he left evidence at the abduction scenes, he was in a state of high anxiety when he carried out the murders.

Turning to the crime scene itself, the profiling characteristics of the 'disorganized' offender seem to hold up pretty well here as well. Experts predict that the assailant will know either, or both, the location of the attack and the victim, and he will leave the crime scene in a random and sloppy manner. Gein knew both Hogan and Worden and the tavern and store in which he killed them. In addition to parking his pick-up right outside the premises while he killed the women, he left empty cartridges from his .32 rifle and the hunting rifle he picked up at Bernice Worden's shop. Bernice Worden's Deputy Sheriff son also discovered a bloodsoaked receipt for anti-freeze at the shop, made out to E Gein and dated the day that she died. The personality profile suggests that the offence will have been spontaneous, that there will have been little conversation between attacker and victim and there will have been sudden violence. Gein breaks slightly from the rails here. Certainly there was sudden violence and it's highly likely the conversation was strained and sparse in both killings. Mrs Worden and her son Frank had noted the handyman's predilection for staring rather than talking. The element of spontaneity is however questionable. Gein undoubtedly fantasized about the attack on Mary Hogan and a degree of planning must have gone into it. In the Worden case though, it is easy to conclude that he acted on the spur of the moment. He was pretending to be interested in

buying the rifle as an excuse to be near the woman he craved
and he decided there-and-then to slip in the shells, kill her and
take her body back to his farm. Crime scene analysis shows the
'disorganized' offender will leave evidence at the scene (as
Gein did), will seldom use restraints (he didn't), will depersonalize the victim and commit sexual acts after death (as he did).
Psychologists believe that Gein killed for companionship. They
interpret the necrophilic acts with those he murdered and those
bodies he robbed from their grave, as his twisted way of
creating lasting friendships with women who reminded him of
his dead mother. The depersonalization comes in the fact that
most murderers, when asked how they managed to mutilate,
decapitate and dismember their victims, claim that by this point
they had stopped seeing the victim as another person and were
simply venting their fantasy and rage on an object. In these
cases, specific areas of the body are often picked out for
extreme brutality. It's likely that excessive wounds to the face
may well indicate that the attacker knows the victim or even
that the victim looks like someone that the attacker knows and
this has caused the assailant some psychological distress. The
Sheriff's men who searched Gein's home said it was like a
human abattoir and it was noted that some of his victims had
been hung as though they were carcasses of meat.

Like Bundy, the offender category doesn't fit perfectly. Gein
didn't leave the body at the death scene as predicted by the
profile and he didn't leave it in full view as is often the case
with 'disorganized' offenders. Research has shown that when
offenders of this category do remove the body of a victim, it is
because they want to spend more time with it and will
then indulge in sexual acts. The FBI have noted mutilation
to the face, genitals and breasts, disembowelment, amputation
and vampirism. It's also been known for such killers to
ejaculate into open stab wounds in the victim's abdomen and
urinate, defecate or masturbate in the victim's home or on items
of clothing.

As a means of a working illustration, students of criminal
investigative analysis at the FBI Academy in Quantico, are

told the following case example of how a profile was drawn up of a 'disorganized' murderer and was contributory to an eventual arrest.

A man returning home from work in the early evening found his wife's body in the bedroom. She had been shot in the head four times and then disembowelled with a knife from her own kitchen draw. Autopsy reports showed that the first cuts had been to the abdomen and then her intestines had been pulled out of the body cavity. Animal faeces had been forced into her mouth, garbage was strewn around her and the home. A yogurt cup was nearby and had been used by the attacker to collect blood which he then drank. Time of death was fixed at some point in the morning, probably as she went out to empty the rubbish.

On the same day, a house burglary was carried out just a quarter of a mile from the murder. Again rubbish was thrown around the house and it was apparent that the intruder had urinated on female clothing that he had found and had then defecated in the home as well.

Two days later, the skeleton of a dog was found in the same area. Ballistic experts worked out that it had been shot in the head with the weapon that had killed the housewife. The dog had also been disembowelled.

Four days after the first killing, more bodies were found. A woman waiting to go on a day trip with her female neighbour and a male friend, saw the car she was looking out for draw up onto the neighbour's drive. She went to her own telephone to tell them she was on her way over but no one answered the call. When she looked out of her window the second time, the friend's station-wagon had gone. To satisfy her obvious curiosity, she went over to the house and discovered quite horrifying scenes of murder and mutilation.

Firstly, she noticed the neighbour's 22-month-old infant was missing from its cot. There was a bullet hole in the child's pillow and there was brain tissue and skull remains on the sheets. The female neighbour had been murdered in her bedroom and had been disembowelled from the breast bone to the pelvis. Her internal organs, including kidneys, spleen and reproductive organs had all been removed and mutilated.

The woman's exterior vaginal area was untouched but there had also been an attempt to remove an eye and a knife had been thrust deep into the victim's anus. The man had been shot but not mutilated and in the bathroom area more brain tissue and skull was found in a half-filled bathtub. Detectives believed the child had been murdered, its body washed and the corpse of the infant then removed from the scene. A ring of blood was found on the floor, indicating that the offender had used a container to collect some from a body and had drunk it.

The Behavioural Science Unit produced the following profile. "Suspect description: White male aged 25–27, thin, undernourished appearance. Single, living alone in a location within one mile of the abandoned station-wagon owned by one of the victims. Residence will be extremely slovenly and unkempt, and evidence of the crimes will be found. Suspect will have a history of mental illness and use of drugs. Suspect will be an unemployed loner who does not associate with either males or females and will probably spend a great deal of time in his own residence. If he resides with anyone, it will be with his parents; however this is unlikely. Subject will have no prior military history. Will be a high school or college drop-out and probably suffers from one or more forms of paranoid psychosis."

As a result of the profile, police carried out a search spanning a mile in radius around the stolen station-wagon. Within the catchment area, they came across a 27-year-old white male, who was 5ft 11in tall and weighed only 149 pounds. In his possession was a gun which matched the weapon used in the series of murders and crimes. When his apartment was searched various human and animal body parts were found. Medical inquiries showed that the man had a diagnosed history of paranoid schizophrenia and had spent some time in a mental institution after he'd been discovered sucking blood from a dead bird. When he was released from mental care he was found in the desert covered in blood, wearing only a loincloth. He told police that he had been making sacrifices to aliens and flying saucers.

'Organized' and 'disorganized' profiles are no longer talked of with great enthusiasm at the FBI. They're still taught as basic concepts, experienced agents still use them as frameworks for cases but the sophistication of criminal analysis has moved on since their inception and there is a reluctance on behalf of the Bureau to be seen to be standing still. The simplicity of the system has also attracted some international criticism, yet the BSU has always argued that the categories are merely meant as starting points for investigators, not as rigid patterns that must always be followed. The FBI soaks up the criticism and says it's always ready to learn from a psychologist, psychiatrist or police officer who knows better. The truth is, much of the criticism has come from English psychologists involved in forms of profiling for regional police forces and intent on making a name for themselves. The work of some of these so-called experts was found severely wanting when they were subjected to a high-level, top-secret review carried out on behalf of the British Home Office. The FBI system, constantly being updated but still rooted in the pioneering work of the late 1970s and 1980s is still the most authoritative and inspirational that is available to today's law enforcement agencies. There is no doubt that new systems will emerge in the future, especially in Britain and Europe, but for the moment in terms of size and success of their operations, the Americans are way out in front.

# 6

## *Inside The Bunker*

*"Hello from the gutters of New York, which are filled with dog manure, vomit, stale wine, urine and blood." – 'Son of Sam', in his letter to the Press.*

In the heart of the FBI's converted bunker in Virginia, computers hum and telephones buzz and beep. Gigantic maps sprawl across the walls and there's the occasional face of a fugitive pinned on a board or staring upward, absentmindedly from the clutter of an In-tray. This is the base for the National Centre for the Analysis of Violent Crime, a clearinghouse for murder, rape, child sex abuse, arson and bombings. Before you even enter the room you're aware of its importance; there's an intense activity alive in a distant cacophony of voices.

"VICAP, can I help you..." "...was the mutilation post-mortem?" "Was the assault site near a school, how far away are we talking..." "Anal sex, vaginal sex, oral sex... do you know which first?" The questions overlap each other, the answers unheard. This is the heartbeat of the NCAVC, the Violent Criminal Apprehension Programme. Sometimes it quickens with the rigours of new cases, often it's just a steady rhythm, dealing with an awesome backlog of murders and the methodical alchemy of turning paperwork into data. Rows of analysts process thousands of VICAP report forms, juggling detailed computer work while making telephone calls to homicide squads thousands of miles and sometimes several time-zones away.

There are three main aims of VICAP. Firstly, to help link unsolved murders, so investigators know when they are working on a murder that is already part of a serial case that perhaps stretches into several other cities or States. It is particularly adept when the homicides are apparently random, motiveless or sexually oriented.

Secondly, it's proved useful in helping clear up confusion over missing persons, when the circumstances of their disappearance has indicated the use of what the police still like to refer to as 'foul play'. Finally, its aim is to help identify murder victims when normal body identification systems fail. Like Larry McCann, VICAP only gets to come into its own when the average police investigation has failed to come up with the goods.

The success of VICAP depends upon how thoroughly its 188 question report form is completed – strictly in block capitals and only in black ink or pencil. The form is important because it has been copied worldwide, often adjusted for cultural differences, but in the main kept pretty much the same. The first 23 questions cover administrative details, such as the type of crime that's being investigated (missing person, homicide, possible kidnapping, etc). This is what amounts to the nuts and bolts of the case, such as where the victim was last seen. Then, there's a slim opportunity for comment: "Based on your experience and the results of the investigation of this case, do you believe this offender has killed before?"

The second section is devoted to information about the victim. It begins with requests for basic identification details, residence, age, build, height, eye colour, etc.

Like a fingertip search of a crime scene, it progresses methodically through a run-down on any tattoos, any outstanding physical features and then into a precise sub-section on the victim's clothing – the preferred colour tone, whether the style was garish, athletic, conservative or whatever. This area is what investigators refer to as victimology and is rich in clues about the offender's personality and behaviour.

In reality, it is at this point in the questionnaire that the archaeology of homicide begins a well-planned dig into the dark and often startling fantasy world of the type of victim a killer would like to target. There are occasions when it can also be a valuable excavation of the offender's own social status, style of dress and lifestyle.

Section three, questions 55 to 79 are devoted to what is known or has been reported about the offender, any scrap of detail from race, approximate age, height, hair colour, etc, to whether he wore a disguise or walked with a limp. Information here laps into the next area, which comes into effect if there is an offender in custody. It covers cities and States that the suspect may have travelled to (for cross-checking with other killings, as in the Bundy case where the murders were carried out in five States but the various police forces were for some time unaware they were seeking the same murderer) and has a grisly catalogue for any body parts that may have been found in his possession.

Another section deals with the exact geographic location of the crime scenes and another on building up a precise description of any vehicles involved. Recent psychological research has shown that many serial killers are compulsive drivers, sometimes 'cruising' to reach a 'comfort zone' that they will eventually kill in. Sometimes, the serial offender will just aimlessly drive around for hundreds of miles.

Predictably, the most attention is focused on the offender's *Modus Operandi* – his method of operating or his MO. The VICAP form asks detectives completing it to painstakingly trace the crime from the momment the offender first approached the victim, observing whether this was done as an act of deception, perhaps with someone posing as a policeman or a businessman offering the victim a job. Alternatively, it seeks to establish whether the offender lay in wait or attacked the victim while she was asleep. Behavioural knowledge of the attacker is also gleaned from learning if he broke into the victim's home (possibly a burglar with previous convictions), and whether the body was written upon or carved on by the attacker and what was used to carry out the writing or carving.

The pertinence of the section on 'body writing' is illustrated in the case of the Manson Family Murders back in America in 1969. Charles Manson, a self-appointed guru of Californian hippies and some of his devotees, broke into the home of super-market millionaire Leno LaBianca and his wife Rosemary in the Los Feliz area of Los Angeles. Manson led the way, sword in one hand and a gun in the other. After tying up and robbing the terrified couple, Manson left and Mr and Mrs LaBianca were now at the mercy of his crazed followers. Rosemary was forced down onto her bed, a lamp-flex was used as a noose around her neck and she was then stabbed 16 times in the buttocks and a total of 41 times through her breasts, abdomen, face, neck and rest of her body.

Meanwhile, her husband was stabbed four times in the throat with a kitchen knife, which was then impaled in his larynx. He was then stabbed a further eight times in the stomach with another knife. As Mr. LaBianca bled to death, 23-year-old Manson-follower, Charles 'Tex' Watson, carved the word WAR on his abdomen. One of his accomplices, 21-year-old Patricia Krenwinkel was busying herself perforating the couple's bodies with a fork, which she then left stuck in Rose-mary's abdomen. Another member of the 'Family' then dipped his or her fingers in Mrs LaBianca's blood and scrawled DEATH TO PIGS on one wall. On another wall was the word RISE and on the fridge HEALTER SKELTER (a misspelling from a Beatles' song that Manson and his group saw as politically inspirational).

The hideous desires of these offenders to 'vocalize' the meaning of their crimes by writing on their victims and in their victims' blood, had been exhibited just a day earlier in the Hollywood area of LA. 'Family' members had broken into the grounds of 10050 Cielo Drive, the home of 26-year-old actress Sharon Tate, the wife of film director Roman Polanski and star of the big hit 1960s film *Valley of the Dolls*. Before they even got to the house they shot and killed 18-year-old Steven Parent, who was travelling down the driveway in his white two seater car. Then 'Tex' Watson, Patricia Krenwinkel and Sadie Mae Glutz made their way into the sprawling mansion, while Linda Kasabian stayed in the grounds as a lookout. Thirty-five year old Jay Sebring was the next to be shot. The Hollywood hairdresser and close friend of Tate's, made a grab for Watson's .22 Buntline Special while demanding that Sharon, who was eight months pregnant at the time, be allowed to sit down somewhere and relax. The bleeding Sebring was then tethered to Tate and her friend Abigail Folger, the 25-year-old heiress to the Folger coffee fortune, with a length of nylon rope that the intruders had brought with them. Folger's 32-year-old boyfriend, Wojiciech Frykowski, was then stabbed by Sadie Mae. As he fought back, Watson shot him twice and then repeatedly clubbed him in the face with the handle of the gun. Watson next turned his attentions to Sebring and delivered four knife wounds that ended the ex-Navy man's life. Patricia Krenwinkel was involved in a struggle with Folger, until Watson joined in and slit her throat, before stabbing her several times in the body. Amazingly, Watson now discovered that Frykowski was not dead and had made his way to the front door. Here, before he could shout for help, he was cut down and stabbed more than 40 times.

Manson's murderers were now intoxicated with the excitement of their violence and any rational thoughts they'd had were drowned in the adrenalin that washed through them. It's at this point that Sharon Tate became the focus of their bloodlust. Despite pleading for her life and that of her unborn baby, Sadie Mae Glutz and Patricia Krenwinkel now held her down while Watson plunged his knife into her body. Afterwards, the girls ritualistically took turns to pass on the knife and stab Sharon and her unborn child. Glutz then picked up a towel that they had used to help tie down Frykowski, dipped it into Sharon's blood and padded the word PIG onto the wall in the hallway.

The Tate murders were quickly connected to the LaBianca killings, the blood-writing proving the most positive forensic link. Surprisingly though, investigators initially refused to include in the series the killing a fortnight earlier in Malibu, of 34-year-old music teacher Gary Hinman. Again, there had been bloody scrawlings on the wall. This time the words POLITICAL PIGGY had been marked out above the dead man's head. The writings all contained the same kind of political and anti-society themes and should have been good grounds for the Los

Angeles Police Department and Los Angeles Sheriff's Office to compare notes and come up with the conclusion that they were hunting the same people.

Ten months after the LaBianca murders, Charles Manson and three of his followers went on trial. They had been arrested at their commune on the Barker Ranch, a run-down settlement in the heart of California's Death Valley. Detectives investigating the Gary Hinman murder had arrested one of the killers, Bobby Beausoliel and had noted that he had hung around with "The weird hippies who live in the desert." With Beausoliel in custody, they were intrigued by the similarities in the Tate and LaBianca murders and wondered whether their killer's friends could be involved. Eventually, a three day raid on the commune revealed two women who had been hiding from 'Family' members and who had begged the police for help and protection. They told officers that they had overhead Manson, Beausoliel and other gang members talking about the murders. Under questioning, various 'Family' members began blaming each other for the killings. Linda Kasabian turned into the prosecution's principal witness in what was America's longest running murder trial, lasting nine and a half months. Manson, Susan Atkins, Patricia Krenwinkel and Leslie Van Houten were all found guilty and sentenced to death. Their executions were never carried out because California abolished the death penalty a year later. Other gang members, including Charles 'Tex' Watson, received similar life sentences at subsequent trials.

VICAP was not introduced until June 1, 1985, 16 years after the first Manson murder. Since then, its report form has been whittled down from a daunting tome that looked like an early draft of *War and Peace* to a much more manageable but still comprehensive 16 pages. Bearing in mind that the form has to be completed by an overworked, harassed detective, great effort has been spent on making it quick and painless to fill in.

Question 134 wants to know if there were symbolic artifacts discovered at the crime scene. This sometimes goes hand-in-hand with the writings on bodies or walls, but also includes the possibility of defecation by the offender or an unusual ritual such as the burning of candles around the victim, use of dead animals or any strange arrangements of rocks or twigs at the crime scene.

A special section is devoted to 'Offender's Communications' and by this, the FBI is not referring to any conversations between the attacker and the victim; that is dealt with elsewhere. Here, analysts are interested in more obvious communications such as ransom demands and extortion notes. Included in this is communication made perhaps by audio tape (as in the misleading Geordie-voiced tapes sent to detectives in Britain's Yorkshire Ripper case) or any letters by the murderer that have been sent to either the police or the media. There's a long history of killers wanting to communicate with law enforcement agencies, stretching from the original letters of the Ripper in 19th-century London to the modern day.

One of the most interesting murderers to write to detectives was the .44 calibre killer, David 'Son of Sam' Berkowitz. His series of murders began in the boiling summer cauldron of New York City in July 1976 and ended 12 months later after he had shot dead six victims and wounded another seven. At the time, the hunt for this podgy former soldier and occasional arsonist, was the largest murder investigation ever mounted by the New York Police, with a detection bill that was running up at a rate of 90 thousand dollars a day. Three hundred detectives were working on the case, backed up by a team of psychiatrists and psychologists, giving behavioural clues to the killer's identity.

Berkowitz targeted couples in cars, his favourite hunting ground being the Queens area of New York. He began with the murder of 18-year-old Donna Lauria. As she opened the passenger door of a car parked near her house, Berkowitz confronted her, lifted a gun from inside a brown paper bag and shot her twice in the neck. She died within minutes. He then homed-in on the other side of the vehicle and opened fire on the driver Jody Valente. His shooting wasn't as accurate this time and Valente survived. The 19-year-old was wounded in her thigh, then Berkowitz fled. His next two attempts to kill were failures but his victims were left paralysed or wounded.

*(Left)* Dennis Andrew Nilsen, Britain's most prolific killer. Photo: courtesy of the Press Association.

*(Below)* Cooking utensils used by Nilsen to dismember and dispose of his victims. Photo: courtesy of the Press Association.

*(Above)* Yorkshire Ripper Peter Sutcliffe with his wife Sonia. Photo: courtesy of Camera Press Ltd.

*(Below)* Still searching for clues: detectives at the scene of yet another Yorkshire Ripper murder. Photo: courtesy of the Press Association.

*(Above)* Rape kit belonging to serial rapist Patrick Reilly. It includes instruments of torture.

*(Below)* Railway Rapist John Duffy – the first British serial offender to be caught by detectives using a psychological profile.

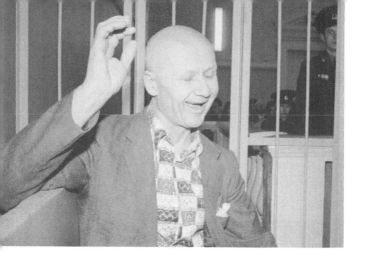

*(Above)* Russian serial killer Andrei Chikatilo killed over 50 people, and now awaits execution. Photo: courtesy of Popperfoto.

*(Right)* Milwaukee 'Cannibal' Jeffrey Dahmer. Photo: courtesy of Popperfoto.

 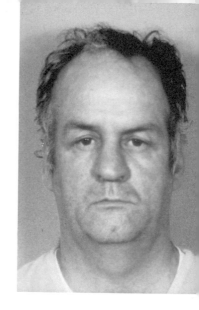

*(Above left)* Artist's impression of Arthur Shawcross.

*(Above right)* The man himself, captured following a bizarre helicopter sighting.

*(Below)* A victim of Arthur Shawcross, abandoned in a river.

*(Above)* Ted Bundy, one of America's most prolific serial killers, pleads for his life before a Florida jury. He was executed in 1989. Photo: courtesy of Popperfoto.

*(Below)* 'Son of Sam' killer David Berkowitz who shot courting couples in cars in New York. Photo: courtesy of Popperfoto.

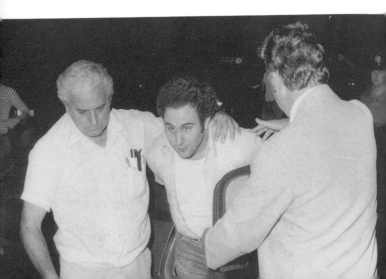

(Left) Edmund Emil Kemper, who shot his grandparents and went on to decapitate eight more victims, including his mother. Photo: courtesy of Associated Press.

(Below) 'Night Stalker' Richard Ramirez was convicted of 13 murders in 1989 and sentenced to death. He is still awaiting execution on Death Row. Photo: courtesy of Associated Press.

*(Above)* Spree killer Charles Starkweather and his 14-year-old girlfriend, Caril Fulgate. Photo: courtesy of Associated Press.

*(Below)* Sexual sadist Bob Berdella who tortured, murdered and dismembered six men. This photo was taken during an interview with the authors.

It was January 30, 1977 that the 24-year-old succeeded in claiming his next life, that of Christine Freund. She was shot dead as she sat in a parked car with her boyfriend John Diel. They had just been to see the recently released Stallone movie *Rocky* and had stopped off for something to eat in Queens. Although 30-year-old Diel survived, his ordeal was not over as he became the number one suspect in his girlfriend's murder.

By this point the same weapon, a .44 Bulldog revolver had been used in the shootings of six people, but the police department still hadn't perceived that they were hunting a serial offender. This is perhaps less astonishing than it at first sounds. About two-thirds of America's annual 25 thousand murders are carried out with some form of firearm and as a result most of the country's crime labs and ballistics experts are working flatout to ease a huge backlog of cases.

The killing that convinced investigators that Diel was innocent and they were in fact hunting a solitary offender, was the murder on March 8, 1977 of Armenian student Virginia Voskerichian as she returned to her home in Queens. It was 7.30 pm when the 19-year-old altered the route she was walking to avoid bumping into an oncoming stranger, only instead of going around her he stopped, levelled a gun at her face and started firing. Instinctively, the young student held her school books to her face but the bullet ripped through them, smashing out several teeth and lodging in her skull. She died almost instantly.

Now, news of an armed serial killer on the loose, was spreading through New York like wildfire and the people feeling most of the heat were the police. Their response was to form an overall task force to co-ordinate the various homicide teams that had been set up to look for new clues.

The publicity given to this initiative was sensational and without even knowing it, investigators had scored a psychological victory over their enemy. There's no doubt that Berkowitz, who avidly followed his own crimes in the newspapers, was upset at the attention the police were now receiving at his expense. He set out to redress the balance.

His first response was to return to the killing zone in which he claimed his first victim, Donna Lauria. Just a few blocks away, he came across 18-year-old Valentina Suriani, enjoying a late night embrace in a car with her boyfriend Alexander Esau. Their kiss was broken by a blaze of bullets from the Bulldog, two ripping into Valentina's head, then two into Esau's skull. At the scene of the murders he left a white envelope in the pool of shattered windscreen glass that surrounded the vehicle.

The letter was addressed to Captain Joe Borelli of the freshly formed Omega Task Force. It was written in bold black capital lettering and was virtually devoid of fingerprints. Experts would conclude that it had been held at the very corners by the tips of someone's fingers. Its contents were harrowing:

I SAY GOODBYE AND GOODNIGHT. POLICE:
LET ME HAUNT YOU WITH THESE WORDS;
I'LL BE BACK! I'LL BE BACK!
TO BE INTERRPRETED AS - BANG, BANG, BANG,
BANK, BANG - UGH!!
YOURS IN MURDER

MR MONSTER.

Although forensically the note offered nothing to go on, psychologists at last had something to get their teeth into. Here was an offender who wished to communicate with the police, who saw the murders as either a form of game or perhaps even a mission to be followed.

His awareness of fingerprinting methods, his planning in taking the sealed letter to the scene and its timing, coming so soon after the announcement of the setting up of the squad, showed the offender was an intelligent and formidable foe. The letter was also littered with grammatical errors and spelling mistakes, the kind of flaws that someone in a professional occupation would have avoided. The puzzle that psychiatrists couldn't answer for detectives was whether he was insane or simply cunning. Was the letter from a madman, or someone already planning a courtroom defence of insanity if he were to be caught?

The letter was kept quiet from the media but its existence was hinted at by *New York Daily News* columnist Jimmy Breslin. Three weeks after posting the first missive, Berkowitz, who by now was irritated at not having read about his taunting of the police, sent another letter – this time to Breslin. The newspaper seized the opportunity to boost its sales and instead of rushing into print, saved publication for almost a week, while every day promoting on its own pages the fact that it had received a letter and was about to make it public. At the request of the police department, one page was withheld. In it, Berkowitz told detectives that to catch him they should look in certain directions.

"HERE ARE SOME NAMES TO HELP YOU ALONG. FORWARD THEM TO THE INSPECTOR FOR USE BY THE NCIC (National Crime Information Centre). "THE DUKE OF DEATH." "THE WICKED KING WICKER." "THE TWENTY TWO DISCIPLES OF HELL" "JOHN 'WHEATIES' - RAPIST AND SUFFOCATER OF YOUNG GIRLS.

But more than anything, the section that interested both the police and the media was the sign-off:

NOT KNOWING WHAT THE FUTURE HOLDS I SHALL SAY FAREWELL AND I WILL SEE YOU AT THE NEXT JOB. OR SHOULD I SAY YOU WILL SEE MY HANDI-WORK AT THE NEXT JOB? REMEMBER MS LAURIA. THANK YOU. IN THEIR BLOOD AND FROM THE GUTTER

"SAM'S CREATION" .44

So, Mr Monster had given himself a name and the press quickly seized upon it, 'The Son of Sam'. It would be many more letters before the origin of the nickname would be established but at least now the two sides in the game had been clearly identified.

The public would be in no doubt that shootings in Queens and The Bronx would be rightly attributed to 'The Son of Sam' and they could judge for themselves just how good a job the other side, the police, were faring in the game. Psychologists also pounced on the way the killer described the killings as "the job," pointing out to detectives that their murderer may well see homicide as his true vocation. Something that he dedicated all his hours and energy to. As a consequence, it was likely that he would probably live locally (people usually live near their job). Berkowitz himself gave profilers evidence of his desire for fame and public acknowledgment after he was arrested. Referring to the Freund and Diel shootings, he remarked: "At this point, I imagine I didn't care very much anymore, for I finally had convinced myself that it was good to do it...and that the public wanted me to do it."

After the Breslin letter, psychiatrists told police they were looking for a neurotic, paranoid schizophrenic who would kill until caught. Detectives also placed high hopes on a warning part way through the letter that seemed to indicate he was about to mark the first anniversary of the death of his first victim. It said cryptically, "TELL ME JIM, WHAT WILL YOU HAVE FOR JULY TWENTY-NINTH?" This was the day that Donna Lauria had been killed. On that evening, the NYPD mounted a massive surveillance operation but to no avail. Within 48 hours 'Son of Sam' had struck again.

Berkowitz had deliberately misled detectives, not only about the date of his next offence, but about the venue as well. For his next attack, he chose a spot 22 miles away. Twenty-year-old Stacy Moskowitz and her boyfriend Robert Violante were gunned down as they kissed in their car beneath the glare of a streetlamp in the backstreets of Brooklyn. Stacy died a day and a half later in hospital, one bullet had just grazed her scalp but the other had lodged in the back of her brain. Robert, who had been shot twice in the face survived the attack but was left blind.

Berkowitz, the illegitimate son of Jewish parents, had killed for the last time. Just ten days later he was arrested outside his apartment block in Yonkers, identified by witnesses at the last shootings. One had seen him throw away a parking ticket and had also spotted him concealing something which she thought looked like a gun. He smiled to cameras as he was led into court for the first time.

Now in captivity, he explained that he had been ordered to carry out the killings by a demon that lived in a neighbour's black labrador. The neighbour was called Sam Carr and the labrador was named Harvey. Berkowitz had feuded with the Carrs for sometime, accusing them of being satanists. He fire-bombed their home, shot their dog and sent them anonymous hate letters. Other neighbours had also received abusive and threatening letters and some had actually reported them to the police. A day after Berkowitz's arrest, a county policeman who had lived in the apartment below the killer, contacted the Omega Task Force and informed them that he too had received obscure and threatening letters from Berkowitz, accusing him of being a spy placed in the complex by Sam Carr to keep a watch on him.

The crazed, furious letters that had been sent for years to neighbours who annoyed him, had been written by the same hand that announced in his letter to the press: "SAM'S A THIRSTY LAD AND HE WON'T LET ME STOP KILLING UNTIL HE GETS HIS FILL OF BLOOD."

If David Berkowitz had been trying to construct a complex case of insanity for his defence, then it didn't work: he was viewed to be sane and was jailed for 365 years. Law enforcement agencies everywhere learned the lesson that killers that communicate with the police possibly have a history of being ardent letter-writers. Certainly these thoughts were in mind as the FBI wrote up its VICAP Crime Report eight years later.

Page ten of the VICAP form begins with a five part section on body disposition, asking initially if detectives believe the offender had moved the body from the area of the death site to the area of the body recovery site. It then explores whether the corpse had been openly displayed or put somewhere where it was guaranteed to be quickly discovered. Whether it had been left with an apparent lack of concern about whether it would be discovered or not, or if it had been deliberately concealed to prevent discovery for as long as possible, was another point in the questionnaire. Behavioural research has shown that the way the body is found can give very clear indications of the type of killer involved. The type of offender that would dismember a victim and then scatter body parts is clearly a different character than one that might dispose of his victim in a deep grave in a remote area of woodland.

Questions 141 to 149 cover the use of restraints on a victim, especially the deployment of a blindfold, what kind of bindings were used to tie a victim up and whether these had been made at the crime scene or had been brought by the offender.

The next section on the VICAP form covers several aspects of the 'clothing and property of the victim'. Questions range from whether the victim was nude, half-dressed or even redressed by the attacker. Analysts are also keen to know whether the victim's clothing was ripped, torn or cut from the body and whether any clothing or other personal items were removed by the attacker. Virtually all these questions concern the fantasy life of the killer. The taking of souvenirs, usually jewellery or underwear, is usually for offenders to masturbate to or simply to mark the killings as conquests. Some British analysts would interpret the cutting of clothing from a victim with a knife or blade of some kind, as signs of escalating violence and indicators of a serial offender, probably with previous convictions for rape.

There are 19 different options under the cause of death category, running from the traditional gunshot and stab wounds to the more sadistic hypothermia, electrocution and scalding. Investigators say they are constantly finding new and staggeringly inhumane ways that victims are killed.

Page 12 of the VICAP form begins with the location of bite-marks on the victim (as proved particularly relevant in the eventual conviction of college girl killer Ted Bundy) and then runs into a disturbing four part discussion on torture. Analysts are also looking for evidence that offenders may have disfigured the body of the victim in order to deliberately delay the identification. The most common example of this is the severing of a head to avoid identification through dental records and the dismembering of hands to avoid fingerprints. The removal of other limbs such as genitalia, nipples and breasts are hallmarks of either sexual sadists or less commonly, lust murderers. The method of limb removal, showing signs of either surgical precision or ham-fisted frenzy, are also of interest in this section and can give clues to an attacker's profession (meat industry worker, butcher, doctor, etc). It can also be an indicator of whether the murderer has killed before.

Someone who carves a chicken for the first time will make a ragged job of removing the wings and legs, but given several more chicken dinners to practise on, he or she becomes far more proficient in the dismembering. Similarly, profilers have found that serial killers have become more competent in severing body parts as they killed more and more victims.

Sexual assault is a crucial focus in the crime report and deals with the penetration of any body cavity. There is some suggestion among analysts that because of sexual taboos in various countries, rapists and killers of certain ethnic origins will penetrate particular anatomical regions in a particular order. To avoid possible 'staging' in future crimes, we have been asked to withhold specific details in this category. It is sufficient to say that even in many consensual relationships some of these acts would still be regarded as illegal. Questions also cover the areas or oral sex, both on the victim and on the offender.

Investigators also ask for details on insertion of foreign objects such as spoons, rocks, knives, bottles, etc into the vagina, penis, anus or mouth of the victim. This kind of humiliating and degrading act is seen as a statement by the killer about the victim and can be a valuable area for research for investigators. As well as ejaculating in body cavities, offenders also masturbate at other parts of the scene and sometimes over the body of their victim. This is of interest to profilers because it enables them to make determinations on the sexual maturity and possible dysfunctions of an offender and also the possibilities of him being involved in stable sexual relationships.

The penultimate page on the form deals with known forensic evidence and the use of weapons. Special attention is drawn to whether a weapon has been manufactured at the scene (a ligature cut from a lamp flex, etc) which is termed 'a weapon of opportunity' or whether a more 'organized' offender has come equipped with his own 'weapon of choice' (a knife, gun or pre-made noose).

The last page is concerned with establishing if the report has been submitted only for information, or if it amounts to an official request for an FBI profile to be produced by the Behavioral Science Unit.

The ultimate category is simply an open list for the investigator to detail any other related cases that are known to him.

Amid the hum of the computers stands VICAP's Programme Manager Terry Green, a veteran detective who greets everyone with a bone-crushing handshake and a deep smile. He summarizes VICAP with a skilled eloquence that has been drilled into all the FBI's front-line managers. "Prior to 1985 there was nowhere that a detective could call, to find out if the type of crime he was experiencing in his jurisdiction was occurring in other places. In other words to take a look at a travelling killer and to be able to link the cases. In the United States our physicians have a centre for disease control, so that a doctor who is treating a case that he has never experienced before can call to find out if anybody else has ever seen this type of disease and how they have treated it. Now we do the same thing for the homicide community, they call here to find out if anybody has experienced a particular type of crime."

VICAP's doors have been, and still are, open to law enforcement agencies throughout the world. It's both reassuring and impressive to see that the skills and systems that have been developed here are not hidden and coveted in the selfish, self-protecting manner found in some research departments, but are shared with anyone who is involved in the traumatic trade of catching killers.

Green, who spent 25 years with the Oakland Police Department in California where for much of the time he was commander of their homicide section, refers to his unit's report form as a VICAP "Protocol." He explains that after completion, it is entered into a computer system called AMOS, an Automated Matching System. AMOS rattles through all the data that's been pumped into it over the last few years and then comes up with an initial list of ten cases that the offence could be linked with (if indeed so many links can be made). If the ten are not sufficient, then the computer will carry out more searches until it is instructed to stop.

"We have a little over 7,000 cases in the system now and we have I believe 262 linked cases, which would be two or more murders attributed to the same killer," says Green. The VICAP database is among the largest in the world, but Green believes it is limited. In a country that on average chalks up more than 20,000 homicide cases a year, he has a staggering task to keep abreast of the constant influx of homicide statistics. "I think we will never be totally efficient until we have all the cases; you need all the murders in the system. You're never going to make a linkage if the case that you are looking for is not in the system. We should have over 36,000 reports in the system. We need a system that is more service orientated, something that can get back immediately to the detective, so that he can punch-up his computer and get some response himself." Green is a great supporter of moving VICAP onto a national system that would be used by all America's law enforcement agencies.

"The numbers of police agencies here are staggering and each one of them is independent of the other and does everything in its own particular way. There's a lot of duplication because of that. A lot of them have their own records system, they'll have their own communications system, there's no national data bank that we can go into, no national computer system that we can link everything up with.

"We have been doing some studies and we've found out that 57 per cent of the murders are committed within 160 cities, so although you are looking at a tremendous number of murders, they are rather compact, so we must look at the ability to link these cities directly to us, through a national computer system."

Terry J Green is also President of the International Homicide Investigators' Association and is an open admirer of the HOLMES national computer system run by Britain's 43 police forces during the investigation of major crimes such as murder, rape and abduction. Green astutely notes that the investigation into the way the Yorkshire Ripper case was handled, spearheaded Britain's use of computerization . "After Peter Sutcliffe, I think that the police in the UK made a dramatic change in the way that they handled these types of investigations and just after the Sutcliffe case had ended we gathered as many homicide detectives as we could from all around the United States who were working in serial murder cases. We were very interested in how they performed, how they co-ordinated their investigation and how they work with other agencies involved in such investigations. As a result we printed up a manual, it's called the MAIT manual (Multi-Agency Investigative Team) and we asked somebody from the UK to come over and make a presentation on the Sutcliffe case, but at that time they were not prepared to do that. Later, I had an opportunity to go to England and talk to some of the people that were involved in that case and heard the tremendous problem that they had with the management of information in the inquiry and whether, if they had been better able to handle it, they would have caught Peter Sutcliffe earlier. They had been using what detectives here call CIB (cards in a box) – they are little index cards with information on, and in the Peter Sutcliffe case they had cards in boxes, stacked in rooms, stacked row after row after row. They had the information in there, but they didn't find it until he had been arrested anyway. The English police learned from that and that's why I think their system is now so good."

VICAP has come a long way from the afternoon of May 29, 1985 when Pierce Brooks first sat in the chair eventually occupied by Terry Green. Brooks is acknowledged as one of the pioneers of profiling in the USA and seeing that first computer analysis take place on the desk in front of him, was something of a personal achievement. Twenty-seven years earlier he had been handling two entirely separate murders when he developed the belief that the killers in both cases had murdered before and were onto at least their second victims. He discovered that there was no national record system that could help him check-out his theory, so he turned to the City Library and went through all the major newspaper murder reports in all of America's major cities. Basically, Brooks set up his own primitive VICAP system. In the 1970s, the FBI man spoke to officials in the US Department of Justice, about establishing a more sophisticated system, and funds were given to him to develop the project along with 20 other experts from law enforcement agencies.

In gathering years of data about offenders, VICAP has helped discern altering trends and patterns in killing. Terry Green assiduously monitors the passing fashions: "I don't know whether murder is becoming more prevalent, it may be that we are becoming more sophisticated in identifying it. Some of our major cities tell us that they don't have serial killers. I dispute that. I think they are not finding serial killers because they are not looking for them. The number of homicides in the United States has increased dramatically.

"In the 1960s we were running at about 8,000, less than 9,000 murders a year and we were clearing about 92 per cent of them. Now, we're looking at about 25,000 murders, so our homicides have increased three-fold but our clearance rate has gone down."

In a statement, uncomfortably reminiscent of that made by Virginia State Profiler Larry McCann, Green observes another disturbing trend. "The term 'recreational murder' is coming up now, that's a pretty expression for what amounts to people who are going out and are killing just for the pleasure of killing." Like McCann, he wears the same quizzical look as he tries to apply a rational explanation to a completely irrational act. He also worries about how big a problem 'recreational murder' is going to become, in a society where people "are killing just to see if they have the nerve to kill, or simply to find out what it feels like."

Undoubtedly, America's gun laws are contributory to their high murder rate. Psychologists liken shooting someone to killing by remote control – just press a trigger and they're dead. It has been found that gun deaths do not usually bring the offender the same kind of trauma as killings where the attacker manually chokes the last breath out of his victim with his own hands. It's now believed that half of all American homicides involve a firearm.

Still, Green doesn't believe countries like Britain, where there's no public right to carry a gun, can afford to be smug about their small murder rate (less than 800 a year). "I think they are going to have some problems that are unique to them but also some problems that we have already faced. We have had people from the UK come over here and look at our systems and what concerns me is that in this new united European Community, once the boundaries come down, I don't see a group that's going to keep track on travelling killers."

Many European Police Agencies share Terry Green's fears and as a result, there are plans afoot to counter the possibilities of someone killing in France and then returning to their home in England or Germany, unchecked because of disbanded customs points where there were once border officials.

"As I understand it, if they have 12 countries each working independently, they're doing the same thing that we would do here with our 50 States, but we at least have the FBI overlooking this entire situation and making linkages in killings. Now, they're going to have exactly the same kind of problems that we've been addressing for about the past five years but without anyone to co-ordinate these types of investigations."

The FBI man is partly right. The sterility of Interpol means ambitious plans are having to be laid to co-ordinate any hunts for a pan-European killer, and while the will is already there, red-tape and a lack of funds means there's a real danger that EC countries won't respond to the problem until confronted York-shire-Ripper-style, with an offender that has claimed untold lives in numerous different countries.

The veteran detective also refuses to believe that the serial killer is either a modern phenomenon or exclusively an American by-product. "The term 'serial killer', is one that has just come up in the United States in about the last ten years, but does that mean that we've only experienced them for ten years, or does it mean that we weren't aware of them but we had them a long time before? I think you're gonna find the same thing in Europe, that when an offence occurs in the UK, it could have been carried out by an offender that came from Germany who has already committed that kind of offence in Germany and perhaps in France and elsewhere as well."

Closer analysis of European crime shows many cultural differences between EC countries and the US. However, there are also many disturbing similarities. Necrophilia, cannibalism and sexual sadism can all be found in the murder cases of today's Europe and are no longer the sole and bewildering province of American crime. Holland and Britain have both already experienced difficulty in detecting what the FBI call 'travelling murders'. These are homicides that have been carried out by professional drivers, such as long-distance lorry drivers, and according to the VICAP Project Manager, European countries can expect to encounter many more similar crimes in the future. "The chosen occupation of today's serial killer is that of a truck driver. These are highly transient killers who travel all over the United States."

Profilers worldwide recognize that many killers prefer to kill in areas that they work or live near, or are familiar with, possibly through work, leisure or past neighbourhoods where they lived as children. These areas are referred to as either 'ground familiar' or 'comfort zones'. The problem in profiling a truck driver is that in some cases his 'comfort zone' can be an entire country. Terry Green quotes a number of cases, including one where investigators believe the death toll could be enormous: "In the case that we are working on now, we have put this trucker in all but three US States. We ran through his truck time-sheets and we found out that there were 800 unsolved murders in areas that we can put this guy in. His 'comfort zone' was most of America. To make matters worse, in these kind of cases, truckers have got travelling crime scenes in the trucks themselves." Frustratingly, there's little left for detectives to base their investigations on in these kind of 'stranger murders', where the victim is picked totally at random.

"It's certainly not the classic type of murder where you solve it by gathering all the family and friends in the front room and go over the case like they do in films. We have about 15 per cent of the murders in the United States where the detective can find no link between the victim and the suspect, so in these cases, even if you brought the victim back to life she wouldn't be able to tell you who her killer was!

It's a person who comes in, commits his crime and is gone, so the old traditional ways of investigating it and looking for the motive, the means and the opportunity no longer exist."

With there being so much emphasis on the advantages of a national computer system, the value of extra data and the introduction of multi-agency manuals, many observers mistakenly believe that the profiling side of the FBI academy is also progressing towards computerization. Unlike VICAP, Green's colleagues in the Behavioral Science Unit, have rejected the idea of investing in expert computer systems. A much-talked-about project called 'Profiler', where investigators fed a VICAP-style form into a computer, along with more detailed crime scene reports, pressed a few buttons and then got an offender profile out of the other end, is now defunct.

Analysts have decided that when it comes to catching the killers that other cops have failed to catch, then the advantages of a computer are vastly outweighed by the intuition, experience and skill of the FBI's team of human mind-hunters.

# 7
# The Mind-Hunters

*"He kept human flesh in the refrigerator and he began consuming human flesh." – Former FBI man Robert Ressler, after interviewing Milwaukee Killer Jeffrey Dahmer.*

On February 9, 1992, St Vincent's Hospital in Melbourne, Australia, was the venue for the biggest gathering of the world's mind-hunters. As rain fell in heavy sheets on the ugly, modern buildings of the hospital complex, detectives, psychiatrists and psychologists were ushered into a square, characterless room. Unsmiling women in black dresses made their way among the damp crowd with trays of tepid orange juice, most resentful of having to give up their Sunday evening. It was a little after 6 pm when the security men who flanked the large doors of Brennan Hall stepped aside and the Minister for Police and Emergency Services, the Honourable Mr Mal Sandon walked passed the crowd and took the stage.

Sandon's uninspired but important speech signified the beginning of the week-long conference on 'Serious Serial Offenders', a conference that had been more significantly timed to bring the world's experts together to help police in Australia launch their own programme for offender profiling. Assembled below the stage in the steamy heat of the tiny hall were many of the pioneers of profiling: Bob Ressler, Roy Hazelwood and Janet Warren from the FBI, Professor David Canter from Surrey University in England and his research fellow Detective Constable Rupert Heritage; Charles 'Chuck' Siragusa, an assistant district attorney, who prosecuted serial killer Arthur Shawcross; associate Professor Steve Hucker from the University of Toronto in Canada; Dr Don Thomson, a barrister from the department of Psychology at Monash University; forensic scientist Dr Rodney Milton from Sydney and Detective Superintendent George Davis and Senior Detective Claude Minisini from Victoria Police in Australia.

As the opening speech ended and the applause died down, the organizing press office made a tacky request. With great effort they had secured a life-size cut-out of 'Hannibal the Cannibal' from the film *Silence of the Lambs*. Now they embarrassingly cajoled the FBI group, who had spent most of the past year trying to separate hard fact from Hollywood fiction, to pose for photographs, with 'Hannibal' in the centre of their group.

Convoys of taxis pulled from the kerbside, ferrying the experts back to the conference hotel in a downpour. Most of the group reassembled in the small, unpretentious bar of The Park on Exhibition Street, shaking off their latest soaking, ordering drinks, cursing the press office and renewing friendships.

Sipping a local lager and wiping the rain-splashes from his tinted glasses was Robert K Ressler, now Associate Director of his own company, Forensic Behavioral Services. He joined the FBI in February, 1970 as a Special Agent and went on to be pivotal in the development of offender profiling. He will always be remembered as the man who coined the phrase 'serial killer'. He was Program Manager of research, development and training at the FBI Academy and eventually Manager of VICAP, the Violent Criminal Apprehension Program, before retiring after 20 years distinguished service. After being an instructor in hostage negotiation in 1977, he began one of the Bureau's most important and controversial projects, the first interviews with a group of more than 30 serial murderers. Bob Ressler can recall all the interviews with uncanny accuracy but there's one moment of recollection that stills sends a shiver down his spine.

It was at Vacaville Prison in California. The interview was over and five minutes had passed since he'd pressed the bell for the guard to come and open the locked cell door. The lengthy discussion with the 6 ft 9 inch, 300lb serial killer had proved a revelation but now there was a sudden and quickly growing tension in the air. Where were the guards? This giant of a man had killed nine people, had severed the heads of all his victims and was noted for his awesome strength and psychopathic tendencies. Almost 15 minutes had passed. Where were the guards? The killer, who also had an IQ of 140, caught the agent's worried glance at a wristwatch, "Relax," he said, "They're changing the shift, probably feeding the guys in the secure areas. It might be 20 minutes before they come and get you." Then he added: "If I went ape-shit in here, you'd be in a lot of trouble wouldn't you? I could screw your head off and place it on the table to greet the guard." The encounter came at the end of a four hour interview with Edmund Emil Kemper in the late 1970s. Ressler says his pulse "did the 100 yard dash" when Kemper pointed out the prestige other inmates would hold him in for killing an FBI agent. "I think he was kidding," he added. "There's no doubt he was capable of doing exactly what he said, so all the time I concentrated on keeping him talking, trying to get this picture out of my mind of those enormous arms grabbing me in a headlock and then just tearing my skull off." Since then, it has become an FBI rule that agents never interview killers alone. This is now only done in pairs.

Ressler finished his beer and began to think about making a call home to his wife in Spotsylvania before grabbing some dinner. He had been on the road a lot in the past few months and had only just returned from interviewing Milwaukee cannibal Jeffrey Dahmer, who killed 17 people. His whirlwind account of some of Dahmer's childhood activities left even the most hardened of minds stupefied.

"The concept that every person who becomes a serial killer has come from a home where sexual abuse and physical beating and that sort of thing are rampant is not necessarily true. Physical abuse can be bad, sexual abuse can be bad, psychological abuse can be as equally bad in the development of a child, but so can non-intervening parents. By non-intervention we include inconsistent discipline, allowing them to do things that they oughtn't to, because mum and dad are just too busy to deal with them, and this can be a real problem with this type of individual."

Lionel Dahmer, Jeffrey Dahmer's father, had a PhD and was a scientist working for a chemical firm. He was very busy working nights and weekends and was often too busy to notice that Jeffrey was in the garage, stripping flesh off animals that he had picked up from the side of the road. When dad did see him stripping down a raccoon or a rabbit he'd say, "Jeffrey, you didn't kill that animal did you?" His son would answer "No dad, I found it at the roadside, it was a road-kill" and the father replied, "Well, fine, but what are you doing there?" Jeffrey's response was ironic: "You know, I'm just interested in the anatomy and I'm interested in the bones and things" and Mr Dahmer would say "That's very good, that's a very good intel-lectual in-quiry." Ressler says the macabre reality of what was happening, was vastly different than that perceived by Jeffrey's father. "Dahmer would masturbate while dismantling these animals, stripping their flesh down while he became aroused by the actual peeling of the skin from the animal. He would masturbate with animal parts and later in his life when he would sexually assault corpses, he would in fact again masturbate during the activity of cutting up the bodies and that sort of thing. He would take the heads and strip away the skin, keeping the skulls. In fact he would spray-paint the skulls to make it look like they had a stone-effect or a kind of flaked covering and then what he'd masturbate with these skulls. He would look at these skulls as a sort of stimulus, which is pretty bizarre stuff. Once I got to interviewing him in-depth, he admitted that he had taken photo-graphs and that the looking at the photographs would also be a stimulus towards masturbation."

Dahmer's masturbatory fantasies seem to have been locked-in on that early fascination with dead things and their total deconstruction. "We found that Jeffrey's fantasies contained those earliest bizarre ideas about anatomy and stripping flesh from animals. These ideas came really before adolescence and his distorted thinking patterns had been supported by the non-inter-vention of his father." As Dahmer emerged as a serial killer, those fantasies were displayed in his behaviour: "He would involve himself in necrophilic acts, not conventional necrophilic acts but dismembering, disembowelling and actually inter-acting with the human intestines through masturbation."

Ressler focused hard on Dahmer's childhood during his interview and concluded that there had been considerable stress upon him as he grew up. "Jeffrey Dahmer's mother had long bouts of depression. That of course created problems; he had mental difficulties throughout his lifetime and those were the things that were becoming a basis for his future behaviour, they were the formative events that were taking him from childhood into adolescence. So, physical, sexual and psychological abuse can be bad but non-intervention with an introverted child can be as equally damaging. The introverted child starts living in a fantasy world at a very young age. There will be developmental failures, problems with him not partici-pating in things and difficulties in developing inter-personal skills. Dahmer in school was very introverted and did not get involved with the other kids, and in fact began doing devious things. For example, one time was when the National Honour Society was meeting and all the kids that had obtained a high scholastic achievement were being photographed. Jeffrey was by this time in his adolescence, 15 or so, and his father had said 'You know, if you put a little more time into your studies, then maybe you'd be in the National Honour Society.' So, when the society students were being photographed, Dahmer snuck up and got in the back row and stood there along with the other kids and was photographed in the school annual as being one of the recipients of the National Honour Society's Awards for high scholastic achievement. When the committee found him in the picture it was too late to paste the picture over, so they just blacked his face out. He'd done it as a kind of joke, to show his parents that he could be in the National Honour Society, but when they blacked his face out, he said it was like they'd erased him, not only from the world but from existence and that troubled him. He realized that it was just something to get him off the picture but he said 'How dare they erase me from my existence', and that bothered him emotionally for years to follow."

Ressler maintained that while Dahmer was becoming a 'loner', he wasn't developing the necessary inter-personal skills that modern society expects. "His parents were pending divorce throughout most of his recollected life and by the time he was 17 he says he felt very alone. His mother was intent on taking his younger brother with her but made no overtures to take Jeffrey and his father wasn't particularly interested in him staying with him either. That was like having a knife thrust through his heart. His father talked about Jeffrey joining the army, going away for a while and growing up and he just got the feeling that apparently nobody wanted him."

From his interviews with Dahmer, Ressler discovered that the future multiple murderer went off to University in Ohio where he spent most of the time as an alcoholic, again trying to avoid the strain of the realities in his life. University is a time when most young people are surrounded with an unbelievable wealth of academic and sexual opportunities. Dahmer was uninterested in participating in either. "Jeffrey Dahmer stated that he had never had a heterosexual thought in his life. At 12 or 13 years of age he began being interested in sexual activity and was always fantasizing about males. At 15 years of age he realized that there were others who were involved in heterosexual dating and that kind of thing, but he says he could not comprehend heterosexual thought, fantasy or stimulation." Ressler then pointed out an early example of Dahmer's infantile but growing urge to kill. "Again at a very early age, still at about 15, he said he saw a movie about a young hitchhiker who was bare chested and had a narrow waist. He had no hair on his chest and he became Dahmer's fantasy model of his ideal mate. This hitchhiker was out on the highway with a bag and Dahmer said that his fantasy started developing along the lines of picking up a hitch-hiker fitting this description, with long hair and slim hips, of taking this guy out and killing him and then having sex with his dead body.

"At 18 years of age, Dahmer was driving down a road one night, and by now he's had three firm years of these fantasies, and he sees a hitch-hiker, bare chested, hitch-hiking down the road and he said, 'It was like my fantasy come true, I couldn't believe it'. He stopped, offered the guy a ride and took the guy to his house. It just so happens that his parents were away that weekend, so the stage was set. He was inter-acting with the guy, having a drink or two for a period of time and Dahmer was enjoying the contact, but the guy said 'I have to leave, I have to go now'. At this point they were down in Dahmer's basement where they had been lifting weights and Dahmer picked up a weight bar and cracked this guy on the head. He then pushed the bar down onto his throat and strangled him to death, afterwards masturbating. Dahmer dragged the body into the crawl space beneath the house, dismembered it as he done with the animals, and stored the parts in plastic bags. After a few days in the summer heat Dahmer realized the smell might soon give him away. He at first buried the bags in a shallow grave. Fearful of discovery he dug them up, stripped the flesh away and spent the next several hours smashing the bones into tiny fragments. He scattered these in the woods behind his house."

Dahmer went on to kill 17 people, a dozen of them over a period of just one year. He progressed from killing several times a month to murdering several times a week, homicide eventually becoming a way of everyday life for him. Bob Ressler was called in by the defence to give a professional opinion on whether Dahmer was insane, but the profiler had to disappoint his paymasters. The former special agent had no doubt that legally Dahmer knew right from wrong. He also felt that there was some form of mental illness that Dahmer experienced and that made him feel as though the killing was justified. The crucial thing for Ressler was that the killer was always sane enough to make attempts to dispose of the bodies and evidence and was never insane enough to kill in front of other people or give himself up to police.

"The themes that developed within Dahmer were those of dominance, revenge, violence and rape molestation. What was not present in Dahmer was sadism, he was not sadistic. After his second victim, the practise he developed was to crush up some sleeping pills that had been prescribed for him, to the point where he had about five or six times the normal dose, and he would mix this into drinks and provide it to his victims. In so doing, he would drug them unconscious and then have sex with their unconscious bodies. Eventually, he would strangle them and then keep their bodies for a period of days while he continued to sexually engage with them. What was important to him was power and control, not torture, but power and control. The mutilation of the bodies was very important to him; it was having absolute control over another individual's life that was becoming increasingly a turn-on to Dahmer.

"By his 11th, 12th and 13th victims he had developed a concept of keeping his fantasy alive more indefinitely. He knew he could not keep his victims unconscious forever yet this was what he wanted. Once he had killed them he had to dispose of their bodies within days. He stripped their skin as he had done with his first victim years earlier. He kept some skeletons because he wanted to recreate them. He would place them in his home where he could view them. He kept the skulls around, he kept human heads in the refrigerator and he began consuming human flesh, eating body parts and getting deeper and deeper into this kind of behaviour. By the this stage he came up with a concept of having a permanent and indefinite sex zombie, and this idea came from within. He said he got the idea that by drilling a hole in the top of their heads, and injecting nitric acid into the brain, he might kill enough of the brain to keep this person in a zombie-state for the rest of his life. Now of course that is not logical or rational thinking anymore but he was completely engrossed and involved in this concept of having a person that would be with him forever and would not go out to work, would not leave the house and would be his alone, for the rest of his life."

Dahmer's desire to have a constant, totally loyal companion, is a sinister echo of the life of British killer Dennis Nilsen. Nilsen was also a homosexual who murdered his victims because he couldn't bear the thought of them going home and leaving him on his own again. Ressler had asked Dahmer a fundamental question: "I said, 'What if you could have gotten a good, compliant male-friend, a homosexual, and just had a good relationship with him?' and he said: 'I thought of that, but I could never have found the person that would not leave my house, they would have to stay there, they'd have to be there for my sexual needs' and he said he wouldn't want to be bothering with them beyond that, adding, 'I wouldn't want to take them out, I wouldn't want them to work, I wouldn't want to take them on vacations.' Realistically this isn't an attainable goal and he recognized that his fantasy could never be achieved normally and therefore he had to pursue it through this bizarre behaviour. With Dahmer, he wanted ultimate control – he was very big on power and control."

Hour by hour, Ressler accompanied Dahmer on that mind-spinning journey from deviant childhood to homicidal adult-hood, never once flinching at the monstrous monologue nor approving of the stomach-churning acts. Impassiveness was the psychological order of the day, as Dahmer catalogued the way he struggled to fulfil his fantasies. "He tried rape, mutilation, necrophilia and cannibalism. With cannibalism you usually find blood-drinking and he tried this but he didn't particularly like it. I've had a number of blood-drinkers and cannibals that I've had to deal with, where in fact the blood-drinking becomes the preferred activity. I have one guy that I worked with in Florida, who for 20 years raped and drank the blood of his victims. He didn't kill them, he extracted the blood surgically with a syringe. The blood-drinking was part of the rape ritual."

As many other killers had done before, Dahmer told Ressler that the fantasy was always better than the act. This usually accounts for the reason why there are progressive acts of violence, increased used of bondage and the introduction of sadism into later killings in a serial murderer's career. From the interviews that the FBI carried out, they discovered a strange paradox. A clear majority of serial killers said they tried to improve their control and power over the victim as the murders increased and they made fewer mistakes. Yet, when their confi-dence to kill was at its highest, even the most 'organized' of murderers started getting sloppy and careless. "Dahmer, I would say in his last four killings, was becoming so careless he was leaving body parts all over the place. He had one body in the bathtub in ice water, trying to preserve him for a few more days, when he had a visitor in his living room. The visitor asked to go to the bathroom and Dahmer said 'Help yourself.' I said 'Jeffrey, you know if the guy had taken a peek behind the shower curtain into your bathtub he would have been a bit surprised', and he said, 'Well, I didn't think he would.' He had people over to the house and he had the head of a human being in the refrigerator, other body parts in the freezer. There were body parts all over the house and his landlord came in on two occasions to investigate the smells and Dahmer just explained that it was the smell from his fish tank and that some of the fish had died. I don't think that landlord was too bright."

If America was shocked from the disclosures of Dahmer's cannibalism, then Russia was reeling from the arrest of serial killer Andrei Chikatilo. His murderous activities had started in 1978, during the fiercely secretive years of Brezhnev. The dead hand of communism had hidden the fact that here was the type of sadistic killer that people had been told only existed in the West. When he was apprehended 500 miles south of Moscow in Rostov-on-Don in November, 1990 the bald grandfather had murdered and eaten the flesh of 52 men, women, boys and girls. He'd raped, tortured, blinded and mutilated his victims before often amputating and then devouring their sexual organs.

He soon confessed to his crimes and took investigators into the woods and showed them the shallow graves where he had buried his victims. He told how he lured his victims to their deaths with the offer of free chewing gum, a meal or a chance to watch a video at his home. "As soon as I saw a lonely person I would have to drag them off to the woods," he said, "I paid no attention to age or sex. We would walk for a couple of miles or so through the woods and then I would be possessed by a terrible shaking sensation." Here, he would bind his victims, cut out their tongues so they couldn't cry out, burst their eardrums and then gouge out their eyes.

Psychological profiling was at the heart of Chikatilo's arrest. With a mounting body count, the demoralized Russian police force had tuned to Rostov psychiatrist Dr Alexander Bukhanovsky. His profile of the innocuous-looking literature graduate was brilliantly accurate. Bukhanovsky said he would be a middle-aged, impotent, heterosexual of above average intelligence, working in a supervisory or administrative capacity. Chikatilo was a former teacher, employed as Head of Supplies at Rostov's Lenin Locomotive Works.

Bukhanovsky told detectives that Chikatilo, like Dahmer was immersed in his own fantasy world. He commented: "His internal world is a thousand times richer than the surface expression of that world." The psychiatrist's profile led to Chikatilo being put under surveillance and he was arrested as he approached a youngster near the woods where he had butchered all his victims. This wasn't the first time he'd been in police custody. He'd been held by detectives after his first killing in 1978 but was released after police wrongly convicted and executed a man they believed to be a better suspect. Another man that they arrested and accused of the murders committed suicide while awaiting trial.

When Chikatilo made his appearance in the shabby Rostov courtroom he had to be kept inside an iron cage. Outside, families of his victims fought with police and prison guards, trying to dispense their own form of justice. As the trial opened, he sprang to his feet and flashed a poster of a naked pin-up girl and a bloodied corpse at his prosecutors, mockingly emblazoned with the words "Greetings to you, Gentlemen."

The psychological profile drawn up by Dr Bukhanovsky impressed a number of people. Chikatilo was so struck by its accuracy that he invited the psychiatrist to his execution. British police were more professionally impressed. In 1992 John Stevens flew to Russia as head of the Association of Chief Police Officers' Offender Profiling Committee and paved the way for a greater sharing of information between Russian and British profilers. Plans were laid for subsequent exchange visits between experts in both countries.

Almost a decade before Chikatilo and Dahmer, Robert Ressler had interviewed Richard Trenton Chase, a man who killed seven people specifically to drink their blood. In some ways this would prove to be vital experience for the FBI man and a form of preparation for the interview he would eventually carry out with the Milwaukee murderer. "This was a vampire killer in Sacramento, who was killing people, taking their body parts and their blood and putting them in a blender to make a sort of brew. In this case he considered this mixture would sustain his life because he believed his blood was turning to powder and this was the only way to stay alive. He was hearing voices, having hallucinations and all sorts of bizarre illusions. He was found guilty in court and ended up suiciding on Death Row. I think any mental health expert now would realize that this man was severely psychotic."

Chase had experienced severe mental problems as a young man, experimenting with drugs, drinking heavily and then being sent to a nursing home for the mentally ill, after injecting rabbit's blood into his veins. While in the home, he would bite the heads off birds that he came across in the gardens and then write about what it was like to kill them and drink their blood. He had also become obsessed with a notion that he had 'soap dish poisoning'. This, he explained, was a drying up of the blood in the veins, caused by using soap that had become sloppy after being left to dry on a sink.

Ressler eventually made the long overdue call to his wife, leaving a moment to reflect on the importance of his contribution as an FBI interviewer. He was the driving force in the FBI's initiative to carry out an initial series of interviews with a group of 36 murderers, 25 of them serial offenders. The Bureau called this the Criminal Personality Research Project and its findings have shaped psychological profiling throughout the world. Like all good ideas, it was a simple one. Ressler figured that if he was to work in the Behavioral Science Unit hunting killers, then he had to know how killers thought, what excited them, what frightened them: in a nutshel,l what made them tick? The young agent decided that the best way to learn, was to go and interview a range of serial murderers who'd all been convicted and had no court appeals still to run. He was embarking not only on something that had never been done before but also something that did not have FBI approval.

Bob Ressler worked on the basis that it was better to say "sorry" than ask permission and be refused. With this in mind, he carried out his first few interviews in secrecy, squeezing them in among his other jobs as a field agent. In the end, it was a struggle to get the Bureau to legitimize his pet scheme. Ressler recalled, "The way the interview project started was that I was on a routine training mission out in the Bay area of San Francisco. I took a couple of extra days to stay out in the area because I knew there were at least a dozen prisons within very close proximity that housed a number of very violent offenders. With the aid of the local FBI people I went to those prisons and I interviewed Charles Manson and some members of what had been known as the Manson Family, including his Chief Lieutenant Charles 'Tex' Watson, who actually committed the homicides. I interviewed Sirhan Sirhan, who shot Robert Kennedy, and I interviewed a man that had killed some farmworkers out in the Sacramento area. What I found was that just in spontaneous interviews, without any particular structure, these people were willing to talk to me and were quite open about what they were saying. I thought at that point that we ought to try to formalize this and get some serious research done."

Eventually, Ted Bundy, (who killed more than 20 women), Ed Kemper, John Gacy (who killed more than 30 boys), David 'Son of Sam' Berkowitz (who shot courting couples in cars) and many more murderers would all confide their criminal secrets with Ressler and his colleagues. The study was a pioneering journey into sexual homicide, passing through the social outposts of rape, torture and mutilation before arriving at what society regards as the ultimate crime, murder.

It was just after the arrest of Berkowitz, that Ressler invented the now famous phrase, 'serial killer'.

"It was in the 1970s and I had been at the Police College at Bramshill, in England, lecturing on a six week course. I went back to the States and was being interviewed by the media when I started to use the term 'serial killer'. I didn't want to use the same term as they did in England (repeat killer) and I wanted something a little more original. As a child, I would go to the movies on the weekend and see serial adventures each weekend, so I started using the phrase and it caught on."

By the time the 36 interviews had been completed investigators had an invaluable data bank from which they would eventually draw rich dividends for their profiling work. All 36 killers were male, born between the years 1904 and 1958, with most of them growing up in the 1940s and 1950s. The vast majority were white and were usually the first or second born in the family. This last fact meant they were generally the eldest sons and in the male-dominated society of America this gave them a position of social advantage upon which to build. In the main, they were found to be clever but underachievers at school, work and in personal relationships. Most were high school drop-outs and only 20 percent of them managed regular employment.

The FBI, like everyone who tries to understand murderers, examined the data microscopically; eager to see if there were any significant, common factors between the killers and also if there were any features that set them apart from the rest of humanity. Of the 36 men, most were said to be of normal height, weight, appearance and looks. A few had some form of physical handicap but the majority were said to be of average to above average intelligence, with a third, such as Bundy and Kemper, actually being credited with 'superior' intelligence.

The first examinations of family background provided nothing startling, except perhaps the normality of the situations experienced by the killers as children. Most of them (20 out of 36) did not come from broken homes and were brought up by two parents not one. It was found, that on average, their fathers were unskilled but were hardworking and enjoyed regular employment. There was no real sign of desperate poverty in any of the cases.

However, while the structure of the family unit was solid enough, real problems developed behind closed doors. Half of the killers' families had criminal histories, 70 percent of the families had a record of alcohol abuse, a third of drug abuse and more than half of the families had experienced some form of psychiatric problems (25 of the 36 offenders would grow up to have psychiatric difficulties themselves).

As a result of all these factors, it's fair to conclude that as children, the offenders may have experienced considerable problems in forming loving and caring bonds with both of their parents. This is an area that most psychologists put great emphasis on. They argue that as children grow up, the quality of their relationships with their parents helps determine how they will turn out as adults themselves and how they will then relate to other people in society.

Against these kind of statistics, it has to be remembered that millions of children grow up with the same kind of experiences and disruptions but do not turn into killers. In many respects, it is still guesswork as to what combinations of hardship, abuse and instability are needed to lay the foundations upon which a homicidal future can be built.

The Criminal Personality Research Project also noted that as children, the offenders were moved around from city to city and state to state, probably much more so than the average child. It's understood this was because of parents searching for work but this may well have contributed to the child's lack of security and stability. In total, only a third of the men reported growing up in one location.

Cruelty, either to animals or to children, is one of a number of similar factors that crop up when profilers and psychologists start talking of common traits among serial offenders. Others include bed wetting, not just as youngsters but as adults as well, and fire-starting as children, possibly leading to arson attacks in later life. The FBI made a studied attempt of sexual murderers to find out what behavioural characteristics were shown by them as children, adolescents and as adults. They discovered that more than 80 percent of offenders said they were prone to day-dreaming and masturbating throughout their childhood, adolescence and adulthood. It isn't only statistics that have come from the programme of interviewing offenders involved in sexual homicide. Investigators have picked up a lot of 'tips' from the experts on the other side of the table. Bob Ressler recalled his interview with David 'Son of Sam' Berkowitz: " He told me that every time he had killed he would go back to the crime scenes, days and weeks later, so that he could relive his fantasies. On occasions he would hit two or three of these locations in one particular evening. Now, what a good piece of investigative advice that is for police officers. Officers can now be walking places where crimes have occurred and on a routine and selective basis take down licence plate numbers or something, and if the same guy keeps turning up at these locations, then they have a suspect that they wouldn't have had before."

While it was found that in almost two-thirds of all the cases the offender had been raised by two parents, it was also discovered that in 17 of the 36 studies, the biological father had left the family home by the time the child was 12. In 21 of the cases, the dominant parent (the one mainly responsible for the rearing of the child, including the discipline) was the mother and in only two of the studies did the offender say there was an equal sharing of parental rearing responsibilities.

Virtually all of the killers said that they did not have what they termed "a satisfactory relationship" with their father. Twenty-six of the 36 said it was cold and uncaring. Only 16 of the 36 had the same condemnation to make of their relationship with their mother. Because most offenders were the eldest born sons in the family (with no older brothers to emulate) and due to the absence of a biological father at a crucial stage of their childhood, it can be safely inferred that many of them grew up without strong male role-models around them. This would have been further complicated by the inevitability that parents with drug and alcohol problems, who were also involved in some kind of criminal careers of their own, probably had little time for ensuring their offsprings were fed a vital diet of love, understanding and moral referencing. While the parents didn't provide role models for sound social development, they were instead possibly providing models for deviancy.

There was also found to be an intense rivalry between the offender and other children in the family, all competing for the love and attention of their parents. In most of the cases, the offender said he emerged without feeling any strong attachments to any of his brothers and sisters. Sometimes, a child that feels unloved by both mum and dad, satisfies that need with the love of an older sister or brother but that did not happen in the cases of any of the murderers.

The murderers also reported what they considered to be continually unjust parental punishment, which was often quite violent or psychologically traumatic, such as being locked in a cellar overnight at a very young age. About a third said they had been sexually abused as children, just over a third reported that they'd been physically abused and almost two-thirds claimed they'd been psychologically abused.

In adolescence, 40 percent of offenders had left the family home before the age of 18 and were in either detention centres, mental institutions, foster homes or state homes. As they became sexually aware, the offenders began to pull away from the normal track of socialization. Instead of dating girls and trying to loose their virginity, around 80 percent of the offenders said they were more interested in pornography and compulsive masturbation. About the same number went on to develop sexual fetishes and 71 percent said they practised voyeurism, mainly as window-peepers. All these aspects of behaviour are reliant on the offender using fantasy to satisfy himself and are predominantly solitary experiences, excluding the involvement of another human being. FBI investigators believe this to be the first stage, where the abuse the offenders experienced as children began to manifest itself in their preference for 'fantasy sex' rather than sex with another person.

In the study of sexually sadistic criminals, it was found that as the offenders grew older and their sexually deviant habits became more steadfast, they became more and more removed from reality. They developed in such a way that they could only sexually relate to the dehumanized genitalia of a magazine page, or the long-awaited but fleeting glimpse of a person through a distant window. Many of those interviewed revealed that they'd never experienced consenting 'normal' sex (heterosexual sex to the point of orgasm) and of those who had, many had not experienced it for the first time until in their early 20s.

One dominant 'link' that does seem to appear in almost all the killers' lives, is that both as children and as adults they never managed to perfect that emotional juggling act of loving someone and in turn being equally loved by that same person. In numerous cases, serial murderers had been found to kill after a relationship they considered important had been ended – usually by the other partner. Similar 'trigger' factors include the discovery of infidelity by a parent they admired (as in the case of Peter Sutcliffe, "The Yorkshire Ripper') or continual parental domination to the extent that the child feels imprisoned by that parental love (as illustrated by Edmund Kemper).

When the 36 murderers were interviewed about their killings, it became apparent that fantasy was laced throughout the act. After murdering for the first time, the men reported that they were deeply preoccupied and turned-on by their memories of the murder. It was also noted that these memories (sometimes used later as masturbatory fantasies) were contributory to the second and subsequent killings.

At the end of the interviews, the FBI came to a number of conclusions: The men had seemingly started life in an advantageous position – they were of average or above average intelligence, were of good appearance and came from average socioeconomic families. It all started to go wrong with the introduction of physical, sexual or psychological abuse, the lack of positive role-models to aspire to, the child's feelings of isolation and the development of a sex life that depended upon fantasy and not reality.

Because of the harsh discipline and lack of parental bonding at home, the offenders believed the world at large, to be unjust and regarded authority as something that was gained through fear and not respect. There was also an overriding feeling that they had no control over their own lives and would consequently retreat into fantasies where they controlled and dominated other people by violence. These fantasies were further fuelled by the offender's preference for solo-sex (what is termed auto-erotic sexuality) so that the violence, aggression and dominance would be 'in-mind' as the man used pornography or indulged in sexual 'peeping'. Many of the offenders admitted that their masturbatory fantasies escalated in violence to include rape, torture and murder. To someone who perceives that they have little control over their own life, a life in a society which they view as unjust and constantly harsh on them, then murder can become attractive as the final and absolute control of someone else's life.

The FBI didn't stop at the 36 interviews instigated by Ressler's initial research. More murderers were also questioned in planned interviews and sessions were then carried out with serial rapists, sexual sadists and child molesters. Having said that, current interviewing of serial killers by the FBI is not unknown but has become rare. Most agents are now simply too wrapped-up in trying to shift a mountain of unsolved murders to afford the time to do the interviews they'd like. Nevertheless, the initial 36 case data base has been substantially extended and updated, with the initial work still standing as the biggest and most authoritative of its kind in the world.

********************

The sharp light of a cloudless new day illuminated the cheerless corridors of St Vincent's Hospital, Melbourne. FBI Supervisory Special Agent Roy Hazelwood, was giving one of a series of interviews to the local television and radio stations that had camped in the building's entrance hall. He reiterated the vital point on criminals returning to the crime scene, remarking that it had been long asserted by Sherlock Holmes before he and his colleagues got wise to the fact. "The murderer, should he return to the scene of a crime, will do so for a variety of reasons: One is to determine whether or not the body has been discovered. Two is to determine just how much progress is being made by the police investigation, and the third reason might well be to relive the murder in his fantasies."

In recent years, Hazelwood has been at the vanguard of the Behavioral Science Unit. As well as his intuitive and expert profiling, his writings on sexual homicide, rape and lust murder have become definitive works. For the sake of the local press, he ran through the basics of profiling: "I should begin by saying that we don't talk about psychological profiling, we've changed that to criminal personality profiling, because we're not clinical psychologists, we are law enforcement officers. We now have this all-encompassing term, Criminal Investigative Analysis, of which profiling is just one element, but still a vital one. A profile is basically a description of an unknown offender which sets forth his characteristics and traits. The purpose of a profile is to give indicators as to age, marital status, arrest history, educational level, military history, sexual dysfunctions, any mental disorder the offender may have had or be having, the type of employment he might be involved in, what his pastimes and hobbies might be, where he lives in proximity to the crime, and when I say that, I don't mean that we say 'He lives at 714 Knock Street' but whether he lives within walking distance of the crime scene, or travelled a great distance to commit the crime. We look at how he interacts with other people, whether he has a sense of humour, what he might like to read, and all that is basically the profile. But those are just the characteristics and traits of the profile; we also give the investigator a reconstruction of the crime in the profile, we tell him how in our opinion the crime occurred, what the sequence of events were between the offender and the victim and then we provide him with information of probable post-offence behaviour." The journalists nod encouragingly but were really more interested in the *Silence of the Lambs* cut-out. Hazelwood courteously declined an invitation to renew his photographic relationship with Hannibal the Cannibal and slipped away to more serious business in the main auditorium.

More than a hundred top criminal investigators from all over Australia and parts of New Zealand were packed into the hall for the lecture Hazelwood was about to give, jointly with Janet Warren. Dr Warren is an FBI Associate, an assistant professor in the General Medical Faculty, Division of Medical Centre Social Work and Department of Behavioral Medicine and Psychiatry at the University of Virginia. They're both among the most accomplished public speakers their professions could find. For more than two hours they shared their research on what they consider the most dangerous of all serial murderers, the sexual sadist.

Assistant Professor Janet Warren set the scene: "In 1984 Roy Hazelwood became involved in a kind of interviewing research with rapists that was similar to the interviews Bob Ressler had done with serial murderers. He went out and interviewed 41 individuals who had carried out at least ten rapes each. Some of these fellas were particularly prolific and had raped up to 80 times. The kind of research that was initiated here was simply going out to a prison cell, sitting down with these offenders and saying, 'I would really like to hear about you and everything you can tell us.' These interviews weren't two hours long, they weren't four hours long, sometimes they would go on for a number of days. In about 1985, I stepped into this historical development and came in looking at the data. We were having all this information piling up from the interviews, all these variables that were fascinating and I began to think that we could look at some of the themes and trends in the behaviour of these individuals."

As the story unfolded, Dr Warren, in a white, short summer dress paced the stage, leaving the floodlit podium and edging nearer to the audience, searching for eye contact among the detectives, evaluating whether she's talking too quickly and assessing their boredom thresholds. She explained that one of the aims of the study was to look at what was happening to an offender at the beginning of his criminal career, during the height of it and at the end when he was caught.

Using statistics, the FBI found that from what they had learned from the rapists, they could look at a particular rape crime and determine whether that particular criminal had committed previous offences. Also, whether he was likely to carry on raping and whether he was likely to become more violent and possibly end up as a murderer. "Whether you listen to serial offenders in their cells, or whether you play around and manipulate the data, you come up with some fairly common and consistent themes. It seems that serial offenders will keep offending, because whether it is rape or whether it is murder, they like to offend, they like to offend very much. They get a great deal of pleasure from what they are doing and they are going to keep doing it as long as they possibly can."

The 41 rapists had carried out a total of 837 sexual assaults and more than 400 attempted rapes. They were dedicated offenders and provided a fascinating study. Hazelwood found that 76 percent of them had been abused as children, 54 percent of them lived in average or above average socio-economic environments, 71 percent had been married at least once, 54 percent had general stable employment, 51 percent had served in the armed forces, 52 percent of them scored above average in the armed forces and 36 percent of them were regular collectors of pornography. In summarizing the findings, Hazelwood discovered that the data contradicted the stereotype of a rapist, who was until then believed to be a loner, an isolated person, living alone with little or no contact with his family. He also found vital indicators as to the type of previous offences that rapists were likely to have committed and here was another shock. Instead of minor sexual offences (such as 'flashing' or 'peeping') the offences fell predominantly into one other specific category, which we have been asked not to name. Janet Warren explained: "We found that these offenders, unbeknown to themselves, follow a specific criminal career. They don't know that they are doing it, they don't know the dimensions of behaviour that they're either staying consistent with or altering from, but you will find that when you look at offenders over a period of time, some aspects of their behaviour stay consistent." Just as the interview work on serial murderers had inspired the interview work on serial rapists, so too did the rape interviews inspire Roy Hazelwood to turn his skills to investigating the lives of the most dangerous offender in the world, the sexual sadist.

Early research into the sexually sadistic criminal showed that from a young age the offender would fantasize about various forms of sexually abnormal acts that in most countries are usually considered illegal. These acts, things like exhibitionism, masochism, sadism, paedophilia and transvestism are referred to as paraphilias. In the sexual sadist it is common to see an offender in his teens fantasizing regularly to three or four of these types of paraphilia. About five years after puberty, it is believed that the various fantasies fuse themselves into more sadistic fantasies and sometimes within a year of the sadistic fantasies beginning, the individual would start trying to act out the fantasy in real life. Dr Warren observed that the criminal sadist would at first take tentative steps, feeling his way from the imaginary world into the reality of offending. "If he could play out parts of the fantasy in real life, he would then go home and masturbate to the fantasy and this would keep the fantasy very, very arousing. Sexual sadists will tell you about the pressures they went through as they progressed from the internal fantasy of sadistic behaviour to actually enacting it in real life. That process may take months, it may take years. It may be that when they are 16, they go to a hardware store and they buy a piece of rope, maybe it's not clear to them at the time why they buy the piece of rope, maybe it's not well-formed in their mind at that time, but they take the rope and cut it into a few pieces and they put it into the trunk of their car. Possibly six months later, maybe a year later, they decide that they might like to go out and buy a knife, that there's a particular kind of knife that for some reason interests them, so they go out and buy the knife and put it in their car. Maybe three months, maybe a year later, they see an attractive woman and for some reason they track her around, not following her home, just following her, but they discover that all this is somehow appealing and arousing to them. Over a period of maybe two years, maybe five years, maybe ten years, you will see the gradual re-enactment of bits of their fantasy, which will ultimately culminate in a crime."

Warren went to some lengths to point out that not all sexual sadists become sexually sadistic criminals; that some sexual sadists contain their fantasies whilst others turn to pornography, sex-dolls or prostitutes to express their desires. "We're not clear what makes the difference between those that go on to act it out and those that go through life keeping it in a world of fantasy. It's our impression that what we are looking at is a pairing of sexual arousal abnormalities of sexual sadism with character pathology. It's likely that when you have a psychopath or sociopath and you have got a sexually sadistic arousal paraphilia then you are really looking at trouble. These are the individuals that might end up having a criminal career."

Where and when it all starts is still something of a puzzle, but one of the earliest examples of the fantasy-life of a sadistic offender has been traced back to his days as a toddler. "The youngest I've heard of concerns a three year old." Dr Warren considerd the incredulous statement for a second, then went on, "I'm not saying this three year old was running around having sexual fantasies, I'm not sure that is at all possible. In the one case that has been studied though, there was a three year old tying strings around his penis and tying it onto the faucet in the bathroom, then tying it onto the drawer in his bedroom and then he would slam the drawer, which of course would be quite painful. When he was about 12, he would hang himself in the bathtub and his mother came in one day and was quite upset when she found her son hanging, with all these ligatures around his neck. He subsequently left home, got into photography and ended up killing three women out in the desert. Again, he used ligatures that were similar to those that he'd used on himself five or six years earlier. So, while it may not have been a sexual fantasy at the age of three, somehow some preoccupations, some interest was existing at that time."

Very much a behind-the-scenes mind-hunter, Dr Warren is as important and certainly as thorough as the more reported FBI profilers. Like her colleagues, she considers the psychological data, not in isolation, but along with crime scene photographs, confessiohs, psychiatric reports, victim statements, prison records, interviews and investigator's reports. Only then, does she feel qualified to talk about the sexually sadistic criminal.

"A very important part of what we looked at and tried to understand was the material actually generated by the offender. These individuals like to create collections, they like to keep trophies of their criminal behaviour, they like to replay all of the experiences that they've had. More often than not, when you investigate these individuals, you'll find that they have audio tapes they've made during their various crimes, they may have video tapes of their murders or whatever they've done. They may have created scrapbooks, they may have their own pornography, they'll have sketches that they've done of their victims or they may even have photographs. For investigating officers it's important that when they go in with search warrants they know what to look for, because it's likely they'll find some of these collections somewhere in the offender's possession."

Roy Hazelwood motioned towards the microphone, a half-gesture but sufficient enough for Dr Warren to understand that he wanted to add a point to her comments. "The majority of these offenders act out symbolically against inanimate objects and we in law enforcement, in mental health practices and so on, tend to treat many of these offences as being 'nuisance sexual offences', for example, offences such as mutilating stolen clothing or women's lingerie, cutting up a woman's picture or her photograph. If you stop and consider that this is simply a re-enactment of his fantasy, then it becomes much more than just a 'nuisance sexual offence'. Well, some officers say, 'but the kid was only 13 years old' – all the more reason to intervene in our opinion. Intervene as soon as possible in their lives.

"Supposing you find sketches, say two or three hundred sketches, such as in a case that I'm working on right now. A lot of these sketches have absolutely nothing to do with the crime, but they give you an idea of what the offender is thinking about, thinking about in an obsessional way. If you stop and consider the fact that what a person sketches, writes or draws is nothing more than a reflection of his thoughts, then by looking at that volume of material and what he has drawn, sketched and written about, then you'll get a good idea of how much he's actually thinking about these types of crimes."

Many sexually sadistic criminals do put their darkest thoughts into actions. One case that stunned America was that of Cameron Hooker. For years he persuaded his wife Janice to take part in sadistic acts. He would tie her up, hang her up naked and whip her, but this was only the beginning of his fantasy. Twenty-four-year-old Hooker was obsessed with thoughts of kidnapping a woman, holding her as a sex slave and brutalizing her. In 1977 he persuaded the woman that had been his childhood sweetheart and was now his doting wife, to help him carry out his kidnap plan. In return, he promised to stop beating and abusing her and she naively went along with his crimes because she believed this would protect her marriage.

Next to the Sacramento River is the small town of Red Bluff, Tehema County. Here, on the nearby Interstate that surges from San Diego to the Canadian Border, the Hookers, complete with young baby dozing in the back, stopped their blue Dodge Colt in the blazing afternoon sunshine. A young hitch-hiker, making her way to see a friend in northern California, rushed to the halting vehicle and gratefully jumped in. It was Colleen Stan's last moment of freedom.

After a short journey, filled with warm welcomes and friendly chatter, the Hookers drove off the main road. Janice began attending to the baby while Cameron got out of the driver's seat and appeared at Colleen's window with a gun pointing at her. Within moments she was handcuffed and blindfolded, then a specially made wooden box was strapped over her head so she couldn't see or hear. The box had been at the centre of Cameron's fantasies and hard work. It looked like a crude, square diver's helmet, bolted shut and was filled to the point of claustrophobia with dense insulation. This was only the start.

Back at the Hooker's home she was led into the basement, where she was stripped, stood on a freezer and chained to a pipe. She was then strapped by leather bindings and suspended from hooks in the ceiling while Cameron whipped her, in between masturbating to pictures of bondage pornography that mirrored what he was doing in reality.

After the whipping she was left hanging naked for some time. She was then taken down and still wearing the wooden head-box, she was put into a large, wooden coffin-like box, which was then bolted up. She was kept in captivity inside Hooker's battered old mobile home for seven years, spending much of it in this kind of incarceration. Even more astonishingly, his brutality towards her had such a brainwashing effect that on one occasion he allowed her home to visit her parents, confident that she would return to him and once more resume her duties as his slave. He had managed this by convincing her that he didn't work alone, that she had been picked out by an international ring of slavers called 'The Company', who would recapture her and kill her if she ever told her parents. Worse than that, her parents would also be killed.

On January 25, 1978 Colleen had been made to sign a 'slavery contract' that Hooker had drawn up in an elaborate plan to show that 'The Company' really existed. In it, she had to relinquish her name and become known simply as K. She had to promise to call Hooker "Master" and always be ready to be sexually or physically abused by him. The contract dictated that she never wore any underclothes and never crossed her legs when she was in his presence. Colleen was left with no option but to sign, yet she still had the spiritual strength to tell Hooker she did not consent to a paragraph that demanded she relinquished her soul as well as her body.

Cameron Michael Hooker was born in Alturas, California and was brought up in an average American family. He wasn't subjected to sexual or physical abuse, there is no evidence of psychological abuse and his parents did not divorce. Observers would eventually put his criminally sadistic behaviour down to 'an accident of internal wiring' but there is more to it than that.

Just as Dr Warren predicted, Hooker had been nurturing paraphilic and sadistic fantasies throughout his teens; years when the gangling youngster was considered 'a loner', and was even banished to parts of the school yard where others would ridicule him and not allow him to join in their games. During these years he also discovered pornography, stashing away secret collections of sadomasochistic pictures, while indulging himself in masturbatory fantasies where he exhibited power, control and dominance over women.

Again, as Janet Warren had indicated, Hooker used to cruise around with handcuffs and bindings in his car, following women for a while, even stopping to take photographs of them, but for ages he managed to maintain his fantasy, corralling it into the safety of daydreams and magazines.

Cameron Hooker was convicted on Halloween Day, 1985 and sentenced to a maximum of 104 years in jail. Hooker's wife Janice had ended it all, by eventually running away from her husband's den of sadism, taking the enslaved Colleen Stan with her. When they first told their stories to the authorities they were met, not surprisingly, with total disbelief. Only painstaking police work and a brilliant public prosecutor managed to crush Hooker's simple defence that Colleen was his live-in mistress, who had been there with his wife's consent and who enjoyed sadomasochistic sex.

Cameron Hooker's case is an exceptional one but it still typifies the sexually sadistic criminal. Dr Warren has worked on far more dangerous examples of sadism. "One individual, who killed a number of times, had an incinerator in his basement for bodies and kept audio tapes of various women screaming. He described sexual sadism in this way: "The wish to inflict pain on others is not the essence of Sadism. One essential impulse, to have complete mastery over another person, to make him or her a helpless object of her will, to become the absolute ruler over her, to become her God, to do with her as one pleases, to humiliate her, to enslave her, to make her suffer, since there is no greater power over another person than that of inflicting pain on her, to enforce her to undergo suffering without her being able to defend herself, the pleasure is the complete domination over another person – this is the very essence of the sadistic drive."

Roy Hazelwood adds to that, "It's extremely important that you notice what this guy said. He said 'to make another person suffer.' It is not the infliction of pain that is sexually arousing to the sexual sadist, it is the suffering exhibited by the victim in response to the pain. The pain can be either psychological or physical, but pain is simply a tool to elicit the desired response of fear, of subjugation, of submission and of course the ultimate fear is the fear of death."

It was to understand the motivations of offenders like Hooker that Roy Hazelwood undertook what was to prove to be an emotionally draining research project into sadistic criminality. It was a series of in-depth interviews, similar to the ones Bob Ressler had conducted, but with different offenders. "Ted Bundy was not a sexual sadist, David 'Son of Sam' Berkowitz was not a sexual sadist, these are not the individuals we are talking about here," stressed Hazelwood. "Almost all of the sexual sadists killed their victims through asphyxiation, and this is something we see with our more virulent sexual offenders. There's not too much potential for interaction if you shoot somebody, but if you have a ligature around their neck, then it's intimate and you can watch them. You can either force them closer to death or bring them back from death, and it seems that process is very important to the sexual sadist."

Hazelwood studied 22 sexually sadistic criminals, who between them had murdered 187 people. He found that often there would be confusion between the terms 'sexual sadists' and 'serial killers'; in fact, only 17 of the 22 sexual sadists that were interviewed were serial killers. Sexually sadistic criminality also is the last bastion of male chauvinism. Researchers were unable to find a criminal female sexual sadist in current or historic studies. All the subjects were white, male and fairly well educated, with some of the offenders having significantly high IQs. They were all regarded as sophisticated offenders who took great care and trouble over not getting caught.

Forty-seven percent of the group came from homes where there had been parental infidelity, 23 percent said they had been physically abused and 20 percent claimed to have been sexually abused as children. Almost half of them were married and 30 percent of them had incestuous relationships with their children. Forty-three percent had graduated from high school and gained

degrees or college qualifications of some kind. They found jobs
as law students, bankers, one was a racing car driver, photographers, cooks and repair engineers.

As Dr Warren later remarked, the offenders appeared to be
perfectly acceptable members of society. "What we found was
that these individuals were involved in the community, they had
regular jobs, they weren't unemployed, they weren't drifters. In
fact 30 percent of them were pillars of the community, which is
slightly unsettling. One fellow up in Alaska ran his own bakery
and was involved in a number of community projects. He also
at one point got his own licence to fly an aeroplane. He would
then go and accost women, get them into the aeroplane and take
them out into the northern parts of Alaska. Then he would
release them onto the tundra with no clothes on and he would
track them with high-powered guns and kill them."

Roy Hazelwood shed some more light into the double life of
the murderous baker. "He used that same aeroplane to fly mercy
missions for sick, old people. At one time he also bagged the
biggest brown bear in the history of the State of Alaska. He was
very charitably orientated too – he killed 17 victims but he let
another 14 go. I was fascinated, because I wanted to know why
he released them and he said 'They didn't meet my criteria for
death.' By the way, this man is married, has his own business,
he's very successful, is a philanthropist and was Catholic
Layman of the Year. So I said 'what's your criteria for
death' and he answered: 'Well, number one they had to
approach me sexually' – so he would go to strip joints and areas
of prostitution etc – secondly, they had to show some disgust
at a sexual act that I demanded. Thirdly, they had to try to
escape. If they didn't meet all three of these criteria then I
would release them'."

Hazelwood's research would show that sexual sadists spent
weeks, months and sometimes even years planning their
offences. This contributed to making them among the most
difficult type of killers to catch. Sometimes working in pairs,
they would alter vans or cars so people such as hitch-hikers
couldn't escape they would dig dungeons in their gardens and

build hidden torture chambers. In all, about 90 percent of sexually sadistic crimes seem to have been pre-planned and there's evidence to suggest that the planning of the act is in itself sexually arousing to the offender.

Dr Warren points out that there are other deadly similarities and traits in sexual sadists. "All the sexual sadists had the money to go about building a torture chamber but many of them would just have an area where they knew they were taking the individual to. This was an area where they would have their pornography, they'd have their weapons, they'd have their torture kits and they would repeatedly murder victims in this same place. Sixty percent of these offenders kept their victims captive for fairly extensive periods of time, often ranging from 24 hours to six weeks. It seems that they were organized well enough to keep the woman and enjoy her, knowing that ultimately they would kill her. Sometimes they would release her but more often they would not. It appears that during that period of having the woman captive, when no-one knew where she was, they had a feeling of absolute control over her and this would be a very important part for them. Eighty-seven percent of them bound, blindfolded and gagged their victims, 77 percent engaged in sexual bondage of one or more victims. When we talk about this activity, we're not talking about a piece of rope that you tie around a woman's hands so she can't hit you, we're talking about very well defined, exquisitely formed bondage of these individuals, so much so, that one of the ways you would know you were looking for the same killer was the sophistication of the way that he would want to bind his women. In these cases, the offenders didn't bind victims to keep them from getting away, nor to simply keep them in one place. Part of the sexual ritual of the offence was using ligatures and binding the victims in a very particular fashion, as a kind of signature. You'd be able to say, 'this is the same guy', because he used the same kind of knots, perhaps with up to 43 ligatures on just one particular woman."

Victims of sexual sadists are often buggered. There also seems to be a preference by the sadist to carry out anal rape before vaginal intercourse. As well as frequently forcing victims to carry out oral sex on them, a high number of offenders also practise 'foreign object penetration', probably in another effort to further humiliate and degrade the woman. It's been found that while carrying out the sexual parts of the attack, many of the sadists become sexually dysfunctional and cannot ejaculate, and this often ends in the offender masturbating over the woman while she is alive, or sometimes when she is dead.

Dr Warren continues: "We also found that about a quarter of the individuals were interested in verbal scripting. Verbal scripting and behavioural scripting are FBI terms for a process by which an offender makes his victims say and act in a particular way. He may make the woman dress in a particular kind of clothing and he may make the woman say particular things over and over again. Alternatively, he may sit the woman down and say, 'OK, I'm going to be with you for the next hour and a half and I want you to say these four or five things repeatedly to me, without me prompting you to do so.' So, you can go from very slight scripting to very complex scripting, but in all the cases these individuals had a very clear idea of how they wanted the woman to look, how they wanted her to dress and what they wanted her to say and do."

With the scripting and costume elements of the sexual sadist, there is frequently a practise of recording their acts, either by stills camera or with videotape. In a sinister way, the sadists go through exactly the same procedure as a film director. Both are caught up in the same business of turning fantasy into reality. The director plans out his camera movements, constructs his sets, hires his stars, costumes his actors, tells them what words to say and when to say them, and then he records it all and replays and edits the work until he's completely satisfied. The sadist plans out the type of victim he's going to capture, constructs his torture room, abducts his victim, forces her to wear specific clothes and say specific phrases, then he carries out his sexual fantasies and takes photographs or video footage so he can replay it and satisfy himself at a later date.

Hazelwood and Warren have poured over the raw data of some of the world's most horrendous crimes, always searching for the glimpse of new information that might give profilers an 'extra edge' on their next case, the kind of 'edge' that could prevent a single murder turning into a series. Janet Warren recalls such an experience as she and Hazelwood worked late one night, 60 feet underground in the tomb-like buildings that have become the home of the FBI's Behavioral Science Unit in Quantico, Virginia.

"I'd gone through many, many boxes of material that I'd been looking at for a number of hours. It was getting late in the evening and there was a manuscript in the boxes of the case that I was working on. I looked at it and it looked like pornography to me. I kind of put it to one side, deciding that I didn't want to spend another four or five hours reading the pornographic writing that this offender had written. Roy came by at that point and said something about reading it, and I said 'Roy, it's just pornography. I'm not going to go through this, I'll go back to his psychiatric records and criminal history information and write his case up that way.' He said, 'read the manuscript' and I said, 'It's late, I don't want to spend the rest of the evening reading the manuscript', but he still said 'read the manuscript'. Well, I started. There were about 250 pages and the hours went by. I finished it and I thought, well at least now I can go to bed. I put it aside and as I lifted up the manuscript and moved it to the other side of the desk, I noticed there was a package of crime scene photographs there. I opened up the package, and began looking through the pictures. What I saw was everything that I had read about in the manuscript. That writing wasn't pornography, it wasn't fantasy, it was a very detailed description of the criminal behaviour carried out by this sexual sadist. It detailed the bodies, the women, the ligatures, the knots; where he made the ligatures, how he left the body, how he cut, how he struck them, how he cut their necks. All of that was exactly what he had been writing in his manuscript and it was at this point that I realized there are parameters of belief, in terms of what these individuals experience that we often don't understand, because it's not part of our experience."

To illustrate this, Dr Warren read some of the manuscript, where the offender was recalling his first killing. This was the almost accidental murder, not of a woman but of a man. "He was hitch-hiking across the country and he was coming down onto the exit ramp of a highway. There was another fella standing there and he kind of went and stood in front of him, and that guy said 'Hey, get out of the way! I was here first.' They got into a tussle and they began to fight physically. The other guy, who was bigger, was starting to get the advantage over him and all of a sudden he grabbed a rock and, well, this is how he put it: '...he dropped like I had shot him. I stood there looking at him on the ground and I was suddenly overcome with feelings of power. I realized I held this man's life in my hands, it was mine to do with as I chose. I thought, I'm like God. I too have the power to give life or take it away. I was drunk with the feeling. I got down on my knees and took the rock and hit him, again as hard as I could. I watched his forehead cave in from the force and the blood and the brains splatter onto the road. His body was kind of twitching and I figured it was nerves. I knew he was dead. I never thought it would be so easy to kill a person, or that I would enjoy it, but it was easy and I enjoyed the feeling of supremacy, a supremacy like I never had known before."

The man went on to kill a number of times before he was eventually caught. There was no accidental encounter with his next victim, this was a planned rape and murder. His account of the rape and strangling was part of the manuscript that had so disgusted Dr Warren and caused her to initially write it off as pure pornography: "I put my mouth over her nipple and brought my teeth together hard. She tried to scream but I had my hand over her mouth. I slid my teeth back and forth in a sawing motion. Her pain must have been truly intense for she blacked out. I pulled out of her and went and got some water. I poured it over her and slapped her until she regained consciousness, she wasn't going to cheat me by fainting." Dr Warren remains impassive as she reads the vividly disturbing script, professionally separating the value of the data from sheer basic disgust:

"He then goes on to strangle her, and as he begins to feel that she may be dying, he again takes the rope away from her neck, breathes air into her mouth to bring her back to consciousness and then goes on with his sexual behaviour. At some point, he begins to orgasm and finds it very arousing. He takes his knife and while he's orgasming, he's cutting her neck and watching her finally die, after bringing her back to life a number of times. He talks about the blood, he takes the blood in his hand, he brings it up to his nose and he says the smell of it was overpowering, 'I put out my hand and wet it with the blood, I put it to my lips and sucked it from my fingers. It was Ambrosia to me'."

The account is undoubtedly sickening but what is more frightening to the layman is that this offender was in all other respects perfectly 'normal'. He was a loving father who never assaulted his wife or baby, a former US Marine, regarded in high esteem by family and friends. Reading his graphic recollection of the murder, made Janet Warren conclude that a person who could find such acts of violence so dreadfully arousing was: "A clinical phenomenon." This phrase seems totally complementary to the unqualified description of Cameron Hooker as "an accident of internal wiring."

********************

It's now lunchtime at the serial murder conference in Melbourne. Warren and Hazelwood say their thank yous and start to leave the packed lecture theatre but they never make it to the doors. As the lights come up and the buzz of the overhead projectors is silenced for an hour, they are descended upon by groups of inquisitive Australian investigators. They never get lunch. The entire recess is spent explaining theories or giving on-the-spot advice to senior officers who have a particular case that is baffling them. In the end, Warren manages a glass of mineral water, Hazelwood slips outside for the cigarette he has yearned for throughout the morning.

For Roy Hazelwood, the day ends much the way it began, in the glare of publicity. It's 7 pm when he keeps his interview date with Central Television for the ITV documentary that was made along with this book. He sits forward in the soft floral chair of a hotel room, elbows perched on a large glass table as he sips a ridiculously expensive coke offered from the room's mini-bar. As the camera-crew re-arrange the furniture around him, searching for the best shot, his finger idly traces through some condensation that has run off the bottle onto the table-top. As the camera lights flicker into life, it's apparent that he's as relaxed here as he is in a lecture theatre or at a crime scene.

The camera 'turns-over', the lighting has had its final 'tweak' and the sound-recordist gives a 'go-ahead' nod. Hazelwood wastes no time getting to the heart of his research. "Fantasy is the most important area in all sexual offences, all sexual offences begin with fantasy. Whether you're talking about the 'nuisance sexual offender' and I detest that term, you know, the window-peepers etc, or whether you're looking at the sexual sadist who keeps his victims in captivity and tortures them, or whether you're talking about the serial killer, it all begins with fantasy.

"Depending upon the intelligence of the individual, the fantasies will be more complex. For example, in order to have a complicated scenario of capture, captivity, torture and murder, you've got to have at least average intelligence to have the continuity of thought for a fantasy like that. So, you can look at the crime scene and determine how rich the fantasy life of the offender is. I recently testified at a murder trial in Georgia, in which an offender kidnapped a woman, took her out and raped her, sodomized her, then left. He came back a short time later and brought teddies (all-in-one styled lingerie) and he made her model these teddies for him, then he raped her again and took her home before killing her. Now, this man obviously has a very rich fantasy life. He also has a collection of teddies, he has a fetish for these items and here fantasy plays a large role. This sexual sadist has a very complex and rich fantasy life and some of your rapists have very rich fantasy lives. If you look at the interaction between the offender and the victim, the more interaction, and by this we mean the more conversation, the more costuming and scripting of the victim, then these are signs that he is acting out the fantasies that he has rehearsed in his mind.

"The human being, male or female, Russian, English, Capitalist, Communist, whatever; we all have the same three components of the sex drive. The first component is the biological component, that's the instinctual urge to engage in sexual activity and that accounts for approximately ten percent of the sex drive. The second component is a physiological component, that is when your glands fill with hormones and you have the urge to engage in sexual activity, and that accounts for approximately 20 percent of your sex drive. At least 70 percent of the sex drive is what we refer to as the psycho-sexual component, that is the mental component of the sex drive. It is the mind that is the primary sexual component in the male or female, not the penis, not the vagina, the mind is the primary sexual organ of the human species. So when an offender talks to a victim, he is attempting to gratify the mental component of the sex drive. Having the victims dress in a certain way does not satisfy the biological component, it does not satisfy the physiological component, what it does satisfy is the mental component, the psycho-sexual component of the sex drive. That is why it is so very important for law enforcement to understand the role that the mind plays in sexual crimes, because you can see what is being played in the mind by how the offender acts with his victim."

Hazelwood takes a sip of the coke, checking that his explanation has been understood. Tapes are changed and a window shut. The gentle breeze blowing in from the tenth floor balcony window has been building towards a gale. Hazelwood is a consummate communicator, reducing the most advanced of theories and most complex of practises into easy to understand language. The camera whirs into life again and he returns to his favourite subject, the sexual sadist.

"A sexually sadistic offender is the most prolific, competent and dangerous sexual criminal that we have operating in America today. Sexual sadism is a paraphilia recognized by the mental health field, in which an individual is sexually aroused or sexually stimulated by the suffering of another person. A lot of people are cruel, a lot of people are inhumane, a lot of people are violent – but very few are excited by their violence, are sexually excited by the suffering of another person. Those people are called sexual sadists. They put more planning into their crimes, they're more methodical, they're more successful and have more victims than any other sexual criminal operating in America today."

As we talked in 1992, Roy Hazelwood was involved in his latest line of innovative research. This time, instead of just talking to sexual sadists and studying their answers, he turned his skills to also interviewing their families, their wives and girlfriends. His aim is to discover how they behaved in everyday life, how they related to their parents and when and where sadism reared its head. The research is ongoing, but Hazelwood already has some clear ideas. "We were very interested in talking to the sexual sadist and we talked to a number of them. We were more interested in gaining access to their personal and prized possessions: what they liked to read, what kind of movies they favoured, what their hobbies were, what their collections consisted of, and most of them talked about that freely, there was no problem about that. Then it came to me one day, that we should be talking to the people who lived with these individuals and who would be willing to speak to us. So, I developed an idea of talking to the former wives and girlfriends of these offenders and I have never been refused an interview, every former girlfriend or wife that I've approached agreed to be interviewed.

"We determined that in each instance, every former wife or girlfriend was also a victim of the sexual sadist, in fact just as much as the 'stranger' victims were. He acted out against his spouse or girlfriend, exactly as he did against his 'stranger' victims. He employed the same fantasies and he behaved in the same way with them. But we gained some very valuable information about their self-esteem, about what made them happy and what made them sad, how they courted, how they interacted with other people, what their opinions were towards law enforcement, towards the criminal justice system, towards mental health agencies and that sort of thing. It provided us with a great deal of insight into these people.

"I will say this, that the interviews with these women lasted approximately two or three times as long as the interviews with the offenders lasted, and they also took a greater toll emotionally. These women had been subjected to horrendous activities, physical abuse, sexual abuse, emotional abuse, sometimes forced to be involved in crimes themselves and now they're suffering today as a result of that."

Hazelwood points out that Bob Ressler's famous study of serial murderers looked at 36 offenders who had killed a total of 127 people, while his study of sexual sadists showed that just 22 offenders had claimed 187 lives. While the likes of serial killers such as Jeffrey Dahmer, Ted Bundy or David Berkowitz are almost household names, few people have heard of sexual sadists such as Cameron Hooker .

"Most serial killers will quickly kill their victims, the sexual sadist likes to keep his victims in captivity, he likes to prolong the suffering. For too long, people believed that it was the infliction of pain that sexually aroused the sadist, but that is not so. Pain is a tool, used by the sadist to elicit the suffering from the victim, to elicit the fear, to create an exhibition of submission.

"A sexual sadist is an individual in which aggression and sexual arousal have become fused, they become one. That is not the same with the majority of sexual offenders – there are a lot of violent sexual offenders but these two elements have not become fused. If we knew what caused sexual sadism we'd be light years ahead of where we are now. We don't know. Only God knows. I certainly don't." Almost on cue, it's time for another tape change.

# 8
## Spree Killers

*"I should have stayed in bed." – Michael Ryan, moments
before taking his own life after shooting his mother and
15 strangers dead.*

The crimes of these killers interrupt television programmes.
They are beamed around the world within minutes. Premiers are
moved to comment on them. The spree killer is so named
because he commits mass murder in a frenzy that spans only
moments or hours and, in some cases, days without the so-
called cooling off period of other serial killers. He is the nightmare that can happen anytime, leaving behind shockwaves of
terror, tragedy and countless unanswered questions.

Nobody can say for certain what sparks off the spree killer.
One incident might trigger a tragic chain reaction. A gradual
build-up of social and domestic pressures could initiate an
explosive release. The reason may be due to genuine mental
illness or a specific medical complaint, or it could be a combination of some or all of these. In most cases the killer is
unavailable for questioning or psychological analysis as he is so
often one of the victims of his own spree.

Mid-morning and the temperature was already rising to 98
degrees across the University of Texas campus in Austin. The
ground-floor receptionist noticed nothing unusual about the
man in overalls who pushed a heavily laden hand-cart carrying
a metal locker and canvas bag into the elevator of the 28-storey
administration building. She assumed Charles Whitman was a
campus workman.

The locker contained a six-mm rifle with telescopic sight, a
sawn-off shotgun, a Remington .35-calibre pump-action rifle, a
.357 magnum pistol, a nine-mm Luger pistol, a 30.06 army

carbine, 600 rounds of assorted ammunition and a Bowie knife. The canvas army duffel bag contained canned food, two bottles of water, a clock, a pink toilet roll and a spray can of deodorant. Whitman was conscious of the heat and it was going to be sticky up on the observation deck.

It was 10:30 am, August 1, 1966, when the elevator took the 25-year-old ex-US Marine to the top of the tower. It had already been a long day for the one-time altar boy and Eagle scout about to embark upon one of the most ruthless murder sprees in US history. The nightmare scenario of an apparently invincible crackshot sniper picking off human targets at will from a seemingly unassailable tower would inspire a string of dubious Hollywood TV films.

During the night Whitman had stabbed his 24-year-old wife Kathy to death. He left a note which said, "I don't want her to face the embarrassment that my actions will surely cause her." Then he had gone round to his mother's apartment and during a struggle stabbed and shot her once in the back of the head. He left a neatly written note by her body. "I have just killed my mother. I am very upset over having done it. However, I feel that if there is a heaven she is definitely there now. If there is not a heaven she is out of her pain and misery. I love my mother with all my heart. The intense hatred I feel for my father is beyond all description." As he left his mother's apartment he attached another note to the door stating she was ill and would not be going to work that day.

After returning to his own house where his dead wife lay, he added to the note which he had written earlier: "3 am. Wife and mother dead."

He spent the rest of the hot summer night and early morning preparing his weapons and supplies. Postman Chester Arrington was probably the last person to speak to Whitman having chatted to him for 25 minutes after dropping off the mail. Years later he recalled: "I saw him sawing off the shotgun. I knew it was illegal. All I had to do was pick up the telephone and report him. It could have stopped him. I've always blamed myself."

The tallest building in Austin was the giant granite tower on the university campus. It housed the library and administration offices along with an observation deck on the uppermost level. He had enrolled as a junior for the summer semester studying architectural engineering and had spent many long hours during the summer gazing up at the tower. Colleagues had just assumed it was his interest in architecture that led him to stare intensely up at the building. None of them knew he had told the psychiatrist at the university health centre of his urge to go up to the tower with a deer rifle and shoot the people below. But he had failed to mention to the psychiatrist that he had been suffering from blinding headaches increasing frequency.

The elevator stopped on the 27th floor and Whitman hauled his equipment up the remaining stairs to the top floor observation deck. He shot Edna Townsley, the 47-year-old registration clerk on the deck, once, clubbed her about the head with the rifle butt and stuffed her body behind a couch. The other sightseers, a family group of four who were making their way up the stairs to the observation deck, did not hear the shot and were completely unaware that Whitman was lying in wait. They walked straight into a fusillade. Fifteen-year-old Mark Gabour and his aunt Margaret Lamport were killed instantly. The boy's mother and brother were critically wounded. Whitman slammed the door shut and barricaded it. He was now alone on the deck with his weapons.

At a height of 300 feet, the deck gave him a clear view over most of the city of Austin so he could sight his weapons on anything within hundreds of yards. The Marine marksman who had handled guns since early childhood was master of all he surveyed.

He had given himself the order to fire at will and scanned the ground for movement. Claudia Rutt, a promising teenage ballet dancer, was picked out through the telescopic sight and was killed instantly with the first shot. Her 18-year-old boyfriend Pat Sonntag threw himself down beside her and was killed by Whitman's next bullet barely seconds later. Another student was blown to death off his bicycle as hundreds more began to scatter for cover. A policeman crept towards the tower and hid behind a statue waiting to get a clear shot at the sniper but Whitman shot him dead. He fired on a small boy then hit Claire Wilson in the stomach; she was eight months pregnant. She survived but her baby was still-born in hospital hours later.

Within minutes bodies and wounded people littered the campus. A woman on the 18th floor of the administration block heard the shots and saw the horror below. She rang a friend in a nearby building shouting: "Somebody's up there shooting from the tower. There's blood all over the place."

A man three blocks away was certain he was out of reach, so he stood out in the open looking up at the regular puffs of smoke which were coming from the top of the tower. A bullet tore into his chest and he was killed instantly.

Frantic police officers set up road blocks and tried desperately to clear 10,000 students and curious sightseers from the area. Whitman had now been firing freely for nearly two hours in which time he had killed 14 people and wounded 31. The campus resembled a battlefield, armoured cars crawled tentatively between the dead and wounded who lay helpless in the mid-day heat. Marksmen hoping to pick off the sniper were foiled when Whitman dropped to the floor and continued firing through drain holes. An aeroplane was sent up in the hope that airborne marksmen could target him, but it retreated quickly when Whitman put a bullet through its fuselage.

Eventually four policemen and a civilian went up to the deck. After breaking through the barricade, Officer Romero Martinez and the civilian Allen Crum began inching their way in separate directions around the observation deck while the other officers covered the exits. Shortly after 1 pm Whitman was surprised by Martinez and fired one shot but missed. Martinez fired six rapid shots into Whitman as officer Houston McCoy emptied his pump action shotgun after kicking down another door. Whitman died in the shoot-out and his body was removed at 1:40 pm.

Born in Lake Worth, Florida, in 1941, Charles Whitman was the oldest of three sons. His father, Charlie senior, was a strict taskmaster who demanded much of his boys and young Charlie was expected to excel. He became an Eagle scout at 12, an adept piano player and worked hard at school, but it was never enough for his father. The boy, along with his brothers and his mother, grew to expect regular beatings.

Young Charles learned how to take his own beatings but he could not bear to see his mother suffer physical abuse. He retreated into himself, bit his nails continually and was resigned to the fact that he would never be good enough for his father. He joined the US Marines in 1959 after graduating from high school. Perhaps it was to get away from the father he had grown to hate or perhaps it was to impress him. Whilst there he took advantage of an educational scheme and the Marines sent him off to college to study engineering. The chosen college was the University of Texas in Austin.

It was here he met and married Kathleen Leissner, from Needville, Texas. After a while she became the target for much of the hostility which seemed to build up within Whitman and he developed a compulsive gambling habit that affected his studies. He was eventually charged and court-martialled for gambling, loan-sharking and carrying an unauthorised pistol, so he dropped out of college and returned to the Marines to complete his enlistment.

However, Whitman went back to the University of Texas in 1964, determined to become a better student and husband. He took extra lessons to make up for lost time and began taking classes in real estate sales in case his degree course did not work out. He also took on a part time job to supplement Kathy's earnings as a teacher and became a boy scout leader.

All this put a lot of pressure on him, and to add to this his mother arrived in Austin in the spring of 1966. She had finally plucked up the courage to leave her violent husband, so Whitman felt an added responsibility to care for her.

Eventually it all became too much. He decided he would quit his studies and leave the wife he loved, in fact leave everything. A college professor persuaded him towards a part-time course while his concerned and confused wife urged him to talk to a psychiatrist. The doctor wrote: "He readily admits having over-whelming periods of hostility." In fact Whitman's dreaded fear was that he was becoming just like the violent and abusive father he loathed. He made a decision, which he clarified in part of his final 'suicide' note: "I can't stand the pressures on me. I'm going to fight it out alone."

Friends reported an aura of serenity about him in his final days, as if he had decided to adopt an air of inner peace. Once he had made his final decision it was obvious that Whitman, through his blinding headaches, was still anxious about causing further problems for the two people he loved, his wife and mother. To him the only answer was to save them the pain and sorrow of the hostility they were bound to face. They had to die. Of course, there was another reason, their deaths would also remove much of the guilt and shame his actions were bound to create within him.

An autopsy on Whitman revealed a tumour in his brain. It had clearly been responsible for his headaches and although it would be too easy to blame this sole ailment for the massacre it must have played some part in creating the terrible traumas and aggressive tendencies that plagued him in his final months.

*********************

Britain's most prolific spree killer came along 21 years after the Texas tower massacre, but the case of Michael Ryan bears many similarities to that of Charles Whitman. Both sprees bore military hallmarks, both involved the initial murders of a close relative, both claimed 16 lives, both occurred in the summer month of August and both ended with the death of the killer.

"Dawn came like any other dawn and by evening it just didn't seem the same day." So said Margaret Thatcher, the British Prime Minister, when commenting on what became known as the Hungerford Massacre.

It began on August 19, 1987, when a 27-year-old 'Walter Mitty' bachelor called Michael Ryan could not decide whether to have a lie-in or give in to a long-held urge to go 'hunting' in Savernake Forest. Ryan lived with his mother in the once

anonymous town of Hungerford. It is a market town in rural
Berkshire lying on the old Roman road to Bath. Mention
Hungerford in the United Kingdom and the word conjures up
immediate images of horror and death.

Ryan was more than a loner, he was a fantasist. He was
unemployed with no friends and certainly no girlfriends. He
told people in his local pub he had been married but his wife
had divorced him because of his adultery. If they bothered to
listen any further, he went on to brag about other conquests. His
love of the military came, he said, from his time as a para-
trooper. He also claimed to be a pilot but it was all lies.

Ryan's only love in life was guns. He collected them and he
could shoot well as he regularly practised at a local gun club. It
seemed to be the only thing that lifted him from the deep
depression he had felt since the death of his father in 1985
which had also apparently intensified his loneliness. He had no
job, no real male friend, no girlfriends and, in his mind, no real
prospect of ever having a girlfriend.

Ryan decided against a lie-in that hot August morning. He
had other things to attend to. With the forethought displayed by
Charles Whitman two decades earlier, Ryan dressed himself in
his camouflaged paramilitary gear, with a bulletproof flak-
jacket and a headband. He packed an AK47 semi-automatic
assault rifle along with an M1 carbine into his car boot. He also
packed a makeshift survival kit including a groundsheet, food,
water and magazines. He picked up a 9mm Beretta pistol, then
drove to Savernake Forest, a beauty spot nine miles away.

Some evidence suggests Ryan had sex on his mind as well
as murder and it may well have been a botched attempt at
rape that triggered the massacres. Mrs Susan Godfrey, a
33-year-old housewife from nearby Reading, had taken her
two children, aged four and two, to Savernake for a picnic. It
was holiday time and the forest was a favourite spot for
family outings. At gunpoint Ryan forced her to strap her children into their car seats and then marched her off into the
woods. She either struggled or ran because, without raping her,
he shot her dead. Leaving the children unharmed he ran to his

car and returned to Hungerford. By now he had passed the point of no return.

This seems evident by an incident at a petrol station which he stopped at en-route. After filling up he aimed a burst of gunfire at a woman attendant, who knew him by sight. Luckily the woman dived unharmed to the floor. Ryan acted as if he didn't care and drove off to his home. Once there, like Whitman, he killed the only two living things who cared for him, his mother and his dog. Ryan set fire to the family home, retrieved and reloaded his AK47, pocketed the Beretta and began a ten-minute stroll through a Hungerford suburb that was to claim 14 more lives and leave as many wounded.

Stunned witnesses recall the events as surrealistic, almost as if in slow motion, a strange dream that was not really happening. Ryan did not have a tower from which to take aim. He calmly walked along tree-lined roads, stopped, took aim, fired and walked on to the next target. An elderly man doing his garden was shot dead; a man walking his dog died when he wandered into Ryan's sights; a motorist on his way to hospital to visit his wife and new-born son was shot dead. So too was an unarmed policeman who arrived near the scene in his patrol car; next were a woman and her daughter who happened to drive by. Others were shot dead as they stood in their gardens and motorists who realized they had driven into a massacre died before they could reverse their way out of the madness. In ten minutes a quiet summer suburb was a scene of silent carnage, twisted bodies lay in pools of blood, and cars had crashed at odd angles with dead drivers still at their wheels. It had all happened so quickly, so matter-of-factly.

Ryan eventually holed-up in his old school while police negotiators tried to reason with him and helicopters hovered overhead. He told one of them: "I should have stayed in bed." In the early evening, after several hours, a shot rang out from a school classroom. After tentative minutes police found Ryan dead. He had shot himself in the temple with his Beretta.

Whitman's death was also a type of suicide, he continued to kill until he left officers no choice but to kill him. He had no intention of surrendering when he was surrounded on the observation deck. Marc Lepine, a 25-year-old spree killer from Montreal, also took his own life.

Lepine, a French-speaking unemployed man who hated feminists, ran amok at the University of Montreal in December, 1989. He prowled the campus with a .22 Storm Ruger rifle selecting only female victims. He shot three women in the cafeteria of the engineering building before bursting into a classroom and separating students into two groups, male and female. He ordered the men to leave before firing on the women killing six and wounding all the others. Lepine went on to shoot three other women dead in a nearby computer room and then began stalking the corridors to shoot those who had fled – and he finally shot himself.

In the cases of Whitman, Ryan and Lepine all three men eventually gave in to pressure in an explosion of murderous rage. Once their twisted statements had been made they were quite prepared to die as there was nothing left to live for. Their careful preparations of weapons and food were as much a preparation for their own deaths. They had no intention of living beyond their awful final gestures.

*******************

The FBI carefully categorizes killers into specific groups. Those who kill four or more people during one incident are regarded as 'mass murderers' and they fall into various categories. Someone who murders four or more members of their family is a 'family mass murderer'. The slaying in the same location of four or more people, unknown to the killer, is carried out by the 'classic mass murderer'. The person who murders four or more people in more than one location without a cooling off period is the 'spree killer' and, of course, the murderer who kills and kills again with cooling off periods in between is the 'serial killer'.

Whitman, under strict FBI groupings, is the 'classic mass murderer', he killed all his victims, except his wife and mother, in one location. Nevertheless we group him as a 'spree killer' because his murders did not take place in mere moments of frenzy. Over a period of hours he shot, reloaded, sought out more victims then shot again, thinking out his warped actions as he waited for the inevitable storming of his citadel.

Similarly, we class another killer who might otherwise be regarded as a 'classic mass murderer' into the 'spree killer' category. His murder of eight student nurses in their two-storey Chicago townhouse spanned three horrific hours. One by one he led the young women into adjoining rooms where he punched, kicked, stabbed and strangled them, clinically and quietly, so as not to alarm his next victim.

The tattoo on Richard Speck's left forearm was a macabre omen, it read simply, "Born To Raise Hell". He had it etched into his skin when he was 19. Years later when he was serving a 400 to 1,200 year prison sentence for his crimes he burned it off with the ember of his lit cigar.

Speck was born in Kirkwood, Illinois, in December, 1941. His father died when he was six years old. He grew up in Dallas, Texas, where at the age of 20 he married 15-year-old Shirley Malone with whom he had a daughter. Speck already had a criminal record with ten arrests for a variety of crimes including criminal trespass and burglary. The marriage broke up with him claiming he had a whore for a wife after finding she had been prone to infidelity. He transferred his hatred for his wife to other women. He was aggressive and violent to most women he came into contact with.

In the mid-60s he headed back up north to Chicago, getting work on the ore boats that plied the rivers and Great Lakes where much of his time was spent reading comics, drinking excessively and popping pills. The violent drifter was fast becoming an alcoholic junkie.

On the night of July 13, 1966, the 25-year-old was hanging around Chicago's National Maritime Union looking for another ship. As usual he was drinking heavily with other sailors when one of them offered him a shot of drugs. He didn't know what it was but injected it anyway. He felt a warm, familiar glow and claimed he remembered nothing of the next few terrible hours.

At about 11 pm he undid a window screen at the back of Jeffrey Manor, a townhouse on East 100th Street, owned by the South Chicago Community Hospital and used as a nurses' residence. Reaching through, he unlocked the back door and searched the ground floor where he found nothing. He took out a gun and a knife and went upstairs. The account what followed was made by the only surviving woman of the nine young nurses who found themselves in the townhouse that night.

Twenty-three-year-old Corazon Amurao, a Philippino student nurse, was awakened by a soft knock on her bedroom door. Her two Philippino room-mates, Valentina Pasion, 23, and Merlita Gargullo, 22, were sound asleep. When Corazon turned the key the door was pushed back and there in the semi-darkness stood a pock-marked man, smelling of alcohol, holding a knife in one hand and pointing a gun in the other. The other two women were roused terrified from their beds. "I'm not going to hurt you," Speck told them, and he ordered them onto the landing. Moving on to the next room he found three other young nurses, Pamela Wilkening, Nina Schmale and Patricia Matusek. "I'm not going to hurt you. I'm just going to tie you up. I need some money to get to New Orleans," he told the six women. Wanting to co-operate with the drunken man the nurses volunteered to get their purses and let him have all their cash. He seemed genuinely gentle and they made no attempt to get away as one by one they went to get their cash and one by one they returned to the room where he sat with his knife and gun. "I'm just going to tie you up," he repeated. "I want to get to New Orleans."

The nurses were all bound by their hands and ankles with torn up strips of bedsheets. He had barely finished tying the last one when Gloria Davy, who was the new president of the Illinois Student Nurses Association, arrived home. She was seized at the door and marched upstairs to join her friends.

Speck now had seven young nurses, most of them in nightclothes bound on the floor at his feet, and one can only assume he was aroused by the possibilities and the power of the situation. The only survivor said he seemed to become agitated as he walked over to 20-year-old Pamela Wilkening, untied her ankles and ordered her to stand up. He ushered her out of the door and closed it. In the next room he stabbed her with the butcher's knife. The other nurses heard a slight scream. It later transpired he had stabbed her in the left breast and silenced her by strangling her with a strip of the sheeting he had used to bind her feet.

The nurses heard the door open downstairs. Suzanne Farris had arrived home with her future sister-in-law Mary Ann Jordan, who didn't live on the premises but tragically had chosen this night to stay there. They walked chatting into the rear bedroom and found the six remaining nurses wide-eyed and bound on the floor. Before they could react Speck appeared behind them and led them from the room, once again closing the door. Corazon Amurao said she and her room-mates heard the same muffled squeals and gasps. Both women had been stabbed, Mary Jordan in the body and eye. Suzanne Farris had put up a fierce struggle and received 18 stab wounds in her breasts and neck and was also strangled before he dumped her body in the bath.

The six women in the other room, still unaware of the horror, heard the taps running, but they didn't realize at the time that Speck was washing blood off himself. Then there was silence for 20 minutes. He came back into the nurses room and selected Nina Schmale, 24. Once again there was the muffled cry, the running tap and a terrifying silence. Nina was stabbed four times in the neck, and so the ritual continued.

The remaining five nurses feared the worse and tried to scramble beneath beds and behind furniture, but Speck checked under the beds and pulled out Valentina Pasion. She too was stabbed to death. Merlita Gargullo was also dragged struggling from beneath a bed, Corazon heard her die in the next room. Corazon, a slightly built woman, had by now wriggled beneath one of the beds in a darkened corner and squeezed herself against the wall.

Speck came back and of the two nurses he could see he took Patricia Matusek to the bathroom, kicked her violently in the

stomach and strangled her. Not realizing one of the nurses was
only visiting the townhouse he had counted eight beds and
tallied them with eight bodies. He thought his eighth victim
Gloria Davy was the last, so he didn't even bother to take her
from the room as he had the other victims. Instead he removed
Gloria's jeans and while a petrified Corazon looked on from her
hiding place he raped her. Corazon would always remember his
tattoo 'Born To Raise Hell'.

Gloria was the only victim to be sexually assaulted, and one
can only assume the murder spree had aroused Speck. He then
took her downstairs and further abused and mutilated her.
Finally he left her, strangled and naked in the sitting room.
Speck returned to the bedroom to make sure no one was left
alive, and satisfied, he left the house.

Corazon Amurao cowered beneath the bed, unsure whether
the killer was teasing her and just waiting for her to crawl out;
she lay motionless for hours. Eventually, at 5 am, she crawled
out, at first in relief and then in horror at the carnage in every
room. From a ledge at the front of the house the first witnesses
heard her scream: "Oh my God, all my friends are dead. I'm the
only one alive."

Speck had meanwhile returned to his 90 cent room at the
Shipyard Inn. He later claimed to be puzzled when the water
turned red as he washed his hands, "It was as if I'd been
bleeding." As he toured the maritime bars the main topic of
conversation was the mass murders and the fact that police were
scouring the area as the nurses had been bound with a sailor's
square knot. Speck, who had jumped bail on a burglary charge
in Texas, did not want to be interviewed by police.

Meanwhile, police looking for the anonymous killer sailor
with the tell-tale tattoo had a vital lead. A clerk at a maritime
union hall remembered the tattoo. A job application form was
retrieved from a waste-paper basket, and it bore the name
Robert Speck. Fingerprints taken from the nurses home
matched those held on police files in Texas. Speck had by now
checked in at another 90 cent room at the Star Hotel on
Chicago's West Madison Street. He had heard the news reports

broadcast his name in connection with the murders which had stunned America. That night he slashed his wrists and ended up in the Cook County Hospital emergency room where he gave his real name and was promptly arrested.

At his trial the jury took just 49 minutes to return guilty verdicts. Speck was sentenced to die in the electric chair. This was commuted to what at the time was the longest-ever prison sentence handed out in the USA, up to one 1,200 years. Despite the sentence, passed in November 1972, Speck became eligible for parole in 1976. He constantly insisted he did not wish to be freed but in 1987 changed his mind and applied for parole. The Illinois Prison Review Board quickly rejected his plea and Speck died in prison from a heart attack in 1991, aged 49.

Although he was only sentenced for the murders of the nurses, Speck is suspected of four other killings, all committed within the three month period leading up to the mass murders. His first victim was Mary Pierce, a divorced barmaid who constantly rejected his advances. She disappeared on April 10, 1966, and was discovered three days later, naked and strangled in a pig-pen behind the tavern where she worked. On July 2, only 11 days before he broke into the nurses home, Speck was fired from his last ship and put ashore at Indiana Harbour. Three girls disappeared from nearby Indiana Dunes that day, their clothes were found in their car but their bodies have never been discovered.

Speck spoke freely to prison psychiatrist Marvin Ziporyn while awaiting trial. The doctor was convinced the killer was genuine about the 'black-out' during which he carried out the systematic and brutal murders in the nurses home. He was also sure that Speck's psychopathic behaviour was mainly due to a series of head injuries which he sustained in his childhood and youth. Drugs and alcohol would have aggravated any brain damage. When Speck was three months old he contracted pneumonia. Doctors told his mother that lack of oxygen to the baby's brain may have caused some damage; as a tot, Speck was knocked unconscious when a shotgun fell on his head and at the age of five he knocked himself out with a hammer and suffered from dizzy spells afterwards. At the age of ten he underwent a personality change after a more serious head injury when he fell from a swing and was unconscious for more than an hour. He became short-tempered and aggressive; at 14 he suffered further head injurys when he fell from a tree and then knocked himself out when he drove his bicycle into a parked car.

He developed a dual-personality. His family recalled him as gentle one moment and enraged and physically violent the next. The violent behaviour increased as Speck grew older and turned to drink and drugs, for which he had a low tolerance, to relieve his persistent headaches.

His dual-personality intensified in the presence of women. His affable nature invited sympathy which enraged him because he felt it sapped his manhood, according to one psychiatrist. Dr Ziporyn speculated that Speck's murderous urges towards the nurses were triggered by just such a demonstration. Corazon Amurao recalled she and her friends showed friendship towards him because they were touched by his initial gentle manner. "This friendliness was another assault on his masculinity and moved him to violence," said Dr Ziporyn.

********************

Ronald 'Butch' DeFeo Jnr tiptoed lightly up the the stairs, both hands clasped tightly around his .35 Marlin rifle, struggling to control his heavy breathing as he crept into his parents' bedroom. He took aim at his sleeping father's broad back and fired twice, his mother sat up as her husband writhed in his death throes. He fired two shots into her throwing her backwards, dead into her pillow. The 23-year-old man calmly moved on to the bedroom of his 13-year-old sister, Allison. She sat up, puzzled and sleepy. 'Butch' shot her in the head at point blank range. He crossed the hall into the bedroom where his two brothers, Mark, 12, and John, seven, slept. Standing between the twin beds he fired once into one brother, turned and fired again into the other; both boys died instantly. 'Butch' reloaded and climbed upstairs to the third floor and the bedroom of his 18-year-old sister, Dawn, and shot her in the base of the skull.

After the eldest son had murdered all six members of his family he went to the bathroom, vomited, showered and dressed for work. On the drive from Long Island to Brooklyn he threw the rifle into a canal. By the end of the day the family home on Ocean Avenue in Amityville was to become world famous.

A weeping 'Butch' DeFeo told police he had found his family slaughtered when he got home from work. At first he suggested to officers that a Mafia contact known to the family may have carried out the murders, but within two days he cracked and admitted he was the killer. "Once I started, I just couldn't stop," he told detectives.

At his trial his defence attempted to prove 'Butch' was insane, he insisted that voices told him to kill. After three days the jury found him guilty of second degree murder and he was jailed for 150 years.

Things had not been good in the Amityville home for a long time before the killings in November, 1974. Ronald DeFeo senior, his wife Louise and family moved into the house called 'High Hopes' in 1965. It was an upmarket move to Long Island for the Italian-American family from Brooklyn and their new ocean-front property boasted a swimming pool and a boat house. DeFeo senior was the service manager at a car dealership firm owned by his father-in-law. He wanted the best for his family and indulged his children, although he and his eldest son didn't always see eye-to-eye.

'Butch' felt he couldn't live up to his father's expectations, so he became violent at home and in return his father used violence on him, which didn't help. After attacking his sister during a family row, 'Butch' was sent to a psychiatrist who noted the overweight teenager was terrified of his father and needed an escape valve for his feelings. There wasn't one and consequently 'Butch' was expelled from various schools and left at 16 without graduating. He drifted from job to job and, to escape from the rows with his father, he turned to drink and drugs and spent long hours locked in his room. During one argument 'Butch', who collected guns, aimed a rifle at his father and pulled the trigger. It didn't go off. 'Butch' tried several times to leave home but even though he was in his early 20s his traditionally-minded father wouldn't hear of it. "I'll give you all the money you want. All I want you to do is live in this house," he told his troubled son. 'Butch', who knew he would be cut off without a penny if he left home, at one stage warned his father: "I'm going to kill you if I stay here."

After the murders and court case made headlines across America and after another family were driven from the Amityville home by strange occurrences a variety of theories were put forward regarding the DeFeo murders. One suggested the house stood on an ancient Indian burial ground which had been cursed after it was disturbed. 'Butch' DeFeo was later to claim he underwent a personality change after moving there at the age of 13. "I became cold and vicious inside." A medium who visited the property two years after the murders insisted people who lived there became possessed by the spirit of a long dead Indian chief. In law however, it was decided the only spirits and demons around were in 'Butch' DeFeo's head.

********************

Not all murder sprees are over in minutes or hours. Some last for days and, like Speck and DeFeo, not all spree killers choose to become victims of their own carnage. Teenager Charles Starkweather and his 14-year-old girlfriend Caril Ann Fugate went on a week-long rampage that left ten people dead. Their victims were aged from two years to 70. Age and sex didn't matter. They killed anyone they came into contact with as they blazed a trail across Nebraska early in 1958.

'Little Red' Charlie Starkweather was a 19-year-old sociopath. He was short in every sense of the word – short in size at five feet two, short sighted, short-tempered, short in education and short on friends. Bow-legged and red-haired, he felt short-changed by society.

His childhood was impoverished. The runt of the litter, he was the third of eight children born in 1940 to parents who struggled to make a living in Lincoln, Nebraska. His clothes were second-hand and he grew up resenting most people, remembering and recalling every perceived sleight against him. He remembered his first day at school as heartbreaking as none of the other children wanted to be near him and he played alone in a sandpit. He said he was mocked and developed a hate "as hard as iron" which drew him into countless schoolyard fights. Years later, while awaiting execution, he wrote in his own bad grammar and spelling: "I fought fast and a little furiously like a maniac in a rage and fury and as I fought sense of outrage grew to striving, to throw, to bend, to hurt and most of all to beat those who teased me...My fighting reputation stayed with me throughout my school years and even after I had stopped going to school that reputation stayed with me, but my rebellion started against the world and the human race when I was being made fun at."

Aged 15, his myopia was discovered too late to salvage an education taught for years from a blackboard he could barely see. He became a dustman, his job in life being to empty the garbage of those better off than him. His anti-social behaviour extended to cursing at passers-by from the back of the garbage truck. In his late teens Chuck Starkweather did his best to dress and comb his hair like his idol James Dean. Of the two men who came from worlds apart, Chuck was the real rebel without a cause.

The only positive thing in Starkweather's life was his girlfriend Caril Ann Fugate. "Being alone with her was like owning a little world all our own," he later wrote. "I forgot about my bow legs when me and Caril was having excitement." He liked the way she swore, wore make-up and slept with him, and she liked the way he lavished attention and what little money he had on her. He thought nothing of buying her jewellery while his clothes came from second-hand stores. He gave up his job so he could take her home from school, which was also an indication of his insecurity. He probably feared she might meet someone else unless he was with her as much as possible. Caril lived with her mother, stepfather and two-year-old step-sister.

Starkweather, always short of money, due to his courtship with Caril Ann, committed his first murder at 3 am on

December 1, 1957. Masked in a bandanna, he held up and robbed a petrol station at the point of a shotgun. Twenty-one-year-old Robert Colvert handed over 108 dollars but was driven to a remote spot and shot in the head. Starkweather later claimed Colvert had fought him and he had shot the man in self-defence. This is unlikely as Colvert was known to Starkweather, who resented him. No one suspected Starkweather as the killer and he derived great satisfaction from this, his first taste of success, a sense of power at outwitting authority. "I learned something, something I already knowed, that a man could have money without haulin' garbage."

He spent the next seven weeks relishing this feeling and most of the time was passed with Caril Ann spending the money and practising his shooting and knife-throwing. The murder spree began on January 21, 1958, at Caril's home. There are two versions of what happened. Caril Ann said her family was dead when she arrived home from school, but Starkweather told a different story.

When he visited Caril's home he spoke to her mother Mrs Velda Bartlett who was looking after her toddler Betty Jean. She told Starkweather she and her husband, Marion Bartlett, did not want him to see Caril again. During an argument she slapped the youth. "She just got up and slammed the shit out of me, in the face." He drove off and returned later only to be literally kicked out of the door by Marion. "Kicked me right in the ass. My tail hurt for three days." He said he returned a third time and happened to have his brother's .22 hunting rifle with him. Caril was in the middle of a fierce argument with her mother who falsely accused Starkweather of getting her daughter pregnant. She slapped him again but this time the youth retaliated and hit her in the face knocking her backwards. Marion Bartlett began struggling with Starkweather who claimed the man went off in search of a weapon, and when he returned he was brandishing a claw hammer. Starkweather shot him in the head. Mrs Bartlett went at him with a butcher's knife and she too was shot in the head and staggered over to the child. Starkweather followed her and clubbed her to death with the rifle butt, and he also clubbed the toddler who started screaming. Starkweather then picked up the butcher's knife to finish off Marion Bartlett who was writhing about, but he threw it at the toddler and hit her in the throat, killing her. He then finished off the father.

After stuffing the bodies into outhouses the teenage couple spent the next week living it up in the Fugate home, and Starkweather said it was the best time of his life with nobody to order him around. They left only when they thought worried relatives might alert police of their concerns. Officers had called once and read the sign on the kitchen door "Stay away Every Body is sick with the Flue." They spoke to Caril who seemed very calm, but other members of the family had their doubts.

The young couple left Lincoln on January 28 and drove to the farm of 70-year-old August Meyer, an old friend of the Starkweathers. Their car got stuck in mud on the farm driveway. "Caril got pissed off because we got stuck. She said we ought to go up and blast the shit out of him because he didn't shovel his lane." Meyer was shot dead along with his dog. Starkweather and his girlfriend ransacked the house for food and money and made off with clothing, a .22 pump action rifle and the sawn off shotgun that they taken from Caril's home.

With the car still stuck in the mud they were offered a lift by a young couple who were everything Starkweather and his girlfriend knew they could never be, and so they murdered them. Seventeen-year-old Robert Jensen and his fiancée Carol King were popular high school sweethearts, intelligent and middle class. Starkweather demanded Jensen hand over his money and drive to an abandoned school, he then ordered him down the steps of the storm cellar and shot him six times in the head. Carol King's death was a source of conflict between Starkweather and Fugate. Both agreed he was in the cellar with her for 15 minutes and at first he said he had shot her but later claimed Caril was the killer. King was found with her coat pulled over her head with her jeans and panties around her ankles. Starkweather said he had been tempted to rape her and had removed her jeans but then Caril had murdered her in a jealous frenzy. The young girl had suffered several stab wounds and mutilation to her groin area, but there was however, no traces of sperm and no indication of sexual attack.

On January 29 for reasons known only to them, Starkweather and Fugate went back to Lincoln and drove past her house which by now was swarming with police. They drove on to cruise the wealthy Country Club section of town, slept in the car overnight and then invaded the home of a wealthy industrialist. Starkweather had once emptied the garbage from the mansion of C Lauer Ward, president of a group of steel companies. The 47-year-old businessman lived with his wife Clara, 46, and their maid Lillian Fencl, who was 51.

Mr Ward was at work when Starkweather and Fugate forced themselves into the house at gunpoint. Starkweather insisted Mrs Ward, not the maid, prepare him some food. "They was real nice to us and I took it while I had it. I knew it couldn't last long." The couple toured the rooms of the mansion, open-mouthed at its opulence.

Starkweather claimed Mrs Ward took a shot at him with her son's rifle so he threw a knife at her which struck her in the back. "She was moaning and groaning. I dragged her into her bedroom and laid her on the bed and just left her there." After killing her dog he returned to the bedroom where Mrs Ward was found on the floor, in a nightdress, with stab wounds to her neck, chest and back. Lillian Fencl was found tied to a bed with multiple stab wounds all over her body, including her arms and legs. After these killings Starkweather and Fugate sat back to await the return of Mr Ward. He was found the next day just inside the doorway. He had been shot in the back and head and also been stabbed. Starkweather and Fugate made their getaway in the Ward's conspicuous black Packard limousine.

With the murder spree death toll at nine, the Nebraska National Guard were called out and heavily armed troopers toured the streets. Conscious of their ostentatious vehicle Starkweather decided they needed another car. He stopped alongside a Buick parked just off the highway. Inside, 37-year-old salesman Merle Collison was sleeping. He was woken by the youth who demanded they swap cars, and when Collison refused Starkweather shot him seven times.

By now another driver had arrived at the scene thinking there had been an accident. Starkweather pulled his gun and a struggle began in the middle of the highway. A Wyoming Deputy Sheriff drove up and Caril jumped into his vehicle shouting: "He's killed a man." Starkweather gave up the struggle for the gun and made off in the Packard towards Douglas, Wyoming. With the limousine leading the way followed by the Deputy Sheriff's car and several other police vehicles, a 100-mile-an-hour chase worthy of the movies began. The convoy slowed slightly in the Douglas traffic but this soon cleared as police began shooting at the Packard's tyres. The cars sped out of Douglas at speeds of up to 120-miles-an-hour before Starkweather stopped and surrendered after his rear window had been shattered by bullets and he had been cut by showers of glass.

He was executed in the electric chair in Nebraska State Prison on June 24, 1959, aged 20. Caril Ann Fugate, who claimed she had been forced to accompany her boyfriend and played no part in the killings, was sentenced to life imprisonment. She was freed on parole in June, 1976, almost 17 years to the day her boyfriend was executed.

# 9

# The Sexual Sadist

*"They were trash before I put them out with the trash." – serial killer Bob Berdella talking about his victims.*

*Interview recorded with sexual sadist Robert Berdella by Mike Morley of Central Television.*

Robert Andrew Berdella is a sexual sadist who aged 35, captured, tortured and murdered six men in Kansas in the late 1980s. He subjected his victims to a catalogue of inhumanities, took photographs and kept meticulous notes on each stage of their agony. Before killing and dismembering his victims, Berdella injected drain cleaner into their throats, sodomized them with a variety of objects and pumped more than 7,000 volts of electricity through their naked bodies.

In July 1992 we flew to Kansas to interview Berdella in the high-security 'lifers' wing at the Jefferson City Correctional Centre. . Berdella had been picked for a variety of reasons, the main one being that he is exceptionally intelligent, with an IQ of around 120. He is also ruthless and cunning. At one point, he hired his own psychologist to help put together a defence that would cheat the State's death penalty.

After fully assessing the strength of the police case against him, Bob Berdella believed the State would only have sufficient evidence to proceed on one possible count of first degree murder. His counsel entered into a plea-bargain with the Prosecuting Attorneys and in return for a life-sentence in jail, he admitted all six killings. This saved the State a small fortune. It avoided any potential embarrassment in court and it allowed detectives to identify all of Berdella's victims and put their families out of the trauma of uncertainty.

There was one other condition to the deal which allowed Berdella to escape Death Row. In December 1988 he had to agree to give a sworn statement, answering any questions the prosecutors cared to put to him. Berdella was true to his word. The deposition lasted three days and went into stomach-churning detail of what he'd done and how he'd done it.

In writing to Berdella, we indicated that we thought his three day interview session was in some ways disappointing and this hit a nerve. Berdella too had felt let down. He told us he'd been looking for the chance to discuss his crimes openly in order to find some answers of his own. Further research also showed that apart from a very basic psychiatric assessment to determine his place in prison, Berdella had received no real counselling. It all added up to the opportunity to carry out a crucial interview with one of the world's most sadistic serial murderers.

Before we even flew from England, we knew there were complications with the interview. Berdella was being sued by some of the victims' families. They had found a loophole in the law that allowed them to take action against him under his household insurance. Their multi-million dollar claim was that Berdella hadn't intended to kill some of his victims – they had died accidentally, as an unintentional result of torture.

This allowed the families to claim on Berdella's insurance, just as someone who had fallen and injured themselves in his garden could have done. This twist had led Berdella to caution that in at least two of his victim's cases he would be guarded about what he was going to say.

There was another worry too. We discussed the case with Paul Britton who interviewed Dennis Nilsen for British offender profiling research. We sought his advice on the possible effects the interview might have on Berdella. If it did manage to bring him face-to-face with the motivations for his crimes and the pleasures he enjoyed, then he could well be traumatized by the result. We worried about leaving such a depressed interviewee in a prison environment where there would be no psychological support for him. Paul, who had carried out many clinical interviews and assessments of psychopaths, murderers and rapists, was also troubled by this. The advice and guidelines that he kindly gave us for the Berdella interview would prove to be invaluable.

Before interviewing Berdella we had arranged to film with Sergeant Troy Cole, the man who headed the task force that caught him. We met in the plush, wood-panelled lounge of the Ritz-Carlton Hotel in Jefferson City. He strode across the opulent room exuding confidence, a well-built detective in his early 40s with a vice-like handshake. First impressions are everything, and everything about Cole was functional. His suit was plain but immaculately tailored and well pressed, his shoes were totally unscuffed and brilliantly polished, his receding blond-hair had been stylishly fashioned into a near Military-length cut.

We drove across town with the detective pointing out where Berdella had lived, worked and played. We touched briefly on the background to the case and Berdella's homosexuality. He was a known cruiser in the red light area down on 10th and McGee, picking up male prostitutes and taking them back to his house for sex. His home on Charlotte Street was full of what Cole called "down-and-outers, no-hopers, chicken-hawks (homosexual prostitutes) and drug addicts."

It seemed that Berdella would allow many people to stay at his house free of charge, if they promised to perform sexual acts with him or carry out menial chores around the dilapidated three-storey home. Berdella was also a small-time drug dealer with a criminal record for dealing. His 'gear' was soft drugs such as valium, marijuana and forms of tranquilizers and sedatives that he would inject into people.

Cole stopped his metallic grey Chevrolet outside 4315 Charlotte and squinted up at the top window. It was from here that Berdella's seventh victim had jumped for his life. Naked, except for a dog-collar, 22-year-old Christopher Bryson had leapt onto the concrete below and staggered to a nearby house to call the Kansas City Police Department.

"I was working what we call 'The Floor' on the Saturday morning of April 2, 1988 when I received a call from a uniformed officer. He told me there was a naked white man who was telling this story about being held captive inside a residence. At that moment I sent a detective out to see if there was any truth in it. When we responded, we found that the young man who had escaped did, in fact, have very severe injuries which were consistent with the story he was giving about being tied to a bed for a number of days and physically and sexually tortured."

Cole admitted he was not sure at the time whether they were not simply looking at a homosexual lovers' quarrel that had gone too far. The scars to the man's body indicated torture, but he may have consented to that torture as part of a sado-masochistic relationship, or he might even have been paid for it as prostitute. This functional detective would not believe anything, unless it was proved to him beyond a shadow of a doubt.

"We were at the house here and were about to check out the victim's allegations when the homeowner, Robert Berdella, returned to the property and wanted to know what all the police were doing around the place. We asked him what his name was and when he told us, we immediately arrested him and asked for his consent to search the building. He refused. We went ahead and got a search warrant and upon entering the residence we found numerous photographs of young white males in various stages of sexual and physical torture. We also found a human skull inside one of the closets."

The photographs had been recovered from beneath a mattress in an upstairs bedroom. As Cole flicked through the poorly taken stills he warned of their graphic and disturbing nature. The first showed Berdella's house, filled with junk, the floor littered with newspapers and dog faeces. Boxes and boxes of jumble and magazines spilled all over the place. High in the corner of a room, at the end of an unpainted wooden shelf was the broken skull of Robert Sheldon, Berdella's second victim. Another shot showed one of the bloodied gags, made from a washcloth and a cord that Berdella had used. He had bound this so tightly it cut through the lips and corners of his captive's mouth. A head and shoulders shot showed an unconscious man with a needle filled with bleach sticking out of his voice-box. Another showed a man naked from the waist down, his arms tied behind his back around a wooden pole and his back arching upwards off the bed in agony. He was gagged and there were ligatures around his neck. From his shoulder dangled a metal crocodile clip and a long wire snaked out of view. The man's face was contorted with pain, his eyes bulging and skin straining from the 7,500 volts being charged through his helpless frame.

Some of the pictures were detailed shots, close-ups of the emaciated faces of the victims or their broken hands. Others Berdella took while sodomizing the men with cucumbers, carrots or his own fists or penis.

There were dozens of photographs, each as sickening as the last. "After seeing these photographs, after recovering them from inside the residence and seeing these individuals in these severe states of torture, a red flag went up. I thought, yeah, there probably is something more to this than just a lovers' quarrel. But, I don't think it was until the next day when we were digging up the back yard of the residence and we dug up a human skull out of that yard, that it really hit me that this was a lot more serious than I had ever envisioned."

Troy Cole still wasn't sure what he had on his hands. The escaped torture victim Christopher Bryson was not a good witness. In order to conceal the fact that he had been working as a prostitute when Berdella picked him up, he lied about several aspects in his statement. Bryson said he'd been given a lift by a man and a woman and had caught the ride in an entirely different and far more respectable part of the City. Still, the detective was sure that if nothing else, there were seven charges of sodomy that could be brought against Berdella, probably two more statutory crimes, of first degree assault (for the batterings and electrocution) and of felonious restraint (for the bindings and gaggings). The police studied the photographs of the tortured victims; those who had been electrocuted, beaten, and violated in a dozen different ways. Identifying them was a real problem. Even when faces were put to some of the pictures, investigators were shocked to find that some of the polaroids had been taken during consenting sexual relationships.

Cole added, "It was the most unusual case I'd ever worked on. It was unusual for a lot of reasons, one being that we had a suspect in custody and didn't know who his victims were. In most investigations you know who the victims are but have no idea who the suspect is. As far as figuring out what made Berdella tick, I don't think that entered our minds until much later in the inquiry. My first concern was to get this guy charged, get a high bond (financial bail limit) and put him in jail where he belonged."

Cole was still a long way off a murder charge. Aside from the nine 'holding' charges, police had to prove that it was Berdella who had taken the sadistic photographs, that he'd taken part in the acts and that he'd forced the men in the polaroids to take part against their wills. There were the skulls in the house, but whose skulls were they? Berdella would argue that he'd innocently bought them for his junk stall and artifacts dealings. There were no other body parts around the house or garden. As Cole put it, "He cleaned up real good."

Speculation began to suggest that Bob Berdella had dismembered his victims after killing them and then fed the human flesh to the giant Chow dogs he bred as a sideline. Forensic searches of the home revealed microscopic traces of human blood, and more splatters and spots were found in the tool shed in the garden and near the dog kennels. It was a start, but there was no real chance of saying which humans the blood had come from.

Attention moved from the photographs to a peculiar diary Berdella had kept. It was strange because it looked as though it had been written in a personal code. Entries included: 11.45 2cc.s ace. No Response. BF. Snoring.12:30 BF 2cc.s Chlora. These abbreviations and notations would eventually be decoded to show that at a quarter to midnight, Berdella had injected his already drugged victim, with two cc.s of the tranquillizer Acepromazine and had then had anal sex with him (Butt Fuck). Berdella recorded that after the assault the man fell asleep and

was wheezing or snoring. Forty-five minutes later he adminis-
tered two and a half cc.s of Chlorpromazine and repeated
the sodomy.

The studied injections and careful notes intrigued Troy Cole:
"In his torture diaries he would write down the various stages of
torture and the types of animal tranquillizers he was injecting. It
was almost like he was playing doctor with the victims. He
would give them enough injections to make them unconscious,
he'd abuse them and then when their health started going down-
hill, he'd start giving them shots of penicillin to try and bring
them back again."

In interviews with Berdella there was only one winner. The
fat homosexual sadist was light years ahead of his interrogators.
Cole says he considered interviewing Berdella to be a complete
waste of time. He says he knew from the start that Berdella was
too bright to let anything slip. He told colleagues they should
concentrate on proving the murders, rather than trying to illicit a
confession. In some ways, Cole looked on confessions as
cheating; he wanted to sew-up an air-tight case on evidence and
send Bob Berdella to the Kansas gas chamber.

In one incident that Cole had advised against, Berdella was
subjected to an intense version of the now exceptionally clichéd
trick of good-policeman/bad policeman. Instead of simply
having Berdella encounter different personalities; in an attempt
to discover his psychological weaknesses and overwhelm him,
they devised an elaborate scheme that they hoped would
provoke a confession. One afternoon, Berdella was taken to a
medical room where a number of Kansas City Police Officers
waited, along with a search warrant for the suspect's body.
They'd obtained from a judge permission to photograph
Berdella's entire naked body (to compare with the polaroid
torture pictures) and also take samples from his scalp, moustache and pubic areas. They made Berdella simulate the positions of sexual abuse in the seized pictures. They showed him
the stills, instructed him to undress and assume a similar pose.
They warned him that if he didn't comply, they'd call in guards
and force him into the staged positions. Throughout this

awkward hour, the policemen reassured Berdella that none of it was meant to embarrass him. They duly reported that the suspect wasn't embarrassed, just slightly irritated.

The next part of the plan was even more ludicrous and even less successful. A theory had been developed that Berdella's ego could be played on if he was shown how important the case had become in Kansas. The star of the unusual photo-call was now chauffeured across town for his next appearance. Doors were opened for him. He was met by courteous police officers who instantly recognized him and passed polite but not ingratiating remarks such as, "Good Morning, Berdella." With more bodyguards than Madonna, he was ushered through to a specially prepared room. Outside hung a large official sign saying 'BERDELLA SQUAD'. Inside, flow-charts and blow-up photographs were pinned across the walls, scores of detectives names (many more than ever worked on the case) were written on blackboards and had been assigned non-existent duties. Berdella was led to a specially arranged interview area, where he was given a large padded seat, his accompanying detectives made to sit on smaller wooden chairs.

He was read his rights and was then politely asked a number of personal questions such as height, weight, marital status, etc.

With the preliminaries over, the detectives moved in on their prey. Now they would know if all the psychological manoeuvres had worked. They cautiously mentioned one of the identified victims, James Ferris. Berdella immediately shut down on them. He told them to cut the chit-chat and get him a lawyer. It had all been a waste of time. Worse still, it had been a clear indication to Berdella that they had little to go on and had been fishing for a lead.

Soon after this, Cole got one of the breaks he was hoping for. Seven of the less gruesome torture photographs were shown on local television stations, in an effort to identify the victims. One man, Paul Howell, recognized an unconscious figure as his missing son Jerry. The rest of the shot, showing that he was bound, gagged and hanging naked from the ceiling by his feet, had been cropped off.

Experts gave Cole another break. Dental checks confirmed that one of the skulls was that of Robert Sheldon. Identification of the other victims followed, slowly and painfully for the families of many missing youngsters who contemplated whether their children had been killed by Berdella.

Eventually, Cole had what he wanted, the identity of a suspect and the identities of the victims he was believed to have killed. They were firstly Jerry Howell, captured on the July 5, 1984, killed July 6, 1984. Secondly, Robert Sheldon, taken captive on April 12,1985 and killed three days later. Then Mark Wallace, captured on June 22, 1985 and killed the day after. Berdella kidnapped Walter Ferris on September 25, 1985 and murdered him two days later. In 1986 on June 17 he took Todd Stoops captive and killed him on July 1. A year later he captured his final murder victim Larry Pearson and killed him on the August 5, 1987.

Berdella had been careless with his seventh victim, Chris Bryson. He had terrorized Bryson so much in the early days of his captivity he was certain the young man would not try to escape. Bryson had told police of his unbelievable ordeal in the house on Charlotte Street and it would turn out to be a chillingly close miss to the same fate already suffered by his fellow victims.

After picking Bryson up on 10th and McGee, Berdella took him to the house and gave him some beer. As the drinking continued, he suggested going upstairs to have sex. Bryson led the way up the narrow staircase and Berdella hit him with a two foot long iron bar, knocking him unconscious. He dragged him into the bedroom, bound him to the bedposts and sodomized him. He also rammed other objects into his anus.

Bryson told detectives he awoke to find his 6ft 2in, 210lb attacker sitting astride him. He was choking for air, trying to fathom why his mouth was stuffed with cloth. Then, as he stirred, Berdella thrust a finger deep into his eye socket. Squirming from the pain of the first attack, Bryson could never have imagined what was to follow. Berdella took a cotton-bud dipped into amonia and forced Bryson's eyelid open. He smeared the bleach across the retina. Berdella had only just

begun. He then battered Bryson's hands, fingers and arms with
an iron bar until his victim could hardly move through pain.
Only now, could the real torture commence.

The young man struggled to remain conscious, believing that
if he blacked out he'd die. Berdella clamped an electric clip to
his victim's testicles and started charging 7,700 volts of electricity through his body. As the shocks surged through him,
Bryson bit hard on the gag trying not to scream. He believed
that any sign of pain merely encouraged Berdella to more
monstrous acts. He was conscious of blinding light and whirring
noises, not shocks from the home-made transformer but the
bulb-flash and electronic recharge of a Polaroid camera. Next,
Bryson felt a needle jab into his tortured and blistering skin.
More sedatives surged into the veins. A second jab, this time
into the neck. The needle was boring deep towards his vocal
chords and a searing heat burned through him. The injection
was 2cc.s of draincleaner. Berdella told him, that if he screamed
or even tried to scream, he'd pump so much bleach into his
voice-box he would never speak again.

Bryson's torture continued for days but became less violent
as he became more compliant with his captor's sexual wishes.
The more he co-operated, the less he got hurt. Berdella
convinced his captive that when he went to work, he rigged the
electrocution device to electrify all the bedroom floor so that
escape attempts were pointless – if he got out of the bindings,
then he'd be electrified. If he beat the electricity trap and tried
to get downstairs then Berdella's gigantic Chow dogs would
savage him to death.

It was with trepidation that on April 2, 1988 Christopher
Bryson made his bid for freedom. By performing all forms of
oral and anal sex with his captor, he'd managed to gain some
privileges. As Berdella went to work, he agreed that the bound
and gagged Bryson could be left on the bed in such a way that
he could watch television and work the remote control handset.
He was still tethered around the neck in a dog-collar, but the
difference today, was that his hands were tied in front of him,
rather than behind him as usual. Minutes after Berdella left,

Bryson slipped the ropes from his wrists. He ripped the dog-leash from the bedhead and then using some matches left nearby, he burned the ropes that bound his legs to the bedposts.

Christopher Bryson never even thought about bypassing the dogs. He made straight for the window, praying that the floor wasn't electrocuted. In a couple of steps he made the window, it slid open and he jumped. The fall broke his foot but after the pain of the last three days it hardly registered. He was free.

Troy Cole clunked the column shift of the Chevrolet into gear and pulled away, heading back to the police station. He summed Berdella up. "He's lower than an animal. He's inhumane." This was the man we were now set to interview.

***********************

Jefferson City Correctional Centre looks like a Davy Crocket fort. It stands on high ground overlooking the pleasant middle-class development of houses, hotels and offices that straddle the fabled Missouri River. Its stone walls are topped with guard towers and the armed custodians are silhouetted against the dazzling blueness of the morning sky. Inside, in a narrow corner of an open canteen, a small table has been pushed discreetly away from the rest. Here, in the visiting area for the centre's 2,000 prisoners, we awaited the appearance of Robert Berdella.

This initial meeting had been planned through negotiations with the Centre's affable Superintendent Michael Groose. We were to be ready and waiting by 9 am, Berdella would be brought to us within minutes and we could have until late afternoon to prepare for the filmed interview the following day. Twenty minutes passed and there was still no sign of Berdella.

Behind a wall of shatterproof glass, prison keys jangled and the unmistakable clunk and scrape of heavy metal bolts announced Berdella's arrival. The killer's grey and thinning hair was swept back in a greasy tangle from his high-forehead, he walked with a shuffling stoop that made him seem much smaller than he is. He wore thick-lensed glasses above a well-trimmed moustache and deliberately avoided eye-contact until he was a foot away from the designated table.

We shook hands, his grip was weak and sweaty, and he sat down without prompting. As he dumped a giant bundle of legal-looking papers on the drink-stained table top he made an apology for keeping us waiting. His voice was low and soft and there was a slight but discernible lisp. Berdella confided that a stomach upset had given him a restless night and he had felt so bad he had been thinking of calling the entire interview off. He just hoped he'd get lots of medicine during the day or he would have to miss the planned interview tomorrow. None of this was a surprise. It was exactly the kind of behaviour we expected. He unfolded some of the heavy block of tied-up papers, explaining that he was involved in litigation against the Superintendent because of breaches of prisoners' rights. He had reluctantly been cast by the other inmates as a 'jailhouse lawyer', championing their causes and continually coming into conflict with the authorities. He also began explaining the 1.5 billion dollar civil suite involving his victims' families. Berdella had already given us a precious insight into his complex character. He'd turned up deliberately late to demonstrate whatever we planned with the prison hierarchy, he alone would decide when things happened. He had blatantly stated that he could call the interview off at any moment, using the invention of a stomach upset to attract sympathy for himself and at the same time create the opportunity to apologize for delaying us. We were to infer that because he turned up, despite the enormous pain he said he was in, then really he was a caring, generous and considerate person. Knowing we would want to talk about his own personal background and his crimes, he'd stolen the agenda from us and launched into his own devastatingly boring stories of prison rules and procedures. At the same time he'd tried to further enhance his own image, by portraying himself as the intellectual inmate who had been adopted as the legal spokesman for the entire prison population. Bob Berdella was interested in control. He was interested in being in charge. He was clearly manipulative and egotistical.

Berdella's monologue burnt out around lunchtime. Instead of trying to overtly swing the conversation towards the sexual sadist's months of torture, sexual depravity and murder, we let him talk his way into it. It was inevitable that when he had talked about everything else, he would turn to the one subject that set him apart.

By lunchtime, Berdella's crippling stomach conditions had miraculously disappeared and we were allowed to buy him vending machine snacks of soft drinks, microwaved pies and pastries and bars of chocolates. He ate everything, then began to talk of how he'd escaped the death penalty.

"We knew from the beginning that the evidence the police had was at best circumstantial, and that even if they got a conviction, it would be hard for them to preserve that conviction through the appeals process. So, even if they'd got the death sentence, then it probably would not be allowed to stand through the appeal review process. It isn't a matter of saying that I cheated the system, because there was no cheating on my part. The system never had the opportunity to go after the death penalty."

The 'informal' interview continued late into the afternoon. The happy, chaotic noise of visiting children running around their father's tables had abated. Most inmates were back in their cells and Berdella began to talk about his upbringing and his family. He felt he'd been a disappointment to his father, who died when he was only a teenager. "I think he wanted me to grow up to be an athlete, to go to ball games with him and that kind of thing." Brought up in a strict Roman Catholic home, he was never able to speak to either parent about sex and never gave them an inclination about his trouble in accepting that he was homosexual. He said he had few friends as a youngster "I felt out of it. I certainly didn't fit in with the cookie-clutter society of Ohio." He continues: "I had a terribly normal, terribly middle class childhood, probably better than normal. I was raised in a good neighbourhood, in a community that believed in schools and the education of their children. So, it is very hard for me to go back and find any fault with the way my parents raised me, or the community that I was raised in. Having said that, the late 50s and early 60s in white middle-class America was a very restrictive time as far as your options were concerned. There was no diversity, no sexual, religious, intellectual or philosophical diversity. So, when I came to Kansas and entered an art institute and lived in a community that encompassed international religions and cultures I had no experience in dealing with such diversity of people. I hit the ground running and learned as I went."

Berdella remembered his first few years in Kansas as among the happiest of his life. He said he found the Bohemian atmosphere and liberated sexuality exciting but was frustrated at art school. He decided he wanted to become an art teacher but there were no specific courses for him to develop along this path, so he dropped out. It was evident that even at this early stage, Robert Andrew Berdella wanted to be in control, he wanted to teach even before he'd been taught himself.

Time was running out – a prison guard indicated we had 15 minutes to wind up our business. Berdella suddenly started to get stomach cramps again, "The old trouble is back" he announced, rubbing his pot-belly. He now considered the following day's interview may be very doubtful. Then, making it clear that he was being brave on our behalf, he thought he might struggle through, if we asked the guard for medicine from the hospital wing. It was an act of clear manipulation. The guard smiled knowingly as we conveyed the request. It was important that Berdella had an incentive to turn up tomorrow, the ultimate thrill for him would be to exercise his power over us by refusing to do the interview we'd flown 6,000 miles for. Just before we parted, we told him some British psychologists had reviewed his case and we'd like to discuss their opinions with him in the morning. Berdella shook hands and left without even saying goodbye. He was deep in thought, working out whether there really was an expert explanation to his acts of sadism or whether we had made it all up. There was only one way for him to find out.

It was time to reconsider the deposition given by Berdella, under oath at the Jackson County Department of Corrections in Kansas City in December 1988. Assistant Prosecuting Attorney

Patrick Hall spent three days chronicling the confession, at one point leaving the courtroom to cry after hearing part of Berdella's testimony.

On the opening morning of the testimony, Bob Berdella spoke contentedly about his early life after leaving art school. Living on his own for so long had made him an accomplished cook and even without any formal qualifications he secured a job as Manager Chef at the well thought of La Tureen Restaurant in the River Quay area of Kansas. He spent five months there before moving on to be the Sauciere at the City's Carriage Club, where he stayed for about a year. After that there were eight more job changes and restaurants in four years. Berdella either left or was fired over what he called "personality conflicts." He eventually decided to set up a small stall in a flea market, selling miscellaneous junk from around the ramshackled old house that he'd just moved into. He supplemented the car-boot rubbish, with small antiques and then progressed to Roman, Egyptian and Mid-eastern artifacts. Bob's Bazaar Bizarre was born.

Attention then focused on his friendship with Jerry Howell, the son of a fellow shop owner and the person destined to become Berdella's first victim. Young Howell and his friends used to swap banter with him and were aware of his homosexuality. "They knew that I was gay. I never really hid the fact. Jerry came up to me one day, and this is not really having any association or relation to him other than knowing him and talking to him, and he basically asked me something to the effect of: 'You know that one friend of mine that you think is so cute?' And I'm going, 'Yes'. He says, 'He's yours for the night for 50 dollars'. I thought it was a joke. I looked at him and said, 'Well, that's about 30 dollars over market'."

Howell continued to 'joke' about the price for the next couple of days, but then surprised and embarrassed Berdella by insisting that he was really serious. "This is the first time that I became aware of any information that Jerry was in any way, shape or form involved with gays. And I don't think he was 18 at this time. It would be something like 16 or 17."

This incident happened about two years before Howell's death. The youngster then left Kansas, only returning after he'd got in trouble with the law as a rent-boy and by getting caught up in street fights. From April until July 1984 he was both a regular visitor to Berdella's house and also his regular sex partner. During the relationship, Berdella supplied Howell, who was a frequent drug abuser, with Valium and marijuana. On one occasion Howell brought a fellow-user to Charlotte Street and Berdella swapped a drug-cocktail of Chlorpromazine, Acepromazine and Ketamine for some stolen goods. These were the anaesthetics he used on his dogs when they were in pain or in labour. They were also the drugs that he would soon use on young Jerry Howell.

Either intentionally or accidentally, Berdella began to emerge as a key figure in Howell's life. He supplied drugs and they shared sex, he loaned money and gave the youngster advice about his legal troubles. He picked up Howell's attorney bills and even paid for his dental treatment. In Berdella's mind, rules were being drawn up, simple ones about doing favours for others and expecting favours in return. He had done lots of favours for people such as Jerry and seldom asked for anything back.

The day after American Independence Day, Jerry Howell broke the rules and lost his freedom. Berdella wanted Howell, who had some knowledge of car engines, to accompany him to look over a Camero that he was thinking of buying. Berdella recalled: "When I picked him up, he announced that he didn't have time to go to look at the cars, that he wanted to get to this dance contest at about seven o'clock, but that he wanted to party before I took him to the dance. And he started asking for drugs. And at that point I just started giving them to him. I had some Valium in the car and some Acepromazine tablets. We got a six pack of Coors, and then we got my house, and he wanted to get more drugged."

Eventually the teenager lapsed into unconsciousness. By the time he should have been at his long-awaited dance, Berdella had given him more shots of tranquillizer.

Hall then painstakingly charted his way through the drug record and began unscrambling the sexual codes in Berdella's torture log. "Nine o'clock and ten o'clock both have the entry F?" the Assistant Prosecutor asked. Berdella replied, "Which would be the abbreviation that I used for fuck."

Hall: "Would that be anal intercourse then?"

Berdella: "Yes."

Hall: "Now, when you tied him down and gave him these drugs that we've talked about, from seven o'clock, was he lying flat on his back?"

Berdella: "No. There is one picture that shows him with his arms to the side, taped around the wrists and then with this velvet cord that I was using. In that picture his feet were already tied. And that picture would have been taken before I would have rolled him over and tied his arms behind his back."

Hall pinned Berdella down on the times that he carried out two anal rapes on Howell, then questioned him over his actions when the teenager began choking.

Berdella: "I had him lying on his front and he started to bring vomit up through his mouth."

Hall: "Now, this is the first time you had ever done this to anyone?"

Berdella: "Yes; that is correct."

Hall: "At that point in time did you realize that Mr Howell was having difficulties and that in fact, by vomiting, he could die?"

Berdella: "Probably, yes."

Berdella explained that after repeated sodomies throughout the night, he slept with the bound and gagged victim and then in the early hours of the morning began sodomizing him again. There followed more injections and more torture. Pat Hall returned to the log. "8.15 am you have the word 'Active'?"

Berdella: "Yes. That's where he appeared to be coming out of it, responding in some ways."

Hall pressed on: "8:40 CF. First of all what's that CF?" Berdella was puzzled, "CF?" Hall asked again, "What does it mean?" Then Berdella remembered, "I believe at the time that was a carrot fuck." The lawyer's mind was reeling, "Can you tell us what you mean by a carrot fuck?"

Berdella: "I used a carrot to sodomize the anus."

Hall: "Had you ever done that on any individual before that day?"

Berdella: "No."

Hall: "Where did you get the idea of doing that?"

Berdella: "I have no direct source. I guess it was what I had in the house that would fulfil the job."

Hall: "It is something that came upon you at 8:40 to stick a carrot up his anus?"

Berdella: "Apparently, yes sir."

Hall discovered that during the following days of torture, Berdella decided that he would never let Howell go. He had started down what he regarded as a one way cul-de-sac. The art school drop-out and former chef had created a sex-zombie for himself. Another human being whom he could treat like a blow-up sex doll.

Hall continued to work through the torture notes, not certain he was prepared for the next set of depraved revelations: "The six o'clock entry, what does that mean?" Berdella unravelled the mystery, "Cucumber rape. Still fighting. And 6:15 there's a notation of one and a half cc.s of the PH medication and the notation that he was still fighting."

Hall: "For the six o'clock, I take it you took a cucumber and inserted it into his rectum?"

Berdella: "That's correct."

Before lunchtime on the first day of the deposition, the two men pieced together the last moments of Jerry Howell's life.

Hall: "The ten o'clock entry is two letters – DD?"

Berdella: "Yes. Dead."

Hall: "Is that all that meant, dead?"

Berdella: "Yes."

Hall: "So he would have died on Friday, July the 6th?"

Berdella: "At 10:00 pm."

Hall: "And what did he die of?"

Berdella: "The best I could tell, either because of the gag, and/or the medications. That he either asphyxiated on vomit or the combination of the gag and the medicines were too strong for him to breathe."

Howell's naked body was taken into the basement and hung upside down from an old ceiling pulley. Berdella photographed the corpse, before he opened deep wounds in the arms and neck, then drained the blood into a giant cooking pot. While the body still hung there he cleaned the bedroom of any signs of possible forensic evidence. The following day, the former chef returned to the basement to set about dismembering his victim. Reluctantly, Pat Hall asked how he'd done it. "What tools did you gather up for the dismembering?" Berdella answered: "A couple of my cooking knives. A boning knife that I had. The chain saw that I used, I think was already in the basement. I originally would have used the chain saw when I like hit the rib cage and my knife wouldn't cut-up."

Sergeant Troy Cole, who was present throughout the deposition had said Berdella's testimony had been delivered almost without a flicker of emotion. "There was no remorse, if anything he enjoyed talking about it." Looking back over the deposition, it's obvious that Berdella drew on his years of experiences in kitchens to guide him through the grisly chore of body disposal. Blood was poured down the household drains and the body parts were wrapped in newspaper, like joints of meat. He then bagged them all up in plastic bin-liners and when the chore was finished, he went straight to bed and slept all night.

Berdella told the lawyers that the following day he had gone to work as normal, but when he returned in the evening he was visited by the dead man's father Paul Howell, "He wanted to know if I'd seen Jerry, and he wanted to know if I had any idea where Jerry might be. The first Michael Jackson tour to come through town was on. I can't remember whether they were supposed to go Saturday or Sunday night – it was probably Saturday. Anyway, Paul was concerned that Jerry hadn't showed up to go to the concert.

Hall: "Did you give him any story?"

Berdella: "Yes. I told him that the last time I saw Jerry was on Thursday and that he was supposed to have gone out to Parkville with me. He then changed his mind, and I dropped him off at the Seven-Eleven on Main, ostensibly so he could use the pay-phone."

Paul Howell would later harbour serious doubts about Berdella's innocence and would visit the police and state that he believed Berdella had killed his son. For now though, he left satisfied but concerned.

The following day, Monday morning, the garbage truck arrived. Berdella deposited his flesh-filled sacks and all the clothes and evidence relating to Howell, in the pile of rubbish being chewed in the jaws of the truck's compressor. All he kept were the knives and chain saw. He would need those again.

Assistant Prosecuting Attorney Pat Hall moved on to Berdella's second victim, Robert Sheldon. He was a friend of a friend, who became a paying lodger at Berdella's home during the Spring of 1985. Sheldon was a heavy drinker and like Howell, he also asked Berdella to inject him with any 'spare' drugs around the house. Sheldon also broke 'the rules'. His drinking would be so bad he would be unable to pay the rent and when Berdella tried to evict him he refused to go.

One night, when Sheldon fell asleep on the sofa in a first floor room, the landlord decided to take another victim. He filled him with drinks and drugs but failed to get the dosages right. Sheldon managed to wake himself and Berdella aborted the plan to capture his lodger.

Berdella told the prosecutors that he hadn't actually found Sheldon sexually attractive but that he had been driven by an urge to "dominate and control" him. "The best way I can interpret what happened was that the impulsive behaviour that began with Jerry Howell became a reality for me. You're looking at what would be some of my darkest fantasies becoming my reality, where I was capturing people, controlling them. You don't necessarily need sexual attractiveness to do that."

Two days later at about 6 pm, Berdella returned home after work to find Sheldon sprawled on an orange couch in a first floor room, drinking heavily. He assessed the empty cans, dirty glasses and opened bottles and calculated that his lodger had drunk six beers and three to four shots of whiskey. He noted it all down. There would be no mistakes this time. "He was obviously a little bit drunk. I gave him five Triavil that I had crushed and put into some Tetracycline capsules."

Berdella gave the sedative to Sheldon under the pretence that it was an antibiotic and would help take the pain out of some insect bites he had complained of. Within an hour the unwanted lodger had collapsed. Now he was booked in forever. Berdella gave him an intramuscular injection of two cc.s of Chlorpromazine. Pat Hall fingered through the new torture notes and inquired about a two word entry that said: 'Photo Eyes'. Berdella explained, "Photo eyes. Open to sound. That's the one shot of him laying on the couch. It appears like his eyes are about half open. The sound of the Polaroid camera was enough to kind of rouse him, just enough to open his eyes a little bit."

More Chlorpromazine was pumped into Sheldon. Another one and a half cc.s in one shoulder, then another two and a half cc.s. By half past eight, Berdella had also started to administer Ketamine, along with yet another jab of the Chlorpromazine.

Robert Berdella waited another hour before making his move. He bound his victim's hands, removed his trousers and tied his legs at the ankles. He spent the rest of the time filling in his log and planning the next stage of his fantasy, "My 9:30 notation is partially tore off, but, it's a notation of 'Moved to landing on second floor. Eyes open. Some vocal'." A triple injection of drugs followed; in addition to the Chlorpromazine and Ketamine, Acepromazine was also pumped into the comatosed body before it was moved into a back bedroom with mustard-yellow walls. Berdella continued, "11:15 is a notation that I butt-fucked him. No resistance or sounds, but he was giving forth a soft snoring." Hall asked if he had been unconscious at the time he'd had anal intercourse with him. Berdella confirmed this and then in a flat unemotional voice returned to his copy of the torture logs: "Then, at 11:25 a notation of DC, which is drain cleaner, to the left ear, er... no the left eye. I'm sorry. That says he had pinpoint pupils at that time. And after the drain cleaner to the eye he was screaming, although a muffled scream, for about one or two minutes." Pat Hall and the rest of the prosecuting team were stunned. Sheldon's pain was imaginable to all of them. More than one person leant forward, head in hands rubbing their eye in imagined pain. Hall asked why Berdella had done it? He answered curtly, "Obviously to damage his eye and cause some pain. Perhaps getting into being able to permanently damage his eyes, which would then have made it easier to keep him and control him."

Throughout the night and early hours of the morning Berdella continued his experimental sadism, injecting drugs into Sheldon's spine and tattooing the word 'Hot' onto the back of his left shoulder. Despite being in a stupor he cried out in continual pain and Berdella made dutiful notes of everytime he pleaded for him to stop. Hall needed further help with the abbreviations: "12:30 pm. By the notation 'BF', you had anal intercourse with him?"

Berdella: "That's correct."

Hall: "You first have, 'there was no reaction'?"

Berdella: "No. At that, no reaction other than a slight, 'Oh, my ass' comment.

Hall: "He shouted out or said..."

Berdella: "Mumbled more or less. No movement other than slight movement in hands. Then at 1:30 anal intercourse again and the notation 'some vocal'."

Hall: "When you were having anal intercourse with Mr Sheldon, how long was this taking? How long were you taking to perform this on him?"

Berdella: "Usually, probably 20 minutes to half an hour. There is a further notation at 1:30 of 'S and W', which means soap-and-water enema and carrot-fuck. Basically, the carrot at that stage was used to cause the enema to take place."

Berdella explained that he didn't find sexual pleasure in sodomizing Sheldon with the carrot, but again viewed its use as:

"gratification on the level of dominance, control." Until the first light of dawn broke into the dingy room, Berdella alternated between abusing his captive with the carrot and buggering him himself. Then he thought of a new way of causing suffering, "I had a caulking gun and I just filled his ears with caulking to reduce the amount that he was able to hear."

Hall: "Caulking, like you would use on your house?"

Berdella: "On windows, yes." Berdella's intention was to create sensory deprivation. It was another weapon in his battle to win total control over his victim. After terrorizing Sheldon by temporarily blinding him with the drain cleaner, he wanted to deafen him as well.

Around 8 am Bob Berdella experimented with hypodermic needles, using them in a cruel form of acupuncture. Instead of finding body spots that could relieve pain, he did exactly the opposite. He rammed the long needles deep under Sheldon's fingernails, reminiscent of an act with bamboo shoots in a Japanese concentration camp. Then he had anal intercourse again with his victim before injecting another six cc.s of three different drugs into his body. Sheldon once more fell into unconsciousness and his attacker went to work.

Berdella returned home at 5 pm and subjected Sheldon to further anal sex. He then battered him with a mallet, injected him with more drugs and took more polaroid photographs. Just before midnight he buggered him again, gave him more injections and then sodomized him with a cucumber. After 29 hours of torture, Berdella at last gave his victim some sustenance, a drink of sugared water. This was followed by more anal sex, another beating with the mallet and also a battering across the neck, with a large wooden stick.

Sheldon was fading in and out of consciousness when Bob brought in his transformer. He jabbed needles into his shoulder and back, ran cables from them to the electrical unit and then dispensed more than 7,000 volts through his body. Berdella took more notes and photographs.

The following morning Sheldon woke Berdella by shouting in pain. He went into the bedroom and beat him unconscious, sodomized him and injected him with more sedatives. Berdella went off to work again. Pat Hall instructed the killer to pick up the story as he returned home on the Sunday evening and found Sheldon still unconscious. Berdella obliged. "He was out. I changed some of the binding and washed him. At 5:45, anal intercourse with no reaction from him." Hall asked how the victim was bound. "I think I still was using some of this black velvet roping that I had," answered Berdella, adding, "and I think on Sheldon I also used, yes, I first wrapped his wrists with tape and then tied the piano wire, then secured the hands a little better with the black velvet roping. So, the reason for having the wires on the hands was to cause nerve damage to the hands."

Hall interrupted, "To cause what?"

Berdella: "Nerve damage to the hands, so that if I did untie him, he wouldn't have control or be able to use his hands."

Robert Sheldon never lived to experience that. The following day he was murdered. Berdella spotted a workman who had begun labouring on his roof in Charlotte Street and so he went upstairs and killed Sheldon. He put a black plastic binliner over his head and tied it around his neck with rope, suffocating him. As Sheldon struggled, sucking in his last gasps of air, Berdella took more photographs.

Over the next 24 hours, Berdella cut him up in his bathtub, drained the blood, bagged up the dismembered pieces and put them all out in rubbish sacks for the garbage van. All that is, except for Sheldon's head.

Hall: "What did you do with the head on Monday night after you cut it off?"

Berdella: "I think I stuck it in the freezer for a couple of days. One evening, I took it out in the back yard and buried it."

The skull was not buried for ritualistic reasons. Berdella had already scalped it and peeled most of the flesh away but some still hung to the sockets. He buried it so maggots and insects would eat away the remaining tissue. Eventually, he returned the severed head to his house and pulled some of its teeth out.

In the summer of 1985, a young man who cut the lawns for Bob Berdella, introduced him to a friend of his called Mark

Wallace. He was destined to become Berdella's third victim. During a severe thunderstorm on the night of June 22, Wallace returned to Berdella's garden and took shelter in the shed, which from his visits he knew was left unlocked. The houseowner's dogs were disturbed, Berdella came out, found Wallace there and invited him inside to dry out. It was the beginning of the end.

Wallace was drunk and depressed. Berdella helped with sympathy, at least six beers and a shot of his tranquillizers. On the second day of the deposition, he told why he took Mark Wallace captive. "Aside from any emotional decisions that would have affected me; anger from some other situation or under duress, it was just that he was there. There was nothing to really link him to my house that night, and he didn't have any family that would come around looking for him."

Callous and uncaring, Berdella had by now perfected the dosage of drugs necessary to render his victim incapable of resistance. In the early hours, the new victim was stripped, then bound and gagged before being moved to the mustard-coloured torture room where Robert Sheldon had been killed. As usual, copious notes and photographs were taken. He was assaulted twice before 6 am. "I sodomized him and front fucked him."

Hall: "And by the front fuck you mean?"

Berdella: "It is just 'going' against the front side of the person and using the groin area."

More anal and frictional sex followed, along with five beatings with the mallet that he'd used on Sheldon. By dawn Berdella noted in his diary that he had damaged Wallace's anal wall and the man was bleeding. He turned to electrocution. The transformer was wheeled in, Wallace was battered about the face and then alligator clips tagged onto his nipples and the voltage charged through him. This was a significant moment for Berdella, "At this point I would have to say that I was beginning to get into sadomasochistic sex."

Hall: "Prior to this, with the other individuals, you did not consider yourself to be getting into sadomasochistic sex?"

Berdella: "I know it would look and sound contradictory. But up until this point, there was a pretty clear separation between inflicting pain and then at another time having sex. It was only I think at this point where I first got into inflicting pain during the period where I was having sex." Berdella was giving his audience a perfect example of how serial killers introduce more and more lavish elements to their crimes as they progress from one murder to another.

The sodomy continued throughout the early morning, along with another two severe beatings with the plastering mallet. By 10 am Berdella noted that Wallace was suffering contusions – large gatherings of blood and bruising on his head. He was close to death. During the day there were more injections, more sodomy, more electrocution and then more of the bizarre 'acupuncture', with Wallace being stabbed in his back with the hypodermic needles.

Pat Hall, Assistant Prosecuting Attorney in Jackson County fixed his eyes on the photographs Berdella had taken during the latest events in his sadistic spree. He asked the offender to 'talk him through'. "The next photo shows me attempting to fist fuck him. He would at that point have been resisting to some point. That may be what I have noted as 'FFF'."

Hall: "And that would be from the front, with your fist?"

Berdella: "Yes. The next photo shows him naked with his hands tied behind him, laying on a blanket. The next photo is the one we discussed with the electrodes. The next photo is showing him on the third floor bound with the rope...I mean, a board between his arms to keep him from rolling. And there is a stick under the cord around his neck that would be gagging him. So that basically, if I needed to very quickly tighten the gag, all I had to do was twist the stick a little bit."

In the perverse portfolio were pictures of a homosexual lover of Berdella's, a former chef who was bound head to foot with a pillowcase tied around his neck. Police and prosecutors had at first thought this was a victim that had been unaccounted for, but eventually traced the man and found he had been a consenting sexual partner. Pat Hall returned to Berdella's notebook. "You came back up at seven o'clock to check on Wallace?"

Berdella: "That's correct."

Hall: "And found at that time he was not breathing?"

Berdella: "That's correct."

He added that he believed Mark Wallace had died from a combination of the beatings, a lack of medication and because of the gag in his mouth, a lack of oxygen. Hall fixed the approximate time of death as 7 pm on Sunday, June 23, 1985. There was now a routine for body disposal. Wallace was dismembered, the parts wrapped in newspapers, dumped in binliners and left out with the trash.

The next victim, Walter James Ferris, was a drug addict and a regular customer at Bob's Bazaar Bizarre. He never visited after September 24, 1985. He went home with Berdella and the two slept together enjoying mutual masturbation. The following day Bob returned to his bazaar. When he came home in the late afternoon he discovered Ferris and a friend of his trying on his clothes in his bedroom. Berdella didn't blow his top. He told them to put the stuff back and then they all went out for a drink together. Berdella returned home alone and went to bed. He was disturbed in the early hours by Ferris and his friend, drunkenly stumbling around in the back yard. They had awoken his giant Chow dogs. By the time their master had got to the porch, Ferris was trying to climb through the window. By now Berdella was incandescent, but he still let Ferris stay the night and went to bed. Ferris had also been talking drugs and every 15 minutes would wander into Bob's room and begin talking.

The following night the two men met up again in a local Kansas bar called the Midnight Sun and once more Ferris imposed upon Bob's hospitality, asking to stay another night in Charlotte Street. Berdella said he then formed the intent to capture Ferris. He put this down to a combination of the aggravating earlier circumstances and the fact that, "he presented himself basically as somebody that nobody would really miss or look for."

Bob Berdella played the congenial host. He cooked his new lodger a dinner of burritos and chili, garnished with a sprinkling of crushed tranquillizers. Within a short while Ferris had collapsed. He was stripped and photographed. Berdella continued the story from the notes he'd made at the time. "At 9:40 I have a notation that I turned him over. There was slight arm movement. At 9:50 I inserted my finger into his anus. There was no reaction." The torture was about to begin again. Berdella: "I then gave him one-and-a-half cc.s injection of Ketamine into his arms, with no reaction. Front fucked. No reaction."

More drugs followed over the next hour. "11:30 to 11:45 I sodomized him, first with my penis, then a cucumber. A notation of slight reaction." Ferris was then regagged more tightly. Berdella brought in his transformer and attached make-shift electrodes in turn to his victim's shoulder, buttocks and testicles. After the electrocutions Ferris lapsed into unconsciousness. Berdella remembered how he woke him. "At two o'clock there's one photo that's a front overhead fuck, which meant that I would have kept him face up to the bed, raised his legs and then inserted my penis in that position."

Berdella turned once more to developing his acupuncture techniques. This time he stabbed the one-and-a-quarter inch hypodermic all the way into his victim's testicles. Within the next two hours, Ferris would be buggered twice more, sodomized twice more with the cucumber and then electrocuted again. The Polaroid camera continued to flash throughout. He was then buggered a further time, sodomized with a carrot and injected with more tranquillizers. It was still only 5:30 am.

Ferris began bleeding, vomiting and trembling. Infection set into some of his veins and he fell into a fever. Berdella gave him Penicillin and continued to abuse him over the next 24 hours. He monitored his deterioration and noted when he cried out for help. The catalogue of obscenities was well underway the following evening, "11:15 to 11:30, finger fuck, carrot fuck, front fuck." And so it went on, until midnight, "When I checked him at 12 o'clock however, he was then dead."

Hall: "You have the notation at 12 o'clock of – '86'?"

Berdella: "Right."

Hall: "Why did you put '86' for dead?"

Berdella: "Basic terminology in the restaurant business which I had been in: 86 meant anything from, 'Throw it out' to, 'Stop the project' – just things brought to an end and/ or discarded."

Walter James Ferris is believed to have died from a combination of overdosing on drugs and asphyxiation (the gag once more depriving the victim of oxygen). He was chopped up and put out with the trash. Berdella kept his driving licence as a 'trophy' of his third victim.

In April 1984 a male prostitute and drug addict called Todd Stoops and his addict girlfriend Lisa moved into Berdella's rambling house. The young couple were given the front bedroom on the third floor but unlike other lodgers in the house, they didn't have to pay rent. Stoops had agreed to provide his sexual services free of charge to the landlord. Bob Berdella was besotted by Stoops but was already having a long-term relationship with another of the lodgers, a man called Eric Gibson.

The sexual dealings in Charlotte Street inevitably became an emotional cauldron and finally everyone moved out. After a while Todd and Lisa moved back in but left again after a couple of weeks. Berdella remained friends with the young street hustler and even gave a character reference for him during a court appearance for drug abuse. By now Berdella was well thought of in the local community and he was the major co-ordinator of the Hyde Park Neighbourhood Association, an anti-crime group.

In June 1986, the pillar of the local community was cruising downtown, looking for rent-boys in the red-light area of 10th and McGee. While he was kerb-crawling, he met Stoops and they renewed their friendship. Berdella discovered that Todd and Lisa had split up, Stoops had gone to Oklahoma after the break-up and had then been jailed for drugs offences. The 'cruiser' invited the 'chicken-hawk' back to his house and made plans to capture his fourth victim.

The 21-year-old had been in the house for less than an hour when Berdella crushed sleeping pills into his peanut butter sandwich and glass of milk. He dozed off and enjoyed the last proper night's sleep that he'd ever have. Within a fortnight garbage men would be spreading his remains among tonnes of rubbish in a landfill site. Berdella recalled: "5:50 he was out of it. I then gave him ten cc.s of Chlorpromazine in his buttocks. No reaction. But he was starting to snore and then at that time I sodomized him. No reaction. 6:10, the observation that he was snoring. 6:20, a front fuck. No reaction. 7:00 the photo of me holding his eyes open, showing that the eyes were fixed. 7:15 side fuck. Some vocal grunts. Reaction in his legs. I gave him three cc.s of Ketamine to the neck at that time. 7:40 is when I finally had tied his hands and feet and secured them to the head-board and floor-board. There was no reaction. I again at this time started to use the electricity on him... 7:50 was a front fuck. There was some grunts from him and muscle contraction in his stomach area."

This table of tortures was the pattern for the last 14 days of Stoops' life. Over that fortnight he would be sodomized with carrots and cucumbers, whipped with a leather belt and electro-cuted into unconsciousness. After the electrocution, to deter-mine how stunned his victim was, Berdella would bite hard on his victim's nipples or bend his fingers back to breaking point.

A cloth gag was bound so tightly around Stoops' mouth, that the piano wire holding it in place, bit into the flesh at the corners of his lips and caused him to bleed. The acts of sodomy had also burst his anal wall but rather than deter Berdella, this excited him into more rigorous abuse. Berdella fist fucked him and took polaroids of his large clenched fist rammed up the young man's bleeding anus. "At this point I was trying to terrify him. Had I not ruptured his anal wall and caused him the severe blood loss that he had, he would have reached a point where he would be much more co-operative. At this point, I wasn't even asking him for that co-operation. I was trying to terrorize him."

It was Berdella's intention, that like sexual sadist Cameron Hooker, he would eventually frighten and brainwash his victim into becoming a willing sex slave who would not try to escape even if left untied and alone. For the moment though, he was taking no chances. To ensure that the dying Stoops didn't cry out for help while he was at work, Berdella gave him another injection. This time it was drain-cleaner. Stoops was tied down and the bleach flushed through a hypodermic into his voice box, Berdella taking care not to jab the needle all the way through into his throat.

Berdella sodomized Stoops while watching television. He then tattooed his body and beat him with a belt strap. Sometime during the second week of his captivity Stoops began to behave as Berdella wanted. He was 'taught' that if he co-operated with the sex acts he would be given minor privileges like food and drink, and if he didn't, then he was beaten and electrocuted. Berdella said Stoops was "reduced to a child" begging for mercy and breaking down into tears.

Todd Stoops never became the slave that Berdella wanted. He died of a fever caused by the internal bleeding at 11:30 in the morning on Tuesday July 1. Berdella dismembered his corpse and left it in trash-bags to be collected with the garbage.

The last man that Bob Berdella killed was Larry Pearson, a bisexual prostitute who worked the streets. A friendship had grown between the two men, but Berdella told Pat Hall that he had been angered by an intimate sexual moment: "He came up to my room and I guess we had what he thought was supposed to be sex. Basically, I performed oral sex on him, while he would do a porno magazine. Afterwards he asked me how it was? And I explained that I had nothing to evaluate, because we hadn't done anything. And he was awkward about this afterwards. And so nothing was ever done sexually, until I took him captive."

The Assistant Prosecuting Attorney produced a black spiral stenographer's notebook; it was the recorded life and death of Larry Pearson. In it was every moment from his abduction on the afternoon of Tuesday June 23, 1987 to his murder on August 5. Hall elicited from Berdella an account of the capture, which came after Pearson had told his 'friend' how he had been working in Wichita "rolling queers". He asked the killer: "If you thought back on it, if Mr Pearson had not brought up this conversation about rolling queers back when he was in Wichita, do you think you would have formed the intent? Or did that just kind of trigger it?" Berdella replied: "I guess that was the trigger. I hadn't been thinking about it for days before or anything."

By this sixth murder, Berdella had perfected his trick of slipping drugs into drinks. As Pearson slid into a haze of alcohol and sedatives Berdella injected him with animal anaesthetics and then dragged him downstairs into the basement where he chained him up in a dog collar and bound and gagged him. Pearson was held for 43 days and was by far Berdella's most successful crime. Many of the mistakes he'd made with earlier victims had now been corrected and this was the closest the sadist would come to creating a perfect slave.

The torture was much the same. Drain-cleaner into the vocal chords and electrocution of the body and sexual parts. Simple bindings had been replaced with handcuffs but these later caused cutting and infection problems around the victim's wrists. Pearson's left hand became bloated with blood because of the handcuff and was said to be three times its normal size. Berdella cut off the handcuffs and then battered both Pearson's hands with an iron bar, breaking his fingers.

Having terrorised his victim, Berdella then set about telling his slave the rules he had to obey. "I just explained what was expected of him, what kind of attitude I expected him to have and what kind of attitude I would have." Hall pushed for a better explanation: "And could you tell us exactly what you meant, or what you were telling him about the attitude that you wanted him to have?" Berdella obliged: "That he would be completely co-operative and submissive; that he wasn't supposed to talk unless I was there with him and told him okay and gave him permission. No screaming. That is, if I was up on the first floor I would be down to check on him, and he would not call up to me, to have me come down."

Berdella told Hall that Pearson had become very co-operative after the explanation and added that he believed he would have got the same level of compliance from Stoops if he hadn't have died of internal bleeding before his 'induction' had been completed. Pearson's co-operation was everything Berdella had dreamed of.

One morning Pearson began calling Berdella "Master Bob" and this was soon rewarded with a move from the basement to a bedroom on the second floor. By this point the victim was so terrified, that for most of the time he was only restrained by the dog collar, tethered to the bed.

Pearson behaved so well that Berdella began allowing him to use the bathroom and was even feeding him regularly. "I think there was never any doubt after maybe the first or second day of what situation he was in. He had been plainly informed that he was being kept as a love slave, a sex slave."

By mid-July the slave was allowed to perform oral sex on the master while he watched television. By July 26, Berdella was no longer torturing his captive, he said it wasn't necessary, "The routine was that I'd wake up in the morning and have sex with him, then prepare breakfast for the both of us. Feed him. Tie him down while I went to work or ran any errands that I might have. Got back from work. Came up. Untied him. Gave him a couple of cigarettes to smoke. And I would always bring a cold drink up from the kitchen, while I made supper or made my phone calls or fed the dogs or whatever else I had to do. Then I would usually just go up and spend the rest of the evening with him, unless I had some meeting or errands that I had to run. He was very co-operative."

On August 5 the co-operation stopped. Berdella made Pearson act-out a reverse of the disappointing pre-captivity encounter when Berdella performed oral sex on him while he read a magazine. This time it was Pearson who became annoyed: "I had him perform oral sex on me while I was looking at this magazine. What ended up happening was he then bit me on the penis severely. He was not tethered to anything. When he was doing the oral sex, I usually would just hold the leash in my hand. He bit me. I finally got up off the bed. He was standing there in front of me with some blood dripping out of his mouth. My penis was bleeding at that point rather profusely. I grabbed a rag and held it to my penis while I talked to him."

Berdella says he discovered that the reason for the attack wasn't because Pearson was trying to escape, but because he was giving attention to the magazine and not to him. Berdella tied him down to the bed and then battered him with a tree limb, crashing the large club into his ribs, head, face and legs.

The master needed urgent medical treatment. He was still bleeding when he arrived at the local hospital and they told him they'd have to keep him in for treatment. They applied emergency dressings and agreed to let him go home briefly. Berdella told the prosecutors, "When I got home, I brought the dog in to her pups, made sure she had plenty of food and water to last a couple of days. Went upstairs to check on Pearson. He was completely passed out, either because of the events or the blow to the head, or both. Berdella then decided that Pearson's injuries would take too long to heal and would need too much attention. He tied a plastic binliner around his neck and allowed him to suffocate while he went downstairs and looked after the dogs. Before he returned to the hospital for an operation there was one last thing to do. He went back to the corpse and ran-off three more polaroid pictures.

Three days later Berdella was allowed home. He needed a catheter to urinate through and had to be visited by a nurse three times a day. For once he was the unhappy receiver of drugs and antibiotics. There was another thing: he was struggling with the body in the basement. "I went down and instead of working on a long-term basis, because I was too weak and painful to do that, I would go down and do one process at a time; like opening the stomach and pulling out all the internal parts. Then I'd go down later and start cutting him up." The whole process took days. "Because of my condition I relied on the chain saw a lot more. I would cut down to the bone, and the meat, the muscle and the skin would fall apart..."

All the body parts were bagged up and as usual put out with the Monday morning rubbish, all except one part. Berdella had cut off and kept Pearson's skull with the vertebrae still attached.

By the time the three day deposition at the Jackson County Department of Corrections had finished, several of the State's legal team were drained of emotion and were furious that they'd had to allow Berdella to escape the death penalty. Prosecuting Attorney Albert Reiderer, said he'd have executed Berdella with his own hands, if the law had given him the opportunity.

********************

Monday, July 27, 1992, three-and-a-half years after the deposition. We wait in the prison library for the killer of six young men to be brought down from his high-security wing. Robert Andrew Berdella comes in, still complaining of stomach ache. We shake hands and guide him to a seat.

The library is very different to the modern-looking visitor's canteen. Housed in the old block of the Jefferson Correctional Centre, it is small and dark. Any daylight from its high barred windows has been completely obliterated by row after row of crammed shelves. The first hour of the interview is a waste of time. Berdella is exceptionally hostile and as unco-operative as possible. He begins to loosen up as we deliberately make the questions more 'chatty' and less formal. The teen-years of Bob Berdella are ones of insularity and uncertainty, "I was somewhat a shy and withdrawn individual". He was beginning to outline for us the kind of alienation experienced by so many serial killers. Research has shown that homosexuality or poor sexual skills forces many serial offenders to retreat into the auto-erotic world of masturbation. This was true of Berdella: "Masturbation was much quicker, much easier. In the environment and the community I grew up in, at the school that I grew up at, and in my family background, there was nothing to give guidance to a sexual direction in my life. I didn't even know who the homosexuals were at school. During the periods where I was chasing after guys, I had girls chasing after me. So, I said, OK, I'll try this, then I'm chasing after girls and the guys then start chasing after me. It wasn't until I was 23, 24, that I was comfortable enough to say, 'we're not playing this anymore.' I made my decision, I liked the ones with hairy legs."

Berdella's sexuality was further restricted by the religious attitudes at his school; he developed what he called, "The Catholic guilt trip" about sex. In his late teens he began frequenting gay bars where male prostitutes went after they'd finished their 'work'. He said that while this prevented him from approaching them for sex (they made it plain they were strictly 'off-duty' in these bars) it did provide him with, "a tremendous amount of insight into the actual workings of these people." A decade and a half later, that insight would help him capture, torture and murder some of them.

We moved on to his varied employment record, including volunteer work in a neighbourhood arts centre, his disenchantment with art school itself and his years as a chef. When he was employed (under the control of senior chefs and managers) he nearly always left or was asked to leave because of personality disputes. When he set up in business, and he was in control, then he felt far more at ease. "I established a little stall at one of the local flea markets and damn, I was making money out of it. Within a couple of years I was making as much money running a shop in a flea market as I had been as a professional chef, and I was having fun being able to be my own boss. It wasn't a planned decision, it was an opportunity which presented itself. Like a lot of other situations in my life. I took advantage of it."

Berdella fully recognized the significance of his last remark. This had been his first real introduction to controlling his own life and experiencing the power that came through financial reward and success. As a stall owner, for once he became a focus of attention. People came to see him, he no longer had to hunt down conversations late at night in seedy bars. He also recognized his own opportunism; it was a trait that would later prove fatal as he seized upon chances to take people captive.

The makings of success were all there. A new job and a new challenge. So what went wrong and when? Berdella bought a house that was urgently in need of repair. It was a drain on his financial resources, but the blossoming businessman also saw it as a form of investment. Looking back, he can't see how things turned sour: "I don't know where there was a turning point, where everything started to go bad. I don't know if it was a personal relationship that was going down the tubes, me feeling the flea market was threatened in some way or if I became too concerned about the house. But somehow, I started to see certain individuals as being a threat, an enemy."

Chances are it was all those things and more. Berdella had said that he felt influenced by the restricted sexuality of his childhood and frustrated by not living up to his father's expectations of him. He also indicated that he was 'a child of his age', influenced by the rebellious spell of the '60s, affected by learning nightly of the televised horrors of Vietnam. In other words, Berdella was susceptible to outside influences, at times he felt "things simply got on top of me." This feeling of 'being pressured' is often referred to as 'situational stress' and again many serial killers admit to similar experiences in the build-up towards a first-offence.

Such feelings often centred upon the various lodgers in Bob Berdella's house. Referring to the fourth killing, he distinctly recalls the pressure he felt at the time. "I think I am a very tolerant individual, very resilient. In a lot of these cases I gave these people fair warning. You know, I repeatedly told them to get out of my life, to get away from me. Then, on top of everything else, you find him (Ferris) breaking into your house at four in the morning, and by previous experience you know you can't get rid of him by any other way, so you say, OK, we'll go along this route. I couldn't get rid of these people any other way, I couldn't get them out of my life, so I had to find a permanent solution. Then it just became habit forming."

Stress was one of the main triggers to Bob Berdella's crimes and to some extent he recognized that: "In some situations the stress was directly related to the person that became the victim. In other situations, perhaps the stress was related from a different situation and then this unfortunate individual came along and I was able to victimize that person because I couldn't take the frustration out on the person or the situation that was actually causing the frustration."

For Bob Berdella to carry out his crimes he had to alter his perception of the people he knew. Just as Dennis Nilsen remarked that he had to depersonalize his victims and see them as objects, Berdella also had to see his victims, not as tiresome friends or lodgers but as 'the enemy'. "I no longer saw them as human beings. At the point that I was determined to capture them, I would no longer be thinking of them as a human being. I no longer recognized them as human beings with a right to live."

'Serial murder' has become a generic term for killers who murder more than once. Berdella told us he believed this was a misuse of the phrase: "They should be called multiple murders. My killings were serial crimes because all the people I murdered were part of the same series, they were the same types of people." He added, "They were all people that were living on the outskirts of society. They weren't well integrated. In a lot of cases they were abandoned by their families and by society. I knew them all, they had all; with the exception of one, been to my house at sometime or another."

Just as 'Des' Nilsen had told us that he spared some of his house-guests because something happened to ruin 'the image' that he had of a passive victim, Berdella also spared people for a similar reason. "One of the things that kind of threw the police was that they questioned one or two individuals that they had photos of, you know photographs that I took of them bound and tied and gagged and everything else. These were people that had come in consensually. They had in fact requested that they be tied up. So, the police were totally lost, they said 'you had these individuals there, they were tied up and you let them go?', and I said 'yep'. They weren't in the target group – I didn't see them as a threat, I didn't see them as an enemy, they weren't in the group that I had designated that I was at war with."

Berdella's 'target group' was basically anyone who annoyed him when he was stressed-out. He also deliberately picked a group of people that he thought he could capture without their families wondering where they were. Drug addicts and male prostitutes were frequent visitors to his house and provided him with ample prey. Berdella accepts that viewing them as 'the enemy' was a psychological device he unknowingly (at the time) applied, so that he would not have to come to terms with the strain of realizing he had killed someone. "I had developed a callousness, a lack of caring. I think that is what happened to me, I just stopped caring. I shut down as a human being, I stopped caring."

Berdella drank from a can of coke during a refreshment break, and told us he had indulged in recreational soft drugs such as marijuana and had been arrested and charged with possession. He was given a five year probation order but still associated with addicts and supplied some of them with tranquillizers or shots of the sedatives he used on his dogs. He had problems with his new home as well. He took in lodgers to help pay for its development and repair but many of them turned into bad debts and troublesome tenants. His house was also broken into several times, further increasing the mounting stress on him.

After a raid that had netted his TV and video, Berdella joined the Neighbourhood Association and began organizing vigils and schemes to cut down the level of crime in the area. Just as going to gay bars gave him an insight into the people he would eventually take captive, holding regular meetings with local policemen on behalf of residents also gave him a preview of his other 'enemies', the police. "I had a lot of experience with the police, I dealt with most of the calls between the police stations and the residents who'd been attacked or robbed. It was a thorough insight. It wasn't, however, experience that I went and got for the purposes of creating crimes. It was like everything else. When I started committing crimes I drew on a lot of my previous experiences and previous knowledge. Because of that I was able to find solutions to some of the problems that were presenting themselves as a result of my crimes, and I was better able to avoid detection."

Applying Berdella's comments to his crimes, some behavioural patterns become clear. Being a homosexual who used male prostitutes, he targeted them as victims, knowing most of them wouldn't be traced. Being a chef, who followed recipes and noted down all his culinary experiments (especially when working on something new) he also wrote down all the 'ingredients' he used during his torture sessions. When a victim died, he even wrote the notation '86', chef's shorthand for, as he put it, 'Kill the order'. His expertise with meat was perfect grounding for the dismemberment of six men and his knowledge of police affairs made him forensically aware and helped him clear away all the obvious evidence. Despite butchering six people in his home, it was almost forensically clean when experts examined it. What traces of blood they did find, were only just recognizable as human and no specific blood typing was possible.

Berdella had a very rich fantasy life. It was a life that didn't just come into play during sexual moments, it was ever present and very central to his personality. It too was set-off by stress: "Fantasy was a sort of safety-valve. If I was at work and I saw the manager as being a total ass, I would not take a knife and go up to the manager and stab him... I would however close my eyes and fantasize about this individual, perhaps falling out of an aeroplane. It would be an intentional safety valve, it would be nice to identify what this individual would look like, bouncing off the ground after a 5,000 foot fall. You know, I think this is a proper use of fantasy as opposed to taking the knife and running up to the manager and saying, 'You're really in my face. Goodbye!'"

These day-dreams were frequent with Berdella. He would imagine people in road crashes, or fantasize about a safe, falling out of the sky onto someone's head. Just as he used his imagination to overcome his frustrations, he also used it when he found himself in a situation where he thought his sexual advances would be rejected. "I thought I wouldn't be successful in propositioning someone for a sexual act, then I would have a quick 30 second fantasy about it and go about my business."

I'm going to have to say that I probably had fantasies where I used force and fantasies where I didn't use force. My fantasies

were not rigid and nor were they directed. I think like a lot of
other people's fantasies they might be geared on an article in a
paper, something on the news, a magazine article, a movie that
you go and see or somebody that you notice going down the
street. It's just some kind of repeat play that you keep plugging
different people into."

The violent and sexual fantasies were well entrenched in
Berdella's life. They'd been sown into the fabric of his mind by
early masturbatory habits and were now providing an inner
narrative to the 'repeat play' which was often one of sadism.
When Berdella progressed from mental rehearsal to physical
performance of his sadism, then something quite surprising
happened. "After the first death, the fantasies came to a halt.
They were no longer attractive. They were no longer enjoyable,
they were no longer accepted, so I didn't – to my knowledge –
indulge in them anymore." This is unusual. It is more often
found that after the first killing, the fantasies of murderers
become more embroidered and complex. It's believed that they
are not so readily gratified by the original dream-scenario and
have to make it more intricate and daring to achieve satisfaction. Berdella has an explanation for his case: "I think the
fantasies cut off because the situation no longer was a fantasy. I
was stuck with a harsh reality so I didn't fantasize. I think
perhaps that might be part of it. Having dealt with making a
fantasy a reality and then being stuck with the consequences
and liabilities of that harsh reality, can you just continue to
fantasize? I couldn't." To put it bluntly, Berdella had experienced the 'real thing' and didn't want to idly dream about it
anymore. He admitted: "There's some truth in that. There was
no longer any satisfaction or attractiveness to fantasy, there was
no longer a safety valve. What I am touchy about is that you
have these experts that believe in the 'crescendo theory', that
once started the fantasies become more and more demanding
and they demand release. In harsh fact, with me, the lack of
fantasy became the driving element. I didn't sit down, plan
things and say, 'OK, it's time to have another victim.' I didn't
have an overwhelming desire, I didn't go and roam the streets

for the purpose of looking for victims. These were people, like I say, that came to my house. And they were there at a time when either they, or some other element, kicked me into a high stress that needed release and these people were available."

Since being jailed Berdella hasn't received any 'deconstructive' psychological treatment. Only months of treatment could take apart his warped reasoning and deviant behaviour piece by piece. Whether he could be 'reconstructed' in any normal fashion is highly doubtful.

Two hours into the interview, we were still discussing Berdella's sexual habits. In yet another echo of Nilsen, he commented that in his latter days of freedom he had been hoping for a stable, loving relationship that gave him companionship and loyalty. He also made a few comments that were at first surprising. "I have never found bondage to be that exciting or stimulating. I'm much more turned on by very co-operative consensual, mutually satisfying sex." We asked him how he could reconcile that statement with his acts of sadism. He answered: "I don't have a clue. You know, to put it in rather simple language, tying up and beating somebody is not an aphrodisiac to me, it is not stimulating. It was done to perhaps control these individuals, to modify them, to make them controllable, so they would be consensual."

Once more, it becomes obvious that it is not sex but the more elusive prizes of 'control' and 'power' that are being hunted by the serial offender. Berdella says his quest for 'control' left him blinded to the reality that he might be discovered and so lose all control of his own life, especially that of his own liberty. "I didn't worry about getting caught. If you are capable of making the determination that a person is no longer human, that he is no longer entitled to be treated like a human, then you become incapable of thinking of other rational determinations such as a belief that you might be punished for what you are doing."

At midday, lunch came. Unlike British prison authorities, officials at Jefferson appreciated the psychological importance of Bob Berdella being allowed to stay with us to eat his food. One of the armed guards waiting outside brought in a large tray of cooked food for all of us. Inside a pack of white polystyrene boxes was charred meat that Berdella identified as chicken. They were accompanied by vegetables that had been cooked into culinary extinction, a mash of bleached white potato that tasted exactly the same as the mound of carrots and a pool of gravy that resembled a Kansas sewer. The Central crew struggled through as many mouthfuls as politely possible, finally opting for hunger. Berdella amazingly overcame his stomach problems and finished off several other portions of the chicken.

In many respects, Berdella's behaviour fits the characteristics of the FBI's 'organized' offender profile. During the interview, we explored to what level he had plotted or organized his offences.

"The closest thing I can ever come to saying that I'd planned it, was on the day that I decided to take Larry Pearson captive. It happened as a result of having him live in my house for several weeks. I'd been trying to get him a job, get him to job interviews, get him employed and everything. There was one consensual sex act between us, which wasn't that enjoyable, then he began to tell me about when he was living down in Wichita and him and his friends used to roll queers. Now there was a total combination of the frustrations of trying to deal with him as far as getting him a job, putting up with his behaviour around the house, and everything else that was a burden or pressure on my life, like the gas bill being overdue and everything else. It was the first time I planned anything. I was in the car with him and I drove down to the hardware store and I bought some ropes and bought some chains. He didn't know what I was buying them for."

Berdella organized as he went along. He wasn't acting to a scripted fantasy like Nilsen did, he was triggered by stress into the first steps of his crime and then experimented from that point onwards. "I don't think I was organized at all. If I had been, I'd have gone out and bought a good pair of handcuffs instead of just dealing with laundry rope, sashes or whatever was available at the time. You have to keep in mind that my crimes took up a very small part of my time; this wasn't something I spent three or four weeks doing, I had to fit it in while doing the shopping and running other part-time businesses and while raising the dogs. It really was a case of 'Whoops, oh, come here you, be a victim.' Then out with the trash. You know, it was a very small segment of my life. You see, I didn't plan or organize it the same way that I planned or organized my business. I didn't see it, at that time, as being an important part of my life."

There is a strong feeling here that Bob Berdella is playing down the amount of premeditation in his crimes. A quick re-examination of his actions shows that he always picked vulnerable victims, he always drugged them into unconsciousness and then bound them (taking no chances that he'd have to face a physical fight), he always sodomized them, he always tortured them, he almost always electrocuted them, he always took photographs of them, he always took notes on their ordeal, he always dismembered them and he always disposed of them by the same fashion. It's quite conceivable that with his first victim, Jerry Howell, he was improvizing for most of the time, experimenting just as a chef would with a new recipe. But Berdella's recipe was for slavery not for murder. He got the final ingredients wrong. With his subsequent victims, he followed the notes he had made, perfecting how much drugs to give them and how much torture to use to terrorize them. Had Pearson not been battered to death after almost biting off Berdella's penis during oral sex, or had Bryson not jumped to freedom from the bedroom window, then there's every chance one of them would have become Berdella's long-term slave.

Another indicator of Berdella's level of 'organization' was displayed when he explained why he'd settled on dismemberment as the best means of body disposal. He insisted it wasn't that he got any pleasure out of it and he positively refuted suggestions that he indulged in any cannibalism. He said, "It was the only workable solution. I mean, there were a lot of neighbours around. I lived in a house that didn't have a driveway, it was up on little steps. My car didn't have a trunk and you know, all these little elements had to be taken into consideration. It wasn't like I could drive the car up into a garage and then transfer a body into a car that had a trunk. You know, I lived in the middle of a city, not in the country. So all these are elements that had to be addressed in finding a means of disposal."

Berdella was depressed that his attempts to enslave his early victims had ended in failure and that he could not realize his dream. This is one reason why he writes them off as not being an important part of his life. He's almost as ambivalent about how stimulated he was by the reality of taking someone captive. "I don't know if I could make the determination that it was exciting. Actually, I found a lot of it to be just damned depressing, boring. It wasn't a turn-on for me most of the time. For most of the time, having somebody bound up on your bed is rather a nuisance." What Berdella really wanted was an un-chained slave that still chose to stay with him as the master. "It's a case of developing the dependency of the victim upon the victimizer. I think this became apparent by victim number five, by his willing 43 day co-operation and certainly by victim number six. I mean, after four days the only time he was tied down was when I left the house. I slept with him in the bed. He was right next to me, with the only restraint on him being a dog leash around his neck. His hands were free and his legs were free. If he had wanted to do me harm, all he had to do was roll over, and there I was." We asked why he thought he had not been attacked by the victim? Berdella replied: "At that point, I think he was broken. He was afraid, he was under control." It's worth remembering that his victims were only compliant at this point because of the extreme brutalization he had previously subjected them to.

We turned to the notes he had made and the hundreds of photographs he had taken of his victims. Behavioural analysts would say that the written and photographic recordings were indicative of the offender's habits in normal everyday life, and Berdella's own explanation of the note-taking supports this. "When I raised a litter of puppies, I weighed the puppies and I catalogued their births, dates, times, sex and their rates of growth. When I had sales in my shop, I kept a record of my sales and my purchases; it was just an element of my existence that extended over into my crimes. I've always used the camera to document things, like when I set up a buffet I would take certain photographs for future reference, to study. I think that has a lot to do with my training as a painter or artist. It is a desire to preserve something, even if it is just a working sketch or a working study, for future use."

There were two definite uses to the crime polaroids. Firstly, Berdella used them for stimulation. After the body had gone, he got them out for study and masturbation. He qualified this by saying, "Sometimes I would find them exciting, but for most of the time they weren't stimulating, they were just boring." The second reason was even more disturbing. He showed his victims the pictures of themselves and other victims being tortured. "Was I conscious that I was recording an act? Yes. Was I conscious that at times I was using the recording of that act to further intimidate and control the victim? Yes. If you have somebody bound and gagged and you've shown them that you are willing to put pain upon them to humiliate them, then it is a further humiliation for that person to be photographed while in pain and then to be shown pictures of their helplessness. It's a case of showing that you are in control of the situation and they aren't."

Not unexpectedly, Berdella hates the Kansas City Police Department. He accuses them of incompetence, sexual prejudice and a lack of respect for his victims' families. The real root of his animosity is that they caught him. However, for years he was always at least one step ahead. Even after the disappearance of four men, when police were carrying out house-to-house inquiries, he drew on his experiences of their behaviour and taunted them. "The one time the police came and talked to me, they were obviously fishing. They had heard rumours that I had a torture chamber down in my basement." Berdella believes these were started by Paul Howell, the father of his first victim. "Now, I knew what my basement looked like, it was a cluttered mess which I used mainly for storage and stuff that had been discarded. So you know, the minute they said that, I said 'OK, that's fine, let's go and look in the basement. There. No torture chamber. Are you satisfied?' They said, 'Well, how about letting us look at the second floor? I said, 'Oh, no. You came in here on a fishing expedition, you said that people had been telling you that the basement was a torture chamber. Now, get real. Come back with some legitimate concern, or leave me alone'." Berdella said this experience hadn't frightened him into believing the police suspected him of the murders. To the contrary, he saw it as a clear indication that they had nothing at all to go on. "That's just it, they weren't getting close, they were coming in on a fishing expedition. They hadn't got anywhere with the Howell investigation nor the other investigations."

The fears and anxieties that he'd experienced after the murders of Jerry Howell and Robert Sheldon had vanished by the time he captured Mark Wallace. Berdella had refined his torture plans and was feeling more confident about his actions. "I think at a point, yes somewhere at about the middle stage, I thought, 'If they haven't got me now, I can continue along the same path and take the same precautions and they won't ever catch me'."

Ironically, in the end, it was Berdella's growing confidence and his obsession for recording events that proved to be his undoing. After almost turning his sixth victim Larry Pearson into the slave he longed for, he felt he could correct any final mistakes with his seventh victim, Christopher Bryson. Bryson rightly realized that he would never leave 4318 Charlotte Street alive, unless he escaped. He went along with Berdella and faked the compliant actions of a slave, while all the time waiting for the one chance of freedom.

Even after Bryson had jumped to safety from the bedroom window and told his unbelievable story, Berdella might still have got away with it. His undoing turned out to be the portfolio of grotesque photographs he'd kept, along with the skulls of two of his victims. Without these, the Kansas City Police

Department would never have been able to link the deaths of six men to the former art-school drop-out, occasional chef and flea-market stallholder.

As Berdella returned to his cell he looked drained and depressed. He was no longer mentioning stomach pains but now there was some genuine and much deeper discomfort. Recalling his fantasies and motivations had taken a heavy toll on him. We mentioned his mental state to a guard escorting us to the front gate. He looked a little surprised at our concern, carried on walking and asked, "You telling me Berdella might be feeling suicidal?" We said we didn't know, but thought he looked distinctly depressed and might just need watching. "Shit." said the guard, "If it looks like he's going to kill himself, I'm going to take a long break and let him get on with it."

********************

For months after the interview Bob Berdella continued to correspond with the authors. In October, 1992 his letters stopped. A fax from the jail arrived, indicating that at 3:55 pm on October 8, 1992 he had died of a heart attack after being taken from the prison to a local hospital. Berdella's interview with us had been the first and last time he would publicly talk so openly about his crimes.

# Bibliography

*Behavior-oriented Interview of Rape Victims:* Robert R Hazelwood, Behavioral Science Unit, FBI Academy, 1983.

*Beyond Belief:* Emlyn Williams, Pan, London, 1967.

*Criminal Investigative Analysis:* FBI Academy, Quantico, 1990.

*Criminal Investigative Analysis: A Step Beyond Psychological Profiling:* Larry E McCann, Virginia, 1988.

*Criminal Sexual Sadist:* Hazelwood, Dietz and Warren, FBI Academy, Quantico, 1992.

*Deliver Us From Evil:* David Yallop, Futura, London, 1981.

*Daughters of Cain:* Renee Huggett and Paul Berry, Chivers Press, Bath, 1985.

*Deviant and Criminal Sexuality:* National Center for the Analysis of Violent Crime, Quantico, 1991.

*Encyclopaedia of Murder:* Colin Wilson and Patricia Pitman. Pan, London, 1961.

*Encyclopaedia of Serial Killers:* Brian Lane and Wifred Gregg, Headline, London, 1992.

*Encyclopaedia of Modern Murder:* Colin Wilson and Donald Seaman. BCA, London, 1984.

*Gender, Crime and Justice:* Pat Carlen and Anne Worrall, Open University Press, England, 1987.

*Homicide Investigators Journal:* International Homicide Investigators Association, USA, 1991.

*Hunting Humans:* Elliot Leyton, Penguin, London, 1989.

*Hunting Humans Vol. 1:* Michael Newton, Avon Books, New York, 1990.

*House of Horrors:* John Lisners, Corgi, London, 1983.

*Killing for Company:*
Brian Masters. Hodder and
Stoughton, London, 1985.

*Murder Squad:* Tom Tullet,
Granada, London, 1979.

*Murderous Women:*
Frank Jones, Headline,
London, 1991.

*Perfect Victim:* Christine
McGuire and Carla Norton,
W.H. Allen, London, 1991.

*Rites of Burial:*
Tom Jackman and Troy Cole,
Pinnacle, New York, 1992.

*The Serial Killers:* Colin
Wilson and Donald Seaman,
W.H. Allen, London, 1990.

*The Serial Rapist:* Robert R
Hazelwood and Dr Janet
Warren, FBI Academy, 1989.

*Sexual Homicide, Patterns
and Motives:* Ressler, Burgess
and Douglas. Lexington
Books, Lexington, 1988.

*Somebody's Husband,
Somebody's Son:* Gordon
Burn, Pan, London, 1984.

*The Death Shift:* Peter Elkind,
Corgi, England, 1990.

*The Milwaukee Murders:*
Don Davis, True Crime, St
Martin's Press, New York,
1991.

*The Stranger Beside Me:*
Ann Rule. W.W. Norton and
Co. New York, 1980

*Violent Crime:*
FBI Law Enforcement
Bulletin, Washington, 1985.

*VICAP:*
FBI Law Enforcement
Bulletin, December, 1986.

*Whoever Fights Monsters:*
Robert K Ressler and Tom
Shachtman, St Martin's Press,
New York, 1992.

*Why they Killed:*
Jean F Blashfield, Warner
Books, New York, 1990.

*Written in Blood:*
Colin Wilson, Grafton,
London, 1989.

# Index